FIGHTING OVER THE FOUNDERS

Fighting over the Founders

How We Remember the American Revolution

Andrew M. Schocket

NEW YORK UNIVERSITY PRESS
New York and London

NEW YORK UNIVERSITY PRESS
New York and London
www.nyupress.org

Parts of Chapter Four were previously printed as "Little Founders on the Small Screen: Interpreting a Multicultural American Revolution for Children's Television," *Journal of American Studies* 45, no. 1 (February 2011): 145–163, reprinted with permission from Cambridge University Press.

All photographs were taken by the author.

Stills of the various films discussed in this book are reproduced under the fair use provision of United States Code, title 17, section 107, from the films as noted in "Further Readings."

References to Internet websites (URLs) were accurate at the time of writing. Neither the author nor New York University Press is responsible for URLs that may have expired or changed since the manuscript was prepared.

ISBN: 978-0-8147-0816-3

For Library of Congress Cataloging-in-Publication data, please contact the Library of Congress.

New York University Press books are printed on acid-free paper, and their binding materials are chosen for strength and durability. We strive to use environmentally responsible suppliers and materials to the greatest extent possible in publishing our books.

Manufactured in the United States of America

10 9 8 7 6 5 4 3 2 1

Also available as an ebook

For Sophie and Phoebe, the next generation of revolutionaries

CONTENTS

ILLUSTRATIONS

ACKNOWLEDGMENTS

One of the debates for which we conscript the founders is whether the United States is a nation of individuals or a national community. It comes up when we talk about guns, or health care, or speech, or the Internet and in many other arenas. Of course, we are both individuals and community members. Similarly, this book was borne both of individual and community efforts.

Let's start with the individual, to get it out of the way: all of this book's faults and errors should be blamed solely on me.

Now, for the fun part, in fact often the most joyful ritual in the writing a book: thanking the broader community of institutions and people that made it possible.

First, a truly heartfelt and deep thanks to all the professionals and volunteers who make the movies and TV series, write the books, design the exhibits, interpret the sites, work in the archives, edit the papers, give the seminars, and, not least, reenact the American Revolution. Their inspirational example was part of what kept me going on this project and is a service to all Americans.

Debbie Gershenowitz was the first believer in this project as a book; our conversations were immensely influential on its shape and tone. Clara Platter has expertly taken it from there at NYU Press, with the able assistance of Constance Grady. Dorothea Halliday patiently shepherded the book through production, Jennifer Dropkin's keen copyediting made it shipshape, and Adam Bohannon designed the striking cover. Thanks also to everyone else at NYU Press who has worked on the production, distribution, and publicity of this book. Just like kids, it takes a village to produce a healthy one.

Several units at Bowling Green State University provided money or time for me to work on this book. American Culture Studies and History made for collegial homes. Thanks to my fellow ACS scholars in and about East Hall—Cynthia Baron, Ellen Berry, Chuck Coletta,

Radhika Gajjala, Andrew Hershberger, Jolie Sheffer, Rob Sloane, and Maisha Wester—and to my Williams Hall History colleagues Michael Brooks, Amílcar Challu, Beth Griech-Polelle, Ruth Herndon, Rebecca Mancuso, Scott Martin, and Apollos Nwauwa. Thanks also to School of Cultural and Critical Studies colleagues Vibha Bhalla, Lesa Lockford, Marilyn Motz, Sri Menon, and Susana Peña. The members of my 2010 "Popular Memory in America" course challenged me (in good ways). Additional support was provided from the BGSU Department of History Policy History Program. Special appreciation is due Tina Thomas and Beka Patterson, who both prove that incredible competence and constant good cheer are not mutually exclusive. A fellowship at BGSU's Institute for the Study of Culture and Society provided time to think that sparked the beginnings of this book, and a BGSU Faculty Improvement Leave further launched it. Just as much, my comrades in the BGSU Faculty Association demonstrated that even small revolutions can make a big difference in people's lives.

In 2011, I attended a summer seminar titled "The Early American Republic and the Problem of Governance," sponsored by the National Endowment for the Humanities (NEH). Any views, findings, conclusions, or recommendations expressed in this book do not necessarily represent those of the NEH. The Library Company of Philadelphia—begun by Benjamin Franklin and still going strong—provided a great home for the seminar, expertly facilitated by John Larson and Michael Morrison. The participants of that seminar provided lively conversation and feedback on my ideas. I gave a paper on *Liberty's Kids* at the Upstate Early American History Workshop, arranged by Doug Bradburn and commented upon by Andrew Fagal, and another that was the basis of my analysis of political speeches at the Newberry Seminar in Early American History and Culture, graciously facilitated by John Donoghue. Both audiences gave insightful feedback, as did the attendees at a roundtable at the 2012 annual conference of the Organization of American Historians. Thanks to the anonymous reviewers at the *Journal of American Studies* for their comments on my extended consideration of *Liberty's Kids* and for the anonymous reviewers at NYU Press, who helped me to sharpen arguments, jettison dubious claims, and avoid blunders.

I took all the photographs in this book on a Canon Powershot SD1200is. The text was composed in Scrivener, and I used Zotero to manage my bibliographies, both on Mac computers. Special thanks goes to Matthew Weinstein for his wonderful TAMS Analyzer program and for graciously answering my newbie questions. The original versions of the charts were designed in Microsoft Excel.

Many people helped with their insights, advice, encouragement, tips, and suggestions, among them Cynthia Baron, Jamie Bosket, Doug Bradburn, Mike Brown, Andrew Burstein, Benjamin Carp, Susan Castillo, Saul Cornell, James Cuarato, John Donaghue, Joseph Ellis, Andrew Fagal, Shawn Ford, Woody Holton, Nancy Isenberg, Miriam Kleiman, John Larson, Jesse Lemisch, Sandra Mackenzie Lloyd, Jennifer Lupinacci, Scott Magelssen, Mike Maliani, Rebecca Mancuso, Daniel Mandell, Doug McIntyre, Mike Morrison, Matt Murphy, Kevin O'Donnell, Jack Rakove, Carol Sheriff, Barbara Clark Smith, Holly Snyder, R. Scott Stephenson, J. Frank Winslow, Thomas J. Winslow, and Kevin Young. Special thanks to Thomas J. Brown for generously supplying his compilation of New York Times best sellers related to the American Revolution and to W. Fitzhugh Brundage for sharing the notes for a talk he gave at the 2012 Organization of American Historians annual meeting. The Second New Jersey Regiment, Helm's Company, graciously and openly shared their insights with this fellow Garden State native.

Although I was able to do most of my work without travel, friends in various places shared their hospitality and conversation, including Bob and Laura Colnes, Jim Eismeier, Beth Gale, Rob and Kim Galgano, and especially dear friends Leigh Ann Wheeler and Don Nieman, who have graciously been a sounding board about this book for years and who have become family. May you all find a way to do research in northwest Ohio, so I can return the favor!

One of the most emotionally significant moments in my career was at an academic conference just after I finished my Ph.D., when Alfred Young was the first scholar to publicly praise my work. More recently and more directly relevant, Al provided generous and detailed conversation concerning parts of this book. He'll be greatly missed. David Waldstreicher offered detailed, constructive, and insightful reviews at several stages of the project, demonstrating both his keen editorial eye and his broad knowledge of the historical and present issues at stake; this book is greatly improved as a result.

Ron Hoffman and Sally Mason, as always, provided mentoring, a home away from home, encouragement, and, not least, wonderful anecdotes. No matter how much I read about the American Revolution, it's still a subset of Ron's amazing grasp of the scholarship. His work and ideas and example have been central to my life as a historian.

Maybe this book would have been possible to write without friends and community, but it would have been much less enjoyable and meaningful. Thanks to the entire fellowship at Maumee Valley Unitarian Universalist Congregation, especially Rev. Lynn Kerr; to fellow agitators Candace Archer, David Jackson, Lori Liggett, Becky Mancuso, and Joel O'Dorisio; longtime Lakers Jim Eismeier, Mike Mazur, and Kevin Scholten; to District of Columbia (and now New Jersey) mayor Bob Colnes; and to fellow former (Williams)burgers Anthony DeStefanis, Rob Galgano, and Lynn Nelson. Becoming part of the BGSC and BGSU soccer community has been a gift, as has the BG poker game. Matt Webb and Jeff Rybak provided great stories and conversations in Ohio (and with Jeff, one evening in D.C.); thanks for the love of my BG brothers, Paul Cesarini and Ted Rippey.

I got my joy of reading from my father, Jay Schocket, and my joy of movies from my brother, Barry Schocket. My mother, Sandy Schocket, is where I got my joy of words. Just as I finished this, my second book, she completed her third; time for me to get back to writing. Thanks also to Lyn and Rob Houk, for their encouragement, interest, and good cheer.

Sophie and Phoebe played soccer and basketball, read books, watched movies and *Liberty's Kids*, ate ribs, played Wii, made bracelets, walked around cities, listened to Bruce Springsteen, built lego houses, cheered for the Mud Hens and Mets and Giants and Devils and Thorns, and did a thousand other little things with and for me. From the beginning of this book and long before that, Deborah has been my sounding board, my support, my editor, my friend, my partner, my love.

Introduction

If you live in the United States in the twenty-first century, you can't escape the American Revolution. Take a drive. Chances are, streets or neighborhoods in your town bear the name "Washington" or "Jefferson" or "Franklin" or "Adams" or "Madison" or "Hamilton," and you live in or near a city or county named for one of the famous founders. Walk by a bookstore or your local library. You'll find a display featuring the latest best-selling founder biography. Take a look in your pocket, and see whose faces stare back at you from the bills in your wallet or the coins in your purse. Mail a letter. Maybe you'll be affixing a "forever" stamp adorned by the Liberty Bell. Got a three-day weekend? Might be Presidents' Day or July 4. If you turn on the TV you'll be greeted with commercials featuring actors in Washington costumes selling you something. Change the channel. Sooner or later, you'll be treated to political campaign commercials that remind us of what the founders wanted for our country and how the candidates honor their intentions. And if you travel to the nation's capital, you'll encounter the founders everywhere. Look up to see the Washington Monument, stand in line at the National Archives to see the Declaration of Independence and the Constitution, stroll into the Capitol's rotunda to see Jonathan Trumbull's twelve-by-eighteen-foot paintings of four scenes from the founding period. Wander to the other end of the Mall to gaze at the Jefferson Memorial, across the tidal basin. Get lost in the nearby maze of roads and you might even stumble upon the forlorn memorial to Jefferson's lesser-known Virginia colleague, George Mason.

My favorite place on the National Mall—one of my favorite places in the world, actually—is in the area called Constitution Gardens. North of the Reflecting Pool that stretches between the Washington Monument and Lincoln Memorial, greenery surrounds a pond maybe an acre's size.

A low footbridge leads to a small, kidney-shaped island. Arrayed in an arc, fifty-six low, polished granite markers, one for each of the signers of the Declaration of Independence, sit grouped according to state delegations. Each stone bears an engraved facsimile of a delegate's signature and his name in block letters. Just a few hundred feet from the rush of busy Constitution Avenue, Signers' Island allows for quiet contemplation. I loved coming to this spot during my years working in Washington, D.C., when I first got the bug to be a professional historian and to specialize in the nation's founding period. I wanted to know how and why the structures and ideas from the founding era came into being, the ones that these men whose names graced the markers had a hand in building. In graduate school, I was fortunate to have Ronald Hoffman as my advisor, a man perhaps as well read on the American Revolution as any other historian. Summers and eventually weekends during the academic year I worked at Colonial Williamsburg, interpreting the Revolutionary era to the general public and school groups. My dissertation and then my first book were about the founding of corporate power in America—something that people had assumed happened sometime late in the nineteenth or early in the twentieth century but, as I argued, was part of the founding bargain of the United States. I teach the Revolution to college students, read about it with my two girls, and, as a citizen, see references to the Revolution in myriad facets of American life. While I still have the passion to research the Revolution itself, I came to realize that I am doing so in a context in which anything written or spoken about the American Revolution inherently holds political and cultural implications.

Despite being a process that occurred more than two centuries ago, and memorialized everywhere, the American Revolution continues to be a subject of controversy. It's rarely the subject of open debate. But the way Americans show it, talk about it, and write about it reveals that we are deeply divided about the Revolution's meaning. Republicans use it one way in speeches, Democrats another. Moviemakers and television production teams engage in spirited discussion about how to portray the Revolution on the big and small screens. Historians trade subtle barbs in their footnotes or, occasionally, open jabs in interviews and opinion pieces. The professionals who design and work in historical sites agonize over what they will show and what they won't, and residents of the communities that host those sites sometimes engage

Figure I.1. Signers' Island: The arc of stones on which are carved the names of the men who signed the Declaration of Independence.

themselves in the process. To show where they stand on pressing political issues, entire social movements name themselves after particular groups of Revolutionaries or Revolutionary-era events. Judges write opinions and legal scholars write law review articles that cite seemingly obscure documents from the 1780s and 1790s. True, other historical events also attract controversy—sometimes the Civil War, World War II, or the Vietnam War—but not across the broad spectrum of American geography, culture, and politics the way our founding period does. The American Revolution might be long over, but to Americans, it's not settled. Considering how historians have interpreted the Revolution, and how I encounter it, I realized that I was looking through the haze of my own preconceptions and view of the world. So, too, were other historians. So, too, are we all. And the more I thought about it, the haze is not even natural; it's more like the "smoke" from a dry ice machine—in other words, a haze largely of our own making. This book attempts to clear the air, if only a little.

Fighting over the Founders illuminates Americans' views of the past as well as the present and plumbs our central conceptions of what our nation means. Is the United States a nation in decline from a golden past, a founding moment of perfection that we can only strive to emulate but are fated to miss the mark? Or did the flawed founders set a standard that they failed but that we are continuing to struggle to approach? How are we to balance the tension between our heritage of individual freedoms and our sense of common purpose toward each other and our country? What is the proper role of government, and what are its limits? What is the nature of belonging to our country—who belongs, and who doesn't? How do we negotiate between the enduring wisdom of the founding fathers and their only-human inability to see fully their own time or the future? These are the kinds of answers that we seek every time the American Revolution comes up, whether we're watching a movie, reading a book, attending a march, pleading a case, or going to a historic site. The American Revolution is so distant from us that, in a nation of now over 315 million people, no more than a handful of our grandparents' grandparents could have remembered it, and it is far enough away that we can easily bend its interpretation to meet our purposes (whether intentionally or inadvertently). But because of how well documented our founding generation is, and how its figures and events so suffuse our popular and political culture and even our daily life, the Revolution is one of the prime ways that we ask, answer, and debate these questions. We live in the founders' world, just as they live in ours.

This book aims to untangle the ways that battles over the contemporary memory of the American Revolution serve as proxies for America's contemporary ideological divide. One strand of contemporary Revolutionary memory, which I call "essentialism," relies on the assumption that there was one American Revolution led by demigods, resulting in an inspired governmental structure and leaving a legacy from which straying would be treason and result in the nation's ruin. The essentialist view suggests a concept of history as a single text with one discernible meaning and so is inherently conservative in its outlook and in its prescriptions for the Revolution's contemporary lessons, which often emphasize private property, capitalism, traditional gender roles, and protestant Christianity. I use the term "essentialist" advisedly, as it's a term that refers to concepts with a long history. The ancient Greek philosopher

Plato proposed that all sets of objects have a true, eternal form, and each individual instance of the set is a copy that has some essence of that form. Every tiger is a manifestation of tigerness, every oak tree is manifestation of oaktreeness, and so on. In more modern times, the idea has been used and challenged in many fields, among them psychology, philosophy, and biology. It continues to hold currency among many Americans: the notion that men and women are necessarily different and have inherent behavioral patterns ("men are tough," "women like to gossip") is a kind of essentialist thinking. I'm applying the term "essentialism" to a strand of contemporary memory of the American Revolution in the sense that the Revolution, too, is often portrayed as having one, true, knowable, unchanging meaning for us now and forever: an essence. In the coming pages, I also describe the essence that many politicians, writers, museums, activists, and reenactors express, wittingly or not. From a purely essentialist standpoint, the suggestions that George Washington was not a hero or that Great Britain was not tyrannous are not interpretations to be debated; they're flat-out wrong.

At the other end of the spectrum, those Americans espousing what I label the "organicist" interpretation of the Revolution agree with essentialists in that the nation has changed over the last two centuries, but they have a different sense of how we think of the past. For organicists, there are many pasts that may share elements but no one fixed truth. Rather, the past must be interpreted to be understood. According to this train of thought, you and I might have different but, depending on the evidence, equally compelling conceptions of the American Revolution: you might insist that white Virginians revolted primarily because they wanted to keep their slaves, and I might insist that white Virginians revolted primarily because they resented British governance, and we could both have a legitimate claim to be debated. While the essentialists see a Revolution with a perfect result, organicists believe that Americans are ever in the process of trying to complete a Revolution that the founders left unfinished. They see themselves furthering the never-ending task of perfecting the union through an inclusive multiculturalism that looks to celebrate historical agency in the Revolutionary era and embodies, not eighteenth-century actualities, but the lofty words associated with the Declaration of Independence. I chose the term "organicism" because it fits this view of history itself, as something that changes over time, in step with differing conditions, almost like a living thing. It's a less perfect fit than "essentialism." Very late in the process of writing this book, Clara Platter (my editor) and I discussed the suitability of other terms, like "pluralism" or "evolutionism," but they had their own drawbacks. We also discussed using a phrase, but that would have been stylistically messier than using one word as an easy shorthand. Plus, I was already in print using the term "organicism," so organicism it is. In writing as in life, sometimes we seek the best fit, rather than perfection.

Many Americans and foreign observers have noted that we seem to be the only country whose citizens want to be in conversation with our founders, as though men dead for two centuries would still have much to tell us. There's more than a little truth to that charge, to which some Americans reply that the United States is exceptional among nations and that our founders possessed uncanny sagacity that transcends time and space. Both sides are partly right. Neither the United States nor its founders hold a monopoly on wisdom, political or otherwise, and a quick look at a globe shows that there are many democracies no less functional and no more dysfunctional than ours. Furthermore, all countries have their heroes, their exemplars who appear on stamps and money, are the subjects of biographies and movies, get mentioned in political speeches, and become cast in bronze. The United States is not the only country that engages in what sociologist Robert Bellah called a "civil religion." Nonetheless, the American Revolution was indeed unusual, as is its relation to the American present. Unlike many other countries, the United States can point to a period of less than two decades as its seminal founding moment. Most other nations have either multiple founding moments or have lived through various evolutions. Unlike the United States, most countries trace their origins to ethnicity and language, rather than to the establishment of a particular political structure. The United States retains its governmental form from the federal constitution that served as the Revolution's crowning achievement, and so its citizens look to the people who established that form as authorities on it. Most other countries have been through multiple iterations of their national governments. The founding generation of the United States was a particularly articulate bunch, whose vast public and private writings have been preserved, ever at the ready. Few other nations have a single generation of leaders that happen to have left such a wordy legacy, always available for apparent authority and, perhaps, exploitation.

Americans debate that legacy because we perceive a lot is at stake. In any society, ownership of an authoritative past provides a powerful political rhetorical weapon. Ernst Renan, one of the first analysts of nationalism, proposed that a nation is composed of two principles: "One is the possession in common of a rich legacy of memories; the other is present-day consent, the desire to live together, the will to perpetuate the value of the heritage that one has received in an undivided form." More recently, theorist Benedict Anderson conceived nations as "imagined communities." Countries are too big for people to know more than those in their local communities. What binds them, then, is a sense of common belonging, and among those things that people in a nation share is a store of memories. In all nations, the ability to claim an authoritative version of crucial national memories makes for powerful ammunition in fundamental debates. Defining memory defines the nation, and defining the nation means the privileging of some values and policies over others. We've long sparred over government's role in economic and civil affairs. Did we have a primarily limited Revolution, dedicated only to independence, or a broader Revolution that was also about equality? The Revolution's richness as a historical process, its broad cast of characters, and the expansive scope of its contrasting principles offers a great deal for us to latch onto. In speech, poetry, and literature, a "synecdoche" is a part that stands in for the whole. In American civic and cultural life, the Revolution stands as the perfect synecdoche for the nation, specific enough for us to be able to use its words and deeds but distant enough so that the differences in detail between the eighteenth century and today can be glossed over.

Our recent rise in interest with the American Revolution coincides with anxieties concerning nationalism. The phenomenon of Revolution-related best sellers and movies arrived at the cusp of a cultural moment in which Americans increasingly associated patriotism with militarism—a typical reaction of a nation at war, and one that the United States has experienced before. The biggest scare in the headlines during the summer of 2001 was shark attacks, notwithstanding that the probability of shark attacks continued to be far lower than being struck by lightning, even for beachgoers. But after September 11 that year, an unabashed American patriotism combined with a faith in violence to achieve security washed over the airwaves. The rhetoric of fear to be resisted by violence resonated in American news media. The U.S. Department of Defense's brilliant policy of "embedding" reporters with military units during the U.S. invasion of Iraq led to breathlessly supportive press coverage, especially because the practice lent itself to focusing on human interest stories rather than investigative reporting. Military press conferences held in a quarter-million-dollar TV-network quality briefing room from Qatar further glamorized a war while minimizing its negative consequences. Perhaps there was no better example of governmental media manipulation than the Bush Administration policy of forbidding press photography of American servicemen's coffins. Lest we think these attempts by the federal government to influence public perceptions during a war were either new or overly partisan on the part of a Republican president, we should remember that the Democratic Roosevelt Administration pioneered similar strategies during World War II. As we will see upon examination of the film *The Patriot*, national defense sometimes become conflated with national values. Recent invocations of the American Revolution can serve as bellwethers in the greater cultural debates concerning whether varying opinions and the challenging of leaders weaken the nation or contribute to American vitality.

For the pluralistic nation that is the United States, the tussle over the Revolution has also increasingly become a debate about belonging. As such, the Revolution has served as a roundabout way to debate the merits of multiculturalism, that is, the idea that citizens of an ethnically, racially, ideologically, and religiously diverse nation like the United States should embrace and celebrate its many pasts and presents, rather than cling to one story for everyone. Is our country primarily white, primarily Christian, primarily heterosexual? If so, then we might emphasize the founding fathers; if not, then we might consider many other Revolutionary-era Americans. Opponents of multiculturalism argue that it unnecessarily divides Americans rather than emphasizing their commonalities. In some ways, multiculturalism's friendly critics have offered more trenchant critiques. They charge that its categories are too rigid or so socially constructed as to be meaningless, that it fails to account for multiethnic people; that it further privileges gendered cultural norms; and that cultural diversity has often been pursued at the expense of class diversity, especially among whites. The engagement with multiculturalism in the academic study of the American Revolution has resulted in the broadening of topics of inquiry and thus broadening understanding, as well as, in some cases, fundamentally altering considerations of what caused the Revolution. The main challenge with the application of a multicultural ethos to interpretations of the American Revolution is that multiculturalism is a social and philosophical sensibility, rather than an explanation of historical process or reality. By the same token, a past that only celebrates the founding fathers is no more representative of the fledgling United States, a nation born with about 2.5 million people, women and men, over a quarter of whom were people of color, and who worshipped in many religious denominations (or chose not to worship at all).

Those battles over the Revolution's meaning raged even before the ink was dry on what we now consider our sacred founding documents. As early as the 1780s, farmers protesting against raised state taxes and other policies friendly to creditors complained that such policies violated the "Spirit of '76." Alexander Hamilton and James Madison, allies in the writing the Federalist Papers to promote the Constitution's ratification, eventually sparred over the original intention of various clauses. Thomas Jefferson continued calling his enemies "tories" for decades. In the 1820s, wealthy Bostonians began celebrating a hitherto-forgotten local event by calling it a "tea party" so as to downplay the radicalism of the mass destruction of private property. Some abolitionists seized on the Declaration of Independence's promise that "all men are created equal," while William Lloyd Garrison blasted the Constitution as "an agreement with hell" for its entrenchment of slavery. Both sides in the Civil War claimed to be acting on the founders' legacy. Turn-of-the-twentieth-century nativist writers and politicians bemoaned what they perceived as the cultural chasm between the new immigrants and Anglo-Saxon American Revolutionaries. Various ethnic groups countered with founders of their own: Baron Friedrick von Steuben (German), Tadeusz Koscuiszko (Polish), and Haym Solomon (Jewish). Isolationists seized on Washington's warning against "foreign entanglements" to oppose action against Hitler in the 1930s, while those favoring the allies called it a fight against tyranny no less than the Revolution. The founders were both in favor of and against the Vietnam War and civil rights for African Americans and women. Thomas Jefferson applauded President Ronald Reagan's attempts to devolve some federal responsibilities to the states but not his exploding of the federal deficit. And Alexander Hamilton, whose extramarital affair with Maria Reynolds was the first sex shocker in U.S. politics, was both sympathetic with and appalled by Bill Clinton during the controversy over his relationship with Monica Lewinsky. We continue today to enlist the founders for our own political battles and to invoke the Revolution in our culture.

We should not go further without a common understanding of what I mean by the "American Revolution." For my purposes, the American Revolutionary era spans from the mid-1760s—that is, from the passage of the Stamp Act (1765)—through the ratification of the federal constitution in 1788. It encompasses the many political, social, military, economic, and cultural changes people experienced along the Eastern Seaboard in the area that became the United States. My American Revolution did not end with the Battle of Yorktown (1781) or with the Treaty of Paris (1783)—when Britain acknowledged the new nation—any more than the French Revolution ended with the execution of Louis XVI. Instead, the American Revolution continued through the establishment of a broadly recognized, stable national government—thus making the distinction between the War of Independence and the overall Revolution. Deciding when a historical process begins and ends is an interpretation unto itself. If we think of the Civil War as beginning with the firing on Fort Sumter (1861) and ending with Robert E. Lee's surrender at Appomattox (1865), then it was primarily a military struggle; if we think of it as beginning with Southern states' secession (1860) and ending with the close of Reconstruction (1877), then it was about states' relation to the federal government; and if we think of the Civil War as beginning with the *Dred Scott* case (1857), when the Supreme Court declared that the enslaved were not citizens, and ending with *Plessy v. Ferguson* (1896), when the Supreme Court applied the doctrine of "separate but equal," then the Civil War was about African Americans' legal status. I begin my American Revolution with the protests over the Stamp Act because that was the moment at which many colonial British Americans first questioned the legitimacy of British authority over them, and I end it with the ratification of the Constitution because that moment signaled that most Americans—the free white ones, anyway—recognized the new national and state governments as being legitimate. It's an interpretation that also holds the virtue of being in line with that of most historians and the general public.

Just as defining the "then" is necessary, so is defining the "now." This book covers the years from about 2000 through 2012. There are some outliers. With presidential campaigns seeming to begin nearly moments after the last one's been decided, I included candidates' speeches from 1999. Similarly, big-budget movies take years to evolve from a gleam in the writer's eye to a cinema projector's beams, so I cast back into the late 1990s to consider the development of *The Patriot*. Debates over Thomas Jefferson's paternity of Sally Hemings's children heated up with the publication of Annette Gordon-Reed's *Thomas Jefferson and Sally Hemings: An American Controversy* in 1997, the same year that Joseph Ellis's best-selling *American Sphinx* hit the shelves. Those pre-millennial milestones were to some extent related: an election featuring wide-open primaries in both parties, the first blockbuster on the American Revolution in decades, and the reopening of a controversy concerning one of the foundingest of fathers, so to speak. In addition, not long after the turn of the twenty-first century, a controversy erupted over how the Liberty Bell and the first president's house would be interpreted, and David McCullough's best-selling *John Adams* arrived in bookstores. In the 2000s, Supreme Court majority opinions for the first time would showed the full fruit of originalism, and the tea party movement made its appearance at the decade's close. American culture, too, changed significantly in the 2000s, as opposed to the 1990s, with the ubiquity of the Internet and increasing political and cultural polarization. Whether the terrorist attacks of September 11, 2001, and the political and cultural reaction to them were intensifications of trends beginning in the decades before or departures from them, everyone who lived through the 2000s knew that they felt different from the preceding years. For each chapter, I considered my subject matter in the context of what had gone before, mostly relying on the work of previous writers who investigated those times. But in the interest of consistency and brevity, this book sticks pretty much to the twenty-first century.

I'm far from the first to consider our collective memory of the American Revolution. The historian Wesley Frank Craven remarked in a 1955 lecture, "Of the many different ways of calling the common tradition to witness as to the right and wrong of a current issue, none has been so favored among Americans as the simple and direct appeal to a standard presumably raised by the founding fathers." The most authoritative scholar of Americans' memory of the Revolution from the eighteenth century through the Revolutionary Bicentennial in 1976, Michael Kammen, agreed with Craven in suggesting Americans have mostly remembered our Revolution in a conservative way. For Kammen, Americans have cast their Revolution as a national coming of age, rather than as a fundamental debate about rights, liberties, and obligations. But as Kammen argued, that perception has also led to the idea that the United States has remained unchanged since that moment, stuck in amber as a youthful country trying to preserve its innocence (or, perhaps, naïveté). Some historians have chronicled how Americans have remembered particular founders over the decades, noting how Thomas Jefferson and Alexander Hamilton's stars have waxed and waned, not only in relation to each other's, but also in relation to contemporary battles over the size of government and the degree to which it should be active in the economy. Scholars have considered how particular historical sites like Colonial Williamsburg (funded originally by the Rockefeller family) or Independence Hall (operated by the National Park Service) put into practice their sponsors' visions of how their visitors should perceive the nation. Authors have tracked the Revolutionary afterlife of particular events (the Boston Tea Party), documents (the Constitution), and even symbols (the Liberty Bell) to illuminate Americans' mixed anxieties and dreams concerning class, governance, and race, respectively. But, to my knowledge, no one has considered memory of the American Revolution more broadly since the turn of the twenty-first century. That's what this book aims to do.

My use of the first person marks a departure from my previous writing and from nearly all books written by academically trained historians in this country. Compared to sociologists, ethnologists, and cultural critics, American historians are notoriously un-reflexive, and historians of the American Revolution are perhaps among the least reflexive of the bunch. That is, we're taught not to think about our research in relation to ourselves or, even worse, to mention ourselves in our work. One of my graduate school professors counseled us to "remove the scaffolding" from our writing. What he meant was that when we were finished with a piece, we were to go back through it and remove any reference to our thought process so what the reader saw was a perfect edifice, as if constructed out of thin air. He learned that metaphor from one of his professors, Edmund Morgan, who taught dozens of graduate students in his forty years at Yale, and that approach is pretty standard in the profession. The advantage of the method is that it can clear prose to make way for great stories without the distraction of moving between the past and the present. But there's a danger, too. Such fluid history writing gives us the illusion that there is one past that stands on its own, there for the discovering, rather than being shaped by the interpretation of human beings—humans who, despite their best intentions, cannot help but to come to the material at hand with a range of experiences and values. And by not writing out loud about those values, we deny to our readers and ourselves necessary information for evaluating our work: why we include and why we leave out, why we praise and why we condemn. Those are partly judgments of craft, but at one level or another, they are always informed by our experiences, our education, and our values.

So here are mine. I grew up in what most Americans would call an "upper-middle-class" Jewish home in northern New Jersey, but by nearly any quantifiable measure, in other countries we'd be referred to as "wealthy." Both my parents had graduate degrees, and my older brother preceded me to college. I attended a small but high-quality public high school and a very prestigious college (Yale), and afterward I worked in management for a major corporation and then as a database analyst for a Washington, D.C., contractor for the Department of Justice. Living in the nation's capital amid monuments to the Revolution made me want to explore the origins of today's political structures, so I went to the College of William & Mary to study the American Revolution. Since 2001, my wife and I (and now our two daughters) have lived in a small midwestern town with a mid-size state university, where we both teach. Although my graduate training was pretty typical of history, I always had the notion that any complex problem required multiple methods to understand it. My dissertation and first book featured not only the kind of historical methodology that I had learned in graduate school but also economics, the philosophy of technology, a little architectural history, and social network analysis. I leaped at the opportunity to teach in an interdisciplinary American Culture Studies program, and doing so led me to think differently not only about history but also about memory. I've always been fairly liberal in the contemporary American sense, culturally and politically, but I am much less dogmatically so than I used to be, or, perhaps more accurately, maybe I'm just more willing to see multiple sides to complicated questions. I came to this book out of the realization that in order for me and other historians to understand the American Revolution better, we had to become aware of the lenses through which Americans encounter the Revolution today.

One of my goals in writing this book was to take every interpretation seriously. I conducted in-person, phone, and email conversations with scores of public history professionals, movie and TV industry people, historians, and reenactors (and even a brewer). All graciously shared their thoughts. Without exception, they earnestly desired to understand the American Revolution and to portray it accurately and responsibly within the context of their vocation. They had consulted archives, engaged in deep conversations with collaborators and internal reviewers, lavished money (or, in the case of Hollywood, other people's money), and spent months or years working to understand their subjects, often to what might appear to other people as trivial detail. Out of respect for them, I read and re-read speeches and books, visited historical sites multiple times, and played DVDs, hit the "back" button, and played them again. As the pages ahead reveal, I don't agree with every portrayal, and some I take strong issue with. But just as we academic historians preach to our students that people in the past were not less smart than we are just because they didn't have smartphones and that we must try to understand people in the past no matter how much their values clash with ours, so, too, I have assumed that the people who produce the works analyzed here did so smartly and in good faith. I have endeavored to grapple with politicians, speechwriters, screenwriters, authors, reenactors, directors, public historians, and jurists on their own terms. Their expressions of the American Revolution constitute forms of understanding the past, each appropriate to its own medium and logic. History produced by academic historians, too, follows its own logic and conventions to generate products about the human past. Readers will find that I'm least tender with professional historians and legal theorists. Of all the people in this book, we are ones who have chosen a life of ideas and have the opportunity to write at length and with nuance. We work in genres that allow for being thoughtful. When we're not, we should be taken to account.

I began this book with grand ambitions: to write the comprehensive tome on the American Revolution in contemporary America. I would read all the popular books crowding bookstore shelves and Amazon best-seller lists, go to all the historical sites and tourist destinations, cover all of politics, watch all the movies and TV shows and documentaries, and scour the Internet for sites, blogs, and discussions. I quickly realized that such a task was neither possible nor desirable. Material comes out faster than any one person can keep up with. In addition, a broad sweep risked my making generalizations that might be interesting but at the expense of deeper understanding. I decided to be more particular. "Truths That Are Not Self-Evident: The Revolution in Political Speech" concentrates on the speeches and debates of Republican and Democratic presidential primary candidates and nominees. "We Have Not Yet Begun to Write: Historians and Founders Chic" explores best-selling non-fiction books about the Revolution and the founders. "We the Tourists: The Revolution at Museums and Historical Sites" examines historical sites in Philadelphia, as well as Mount Vernon, Monticello, and Colonial Williamsburg. My consideration of the American Revolution on-screen ("Give Me *Liberty's Kids*: How the Revolution Has Been Televised and Filmed") focuses on the biggest productions: *The Patriot*, the *National Treasure* franchise, *Liberty's Kids*, and *John Adams*. "To Re-create a More Perfect Union: Originalism, the Tea Party, and Reenactors" delves into the commonalities and differences among constitutional originalists, minutemen, tea partiers, and reenactors trying to bring the Revolution into the present. Admittedly, there's much that's missed. Other books, other films, other historical sites, other speeches. Readers might want more concerning two areas in particular that this book does not address. School textbooks and curricula have become increasingly politicized, and the founding era has been among the areas of contention for state boards of education. There have also been several video games set in the Revolution. Others writers, though, have taken on those tasks. Besides, if one expands a book to encompass everything, it would never be completed. Whether the following pages do justice to what I have covered is for you, Dear Reader, to judge.

1

Truths That Are Not Self-Evident

The Revolution in Political Speech

One day during the last week of October 2010, as I was opening the mail, a political flyer caught my eye. Political mailings were no strangers that season. Nonetheless, even more than most voters during the Fall 2010 election cycle, residents of our small Ohio town had been bombarded. We had the full slate of candidates at every level except president; levies for the schools, the library, and local emergency services; and a referendum on anti-discrimination ordinances that attracted tens of thousands of dollars in out-of-state money and more letters to the editor of our local paper than any other issue in its century of publishing. Still, this flyer was striking. It featured a colorful shot of Mount Rushmore with an American flag in the foreground. "They," that is, the honored presidents carved into South Dakota granite, "would expect you to vote" to "create Ohio jobs," to "balance the budget," to "provide taxpayers relief," and to "stop government takeovers." Finally, it implored its readers, "Don't let them down!" The photo had been altered to highlight a sunlit George Washington, Thomas Jefferson, and Abraham Lincoln but cast Theodore Roosevelt in shadow—no need for the conservative group that financed the mailing to remind voters of the ambiguity of a Republican president who believed in a vigorous federal government. The whole thing seemed curious to me, especially considering Washington and Jefferson. Neither of them conceived that the government had any direct role in creating jobs. As president, Washington pursued policies that greatly increased the federal debt, rather than balancing the budget, and although the federal debt was reduced during Jefferson's presidency, he was deeply criticized for the extravagance of the Louisiana Purchase. As a general, Washington bemoaned citizens' reluctance to pay taxes to support the Continental Army; would he really want taxes cut now, as the nation was involved in two foreign wars? And how could anyone possibly divine the opinion of men who lived in an age of horses as to their position on the federal bailouts of General Motors and Chrysler? I don't know the answers to these questions. No one does.

One thing I do know is that political parties and politicians do more than enlist the founders to serve their own political ends. They do so in markedly different ways, depending upon where they—the politicians, that is—stand on the political spectrum. This chapter maps the terrain of today's politicized memory of the American Revolution to explore shared expressions, common themes, and ideological differences that have implications not only for how different Americans consider history but also for contemporary policy making, showing how the American Revolution continues to be contested ground. It does so by charting presidential campaign rhetoric, primarily from 2000 through 2012. During the 2008 presidential campaign, John McCain praised "our founding fathers," who "were informed by the respect for human life and dignity that is the foundation of the Judeo-Christian tradition." Conversely, Barack Obama spoke glowingly of "that band of patriots who declared in a Philadelphia hall the formation of a more perfect union." Conservative candidates tend to invoke an essentialist view of the American Revolution. Would-be Republican presidents were often quick to mention the "Founding Fathers" (usually capitalized in official transcripts released by the candidates) and cite their wisdom to suggest that the founding generation, speaking with one voice, offered timeless, inviolable principles that apply directly to contemporary political issues. Essentialism assumes the imperative for a limited federal government and thus the illegitimacy of programs and policies that extend the federal government's purview. Liberal candidates offered potential voters the chance to further "perfect the union" to realize the egalitarian ideals of the Revolution, thus espousing a more organicist view of history and the Revolution. Organicists understand the task of perfecting the union as one that requires new tools for changing political, economic, and social conditions—in ways organicists openly admit the founders would not have recognized. These differing views of the past have profound consequences.

To get a sense of the way the memory of the American Revolution has become politicized across the spectrum of historical expression—including politicians, public historians, scriptwriters and directors, judges and activists, biographers, and even historians—I begin with the most easily identifiable by ideology, choosing to analyze presidential campaign rhetoric. Nearly 250 years after the American Revolution, U.S. politicians still frequently refer to its words, its leaders, and its events, thereby acknowledging and further enshrining its place in national memory as continually contested and politicized. It gets invoked as the ultimate appeal to civic authority, as a challenge to live up to or exceed the founders' vision, and in paeans to patriotism. But the possibilities and therefore the practical difficulties of getting a grip on what's being said are nearly endless. Contemporary news is bathed in political rhetoric. Nearly every day, it seems, the president, 435 members of the House of Representatives, 100 senators, 50 governors, their aides, and all the people intending to vie for those offices are eager to speak, state, talk, and now even tweet. I decided to focus upon presidential campaigns, including both the party primaries and the general elections. Every four-year cycle, up to a dozen candidates hail from at least one of the two parties, and in elections with no incumbent, from both parties. The primary candidates cover the range of what we might call "mainstream" American political discourse. Because candidates are running for national office, they address broad themes, trying to communicate more than their positions on particular policies (sometimes to clarify, other times to artfully obfuscate). They want to convey a more general picture of their aspirations for public policy and for the nation. Their references to the American Revolution become particularly freighted with implications for how potential presidents would pursue policy in the Oval Office and how they believe their views match the nation's voters.

Political polarization, and the partisanship that has come with it, has broadened markedly in recent decades; political scientists suggest that the United States may be more starkly divided now than at any time since the late nineteenth century. That's not to say that Americans have not always been partisan; rather, political division has become measurably more intense. Admittedly, politicians, especially the ones who think of themselves as moderates, have bemoaned partisanship for decades. Lloyd Bentsen chalked up the failure of his 1976 bid for the Democratic presidential nomination to increased partisanship, which was easier than blaming his campaign's lack of organization or his own lack of charisma. But by a variety of measures, partisanship has increased from the

1970s through the 2010s, especially in the 2000s. This accelerated division has occurred both among the people and our representatives, even in the Supreme Court. Casual and systematic observers have suggested many causes, among them the fracturing of the big three networks' former media dominance, the prevalence of self-contained communities on the Internet, and the rise of ideological political spending outside of party control. Gerrymandering has been another widely perceived culprit, although examinations of redistricting as a source of political polarization suggests that Americans are also moving into communities of like-minded people. Since 2000, one would be hard-pressed to find any presidential primary candidate who was more ideologically in tune with the other party than with his or her own. That makes the use of presidential primary speeches an especially good source for considering the intersection between political ideology and interpretation of the American Revolution.

In order to be systematic in my analysis of presidential campaign speech, I began with speeches from the 1968 election. I therefore included speeches before and after the celebration of the nation's bicentennial, just to see whether that massive celebration of the Revolution had any effect (it didn't, as far as I could see). Only the speeches of the two major-party nominees after their official nominations from that contest through the 1996 election were readily available, but that was enough to give the overall study a sense of historical context. From the 2000–2012 elections, I was able to collect a large sample of the speeches and statements of all the Democratic and Republican presidential primary candidates. These speeches ranged in date from when the candidates declared their intention to run for president through when they dropped out or, in the cases of the party nominees, through Election Day. In self-identification, candidates ranged from the further ideological reaches of their party—like archconservatives Fred Thompson and Gary Bauer and ultraliberals Dennis Kucinich and George McGovern—to those attempting to position themselves as centrists—like Rudy Giuliani and Joe Lieberman (here I am using their general political and rhetorical positioning, not the way their opponents or supporters characterized them). Some candidates made their careers outside Washington, such as mogul Steve Forbes and Arkansas governor Bill Clinton, in contrast to longtime Washington hands like the former Speaker of the

House Newt Gingrich and Senator Joseph Biden. A few offered short political résumés, like Herman Cain, who had never even run for elective office, while others like Bill Richardson boasted long and varied political experience (Richardson has served as a governor, ambassador, member of Congress, and cabinet member). Given the realities of our two-party system, and that, in the most recent election cycles as in most in the nation's history, there have been few extended third-party movements, I excluded third-party candidates.

As with any decision of what to research, the selection of presidential speeches held advantages and pitfalls. My collection included speeches from eighty-one campaigns (thirty-eight Republican, forty-three Democratic) and seventy-two individual candidates (all of the presidents who served a first term ran for another, and some of the also-rans failed in multiple tries). The total corpus ran to nearly seven million words, far more than any one person might care to read—even a political junkie, which I'm not—and so I dumped all the speeches into a database. Nonetheless, the analysis below should be considered suggestive rather than definitive. Those millions of words and thousands of speeches come from only a fewscore politicians and their speechwriters. By necessity, a large proportion of the speeches come from a pair of men: George W. Bush and Barack Obama, their parties' nominees in two elections, loom large (although, as it turns out, Bush and his team did not refer that much to the American Revolution). Other candidates, like Rick Santorum and Bill Clinton, stand out because they often brought up the founding generation. So we must take into account the context and tone of these references, as well as realize that we are dealing with the idiosyncrasies of men and women with large egos, some of whom lead lives with few checks on their loquaciousness (Exhibit A: Newt Gingrich; Exhibit B: Joe Biden).

I searched the entire corpus for a variety of terms, names, dates, and phrases that relate to the American Revolution. Some of these were obvious, including people such as Washington, Jefferson, Thomas Paine, and John Adams; documents like the Declaration of Independence, the Constitution, and the Bill of Rights; dates like 1776 and 1789; and phrases like "life, liberty, and the pursuit of happiness" and "we the people." I also combed for terms that refer to the Revolutionary generation, like "founders," "framers," and "patriots." In addition, I looked for people and phrases not usually included among the founders but still from that era, like Crispus Attucks (a person of color who was shot in the Boston Massacre), as well as some that scholars would be more likely to be familiar with than the general public, such as George Robert Twelves Hewes and Deborah Sampson. Not surprisingly, none of these more obscure people showed up in candidates' speeches. Intriguingly, Benjamin Franklin did not show up in many election cycles either, despite boasting what current pollsters would call the highest "name recognition" of any of that generation who didn't become president. I then read through the paragraph containing each occurrence to determine whether it was indeed a reference to the American Revolution. Some terms required some judgment as to what to include and what to exclude. For example, the "Constitution" could refer to the founding document or to the nation's current governing structure. "Washington" could signify the man, the state, or the federal capital (there were over 4,400 hits for "Washington," fewer than a couple hundred of which were really about Martha's husband, and fewer than a handful about Martha herself). When in doubt, I opted for inclusiveness, knowing that such terms can work on multiple levels rhetorically and in audiences' mental associations with them. The data provide a broad and detailed picture of the ways that candidates invoked aspects of the American Revolution.

Not surprisingly, my survey of these speeches revealed a surfeit of references to the American Revolution. The oft-repeated dictum that the United States is more an idea than an ethnic or cultural construct (as opposed to, say, Italy or Russia or Germany) is overblown: try explaining to nearly anyone else in the world the attraction of peanut-butter-and-jelly sandwiches or tractor pulls. Nonetheless, the Revolution serves multiple purposes in the national political consciousness. The American Revolution resulted in the creation of the United States as a nation-state, and it continues under the federal political structure devised by the founding generation. The ideals of liberty and equality, the idea of limited government, and the fundamental notion of a polity of laws stem from the founding period and form a significant portion of national identity. The Revolutionary period serves as the font of many of our politically useful national myths, complete with its pantheon of heroes and villains, causes and stories, and even, in the form of slavery, what so many have called an "original sin." For civic entreaties, it offers

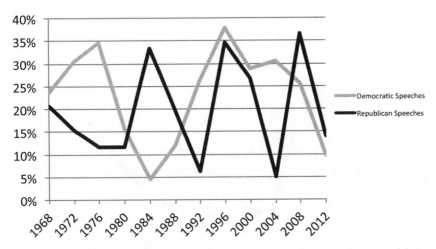

Figure 1.1. Percentage of Speeches in Which "American Revolution" Was Mentioned, by Presidential Election Cycle

personae with idealized characteristics: Washington, the personifica-tion of fearless leadership; Jefferson, the eloquent avatar of democratic idealism and small government; Adams, the persistent champion of lib-erty; and Franklin, patron saint of upward mobility and civic participa-tion. Because these men and their colleagues composed the documents that continue to be at the center of the American governance, especially the Constitution and the Bill of Rights, they can be cited as the ultimate appeal to authority on current policy disputes that involve questions of constitutionality. Furthermore, like the minuteman, the ordinary citi-zen ready to drop everything to serve his country at a moment's notice, they provide examples of civic virtue. And despite belying the politi-cal and social structures put in place in the late eighteenth century, the American Revolution's lofty egalitarian rhetoric provides uplifting elo-cutions from the Declaration of Independence and the Constitution to Paine's *Common Sense* and *The American Crisis*. The Revolution contin-ues its role as a touchstone in American political culture.

There has been no constant quantitative pattern over time to explain how often presidential hopefuls refer to the Revolutionary era. Sometimes many primary candidates from a particular party brought it up, sometimes not. Incumbency seemed to make no difference, nor

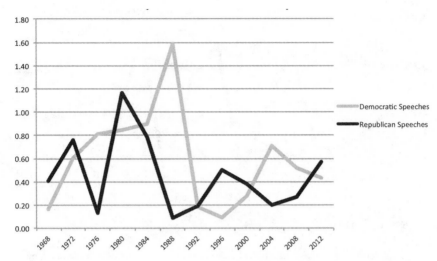

Figure 1.2. Number of "American Revolution" Mentions per Speech, by Presidential Election Cycle

did the party affiliation of the incumbent or challenger. In 1996, Bill Clinton appeared particularly fond of Revolutionary references. And yet, though he sprinkled the Revolution in a greater proportion of his speeches in that election cycle than in 1992, he actually addressed it more intensively within the few speeches in which he mentioned it during his first presidential campaign. George W. Bush, however, invoked the Revolution less often and in fewer speeches during his 2004 reelection campaign than in his first bid for the presidency in 2000. Interestingly, in elections with no incumbent, candidates from the two parties invoked the Revolution at fairly similar rates. There appears to be no significant spike during the 1976 Bicentennial of Independence or near the two hundredth anniversary of the ratification of the Constitution in 1989. If any pattern presents itself at all, it is that candidates in the party out of power generally mention the Revolution more than candidates of the party in power, but not all the time, and not always by much. In short, the overall numbers don't necessarily tell a clear story here.

A more complete picture comes from looking at individual references, how they were used, and in what context. During the 2008 presidential election cycle, candidates of both parties invoked the

American Revolutionary era in nearly one-third of their speeches, Democrats in a quarter of their speeches, and Republicans in over a third of theirs. They tended to do so in several modes. Most obviously, speakers cited the nation's founding generation in an appeal to authority. This could be done collectively, as when Joe Biden noted that "the Framers . . . included habeas corpus in the body of the Constitution itself" in his critique of the Bush Administration's detention policies in the war on terror. They also mouthed the well-turned phrases of particular founding fathers. Rudy Giuliani advocated a strong military by reminding voters that "George Washington told us more than 220 years ago . . . 'There is nothing so likely to produce peace as to be well-prepared to meet an enemy.'" Quoting the founders represents a strong rhetorical gambit, reflecting the assumption that no one can gainsay Jefferson on the meaning of the Declaration of Independence or the members of the Constitutional Convention on the meaning of the Constitution.

Candidates brought up those founding documents explicitly. Sometimes they did so to establish their dedication to lasting American ideals. Fred Thompson told one audience he did not "think the Declaration of Independence and the Constitution are outmoded documents," signaling that he was in favor of traditional approaches to current issues. At other times, speakers invoked these charters because, in title and in content, they resonate so deeply in the American consciousness, as John McCain did when he promised "a national energy strategy that will amount to a declaration of independence from the risk bred by our reliance on petro-dictators." And occasionally they cited the Revolution to parade their patriotism. In a speech at Independence, Missouri, the week before Independence Day, Barack Obama invoked the Battles of Lexington and Concord, when, with "a shot heard 'round the world the American Revolution, and America's experiment with democracy, began." For a politician, talking up the Revolution represents a low-risk speech-writing strategy.

How candidates spoke about the Revolution represented both a historical interpretation and a philosophy of history itself. Republicans generally espoused what I will call here an "essentialist" view of the Revolution. For them, there is a definitive past, a real past, an unchanging past we can study for guidance, wisdom, and understanding. If we as contemporary Americans want to understand the political structures we inhabit, structures that have lasted in their current form longer than any other contemporary democratic republic, then we had best look at the men who drafted the blueprints. The founders knew well enough to draw up a brilliant and durable design and successfully craft the building and, so, can be authorities worth consulting not only on what they built but also on how it can weather new storms. Interpretations concerning people other than the men who wrote the Declaration of Independence and the Constitution are not necessarily wrong, but they are beside the point, just as a newspaper story about people watching a building go up may be nice in telling us about them but would not change what that building looks like, how it functions, or whom we might ask to know about it. And if the building seems not always to function as it should, we might need to redo the wiring or fix the plumbing, but otherwise we should keep the floor plan that has served us so well, work to spiff it up, and restore it to its former glory. When 2008 Republican hopeful Mike Huckabee spoke about the signers of the Declaration of Independence, he paraphrased its last line in imploring his listeners to "pledge our lives, our families, our fortunes, and our sacred honor to that which is true, which is right, and which is eternal." According to this viewpoint, the United States has survived through its fidelity to immutable doctrines central to the American Revolution that continue to be at its essence: national self-determination, the sanctity of private property, suspicion of central government, and a particular form of Christian values.

Essentialism is also a reaction to what most conservatives rightly perceive as the multicultural challenge to their basis of power, especially given the increasing reality of self-identified conservatives who are predominantly white men. Despite this demographic disparity, speakers can no longer overtly praise Anglo-Saxonism or the white race explicitly, as they used to do, without being flogged in the media and, for the most part, rejected at the polls. Most voters, broadcasters, editors, and producers wince at language they perceive as racist. A politician caught using overtly racist language could seriously damage her or his electoral prospects. One of the more memorable of such incidents occurred when Virginia senator George Allen ran for reelection in 2006. Allen was being observed at all public functions by an operative of his opponent, a common practice, in this case by a volunteer, S. D.

Sidharth. At one appearance Allen addressed Sidharth directly, several times calling him a "macaca," which in some contexts is used as a slur against immigrants of color, and implied that Sidharth wasn't American (he was Virginia born and raised). Sidharth's film of the incident went viral on the Internet in a matter of days. What had seemed like an easy reelection bid eventually resulted in Allen's narrow defeat. Half a dozen years later, Allen's career remained defined by the incident. This is not to suggest overt racism on the part of conservatives. That many voters in Virginia switched sides, and that such language is generally unacceptable in public discourse, indicates otherwise. But as sociologist Eduardo Bonilla-Silva has demonstrably noted with his elaboration of "racism without racists," it does suggest that American conservative language, of which essentialism is a part, retains to many of its practitioners and much of its audience an implicit racial tinge.

To avoid electoral suicide, conservative politicians and their speechwriters have resorted to subtle strategies, especially in the context of how they refer to the American Revolution. Essentialists use the Revolution to counter multiculturalism by framing their arguments to promote personal individual freedom, which they characterize as people being able to do what they want politically and economically, including what they do with their own private property. That kind of framing is seductive because it would seem to apply equally to people regardless of race. But some policies that are meant to help people regardless of race, such as food stamps, are perceived by broad swaths of the American public as benefiting some groups more than others. In 2012, Republicans Newt Gingrich and Mitt Romney both invoked the Declaration's "pursuit of happiness" as opposed to what they argued was individuals' dependence upon unemployment benefits. While this may seem abstract with regard to race, over the last decade white attitudes toward unemployment insurance have shifted because of the mistaken perception that blacks are more likely to be recipients of unemployment benefits than whites (in fact, unemployed whites are more likely to apply for and receive benefits than unemployed African Americans and Latinos). Gingrich and Romney's speechwriters thereby task the Declaration of Independence to contrast their candidates' ostensibly hardworking white audiences with putatively lazy black and brown people. I'm not arguing that Gingrich, Romney, or their potential supporters are bigoted. Nor are they unique in using abstract language to forward arguments regarding minority populations: liberals sometimes use the same kind of seemingly neutral language that holds deep policy implications, for example, trumpeting "marriage equality" in the context of allowing same-sex marriage. Nonetheless, essentialist political speech carries perceivable racial undertones.

One seemingly neutral Revolutionary reference carries particularly heavy racial and gendered freight. If any one phrase can be recognized as essentialist, it's "founding fathers." Since 1968, and especially from 1996 on, Republicans have used that phrase roughly four times more frequently than Democrats. The term has a Republican heritage, having been coined by then–Ohio senator Warren G. Harding in 1912. Richard Nixon, no stranger to the use of race in campaigns, brought the implication of the founding fathers as white and well-to-do to the fore in 1968. Criticizing what he painted as opponent Hubert Humphrey's tacit endorsement of the riots in many American cities that summer, which were primarily in African American neighborhoods, Nixon reaffirmed "the right of peaceful protest." Regardless, "in a country whose Founding Fathers had the genius to set up a system that provides a method for peaceful change," Nixon told his listeners, "no cause . . . justifies breaking the law or violence in the United States of America." Nixon offered an image of white founding fathers, dedicated to order, as opposed to violent blacks. Sometimes candidates invoked the founding fathers in ways seemingly interchangeable more innocuous phrases such as "framers" or "founders." In 1996 Republican nominee Bob Dole noted the founding fathers' inclusion of the Tenth Amendment to the Bill of Rights, limiting federal power, and his opponent Bill Clinton claimed the founders as progressive members of the "'we can do better' crowd." But usually, use of the term "founding fathers" was bound up with connotations related to not only to race and gender but also to ethnicity, class, culture, and economics. John McCain's 2008 talks to the National Rifle Association (NRA) invoked the support of the "founding fathers" as apostles of personal gun rights, having written them into the Second Amendment. While not mentioned in a racial context, McCain's formulation surely played well to an organization primarily white and male, a large proportion of whose membership engages in sport hunting as a ritual of masculinity, and whose advocacy is bound up in the Bill of Rights.

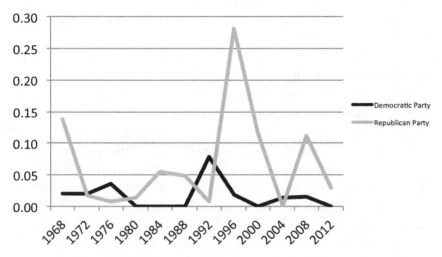

Figure 1.3. Mentions of "Founding Fathers" per Speech, by Presidential Election Cycle

More often than not, the use of "founding fathers" came with racial strings attached, in a way that could appeal to white voters without explicitly mentioning racial categories. Occasionally the image of white men became overt, never more so than in a 2008 Mitt Romney address to the Family Research Council, an advocacy group dedicated to promoting what it calls "traditional," heterosexual family structures, with men generating income and women respectfully raising children at home. After deploring the high percentage of African American households headed by single women, Romney argued that "a nation built on the principles of the founding fathers cannot thrive when so many children are being raised without fathers in the home." Intended or not, the contrast between apparently heroic white men and ostensibly delinquent black ones could not have been more stark. Ironically, this passage began with the assertion that "one of the biggest threats to the fabric of our society is out-of-wedlock childbirth." Had Romney spoken the phrase "founding fathers" in the same sentence as one concerning "out-of-wedlock childbirth," perhaps the audience might have come away with a much more ambiguous message, given what we now know about Thomas Jefferson's children with his slave, Sally Hemings. The use of "founding fathers," especially as opposed to the more neutral "framers" or "founders," necessarily suggested a romanticized, white, male-dominated past that some Republican candidates clearly believed held considerable appeal for their audiences.

Candidates also drew upon the founding fathers' masculinity. In many speeches, the "founding fathers" as male and white remained tacit, at least to the extent that any reference to "fathers" can possibly be more implicitly than explicitly gendered. But candidates were not always shy in pointing out that the founding fathers were indeed men. In 2012, African American Republican Herman Cain, running on his record as a corporate executive, announced his candidacy by touting his opposition to what he characterized as the federal government's encroachments on businesses and individuals. "The founding fathers did their job," Cain said, "We have to do our job and be the defending fathers," segueing to a discussion of his own children and the society that they would inherit. It's hard to imagine that appeal carrying much weight with female voters, and, after a brief surge, Cain's campaign failed to gain traction with male voters, either. Tellingly, in 2008 Hillary Clinton mentioned "founders" six times, but nary a one did she call a "father." Over the last couple of decades, gendered voting has become increasingly skewed in presidential elections, with men more likely to vote Republican and women more Democratic. The essentialist invocation of "founding fathers" does nothing to break that pattern.

Essentialism became most pronounced with the assertion that the United States was founded as a Christian nation, on precepts consistent with a certain brand of twenty-first-century, conservative evangelical Christianity. Appealing to the founding patriarchs has often gone hand in hand with the notion of an eternal, essential American Christian religion. This kind of reference was wholly the province of socially conservative Republicans. In 2000, Republican primary candidate Gary Bauer, who headed up the Family Research Council, warned one audience that "too many people that have forgotten that our liberty comes from God and not from any man." He was there to remind them that "all the Founding Fathers knew that a miracle could only make it if it had God's blessings." Eight years after Bauer's failed Christian-tinged campaign, Republican Fred Thompson tried a similar message (and got similar results). Thompson told his listeners that "we had a group of Founding Fathers who knew the scriptures, who knew the wisdom of the ages." These founders, Thompson argued, "announced to the entire world that we believe and we acknowledge and we know in this country that our basic rights come from God and not from any government." During the 2012 campaign, Rick Santorum invoked the Declaration of Independence as stating that "we are going to be a country with limited government and believing in free people to be able to form families, and communities, and churches, and educational institutions, and hospitals, and be able to build a great and just society, a free society from the bottom up." That would appear to be neutral. But for Santorum and his supporters, that reference was coded to apply to major issues in his campaign like allowing local institutions to reinstitute school prayers, exclude same-sex marriage, and refuse to perform abortions. Such appeals to religious founders were used to justify a range of conservative cultural causes.

A comparison with other nations' foundings would dispel the notion of a purely Christian American founding faster than you can look up "disestablishmentarianism." In the eighteenth century, nearly every European national government took some form of monarchy, and monarchs were either the head of their churches (as in England) or at least in theory sanctioned by the heads of their churches (as French kings were by the pope). During the French Revolution, the Catholic church was banned, and the revolutionary state seized church lands: a secular revolution. In a less radical vein, the only religious reference in the Declaration of Independence is in the preamble, with a nod to the "inalienable rights endowed" by a "Creator." The scarce mentions of faith in the Constitution are in Article 6, which bars religious tests for office at the federal level, and, of course, the First Amendment, which provides for freedom of religion and prohibits any official state religion. Christian? That seems a stretch. Many states did keep colonial laws on the books, some until the 1820s, that funneled tax money to support churches or required an oath or affirmation of Christian piety in order to hold public office. To see what a truly Christian constitution from the American Revolutionary period looks like, take a gander at the 1791 Polish constitution. Its preamble opens with "In the name of God, One in the Holy Trinity." Its first substantive section is titled "The Dominant Religion," which establishes "the sacred Roman Catholic faith with all its laws" and which forbade conversion from Catholicism to any other faith. In Poland, Christianity was the law; in the United States, a popular choice, but still just a choice. Admittedly, the role of religion in the founding is complicated, and over the last few years there has been increasing scholarly attention given to the degree to which Christianity played a role in the Revolution. But at the federal level, the evidence in the documents indicates that there was to be no official religion of the land. Essentialism's emphasis on a Christian republic represents a wish to provide Revolutionary cover for contemporary policies.

While the campaign prevalence of faith in the "founders" was fairly constant, sometimes a particular one gained currency in an election. If any of the Revolution's leading men served also served as an essentialist icon in 2008, it was John Adams, whom Republicans named in nine different speeches. Republican hopeful Tom Tancredo placed Adams in a holy trinity of conservatism along with Margaret Thatcher and Ronald Reagan, although with little elaboration. Maybe, aware of the founder's resonance with more conservative voters, Republicans were more likely to invoke his name. Maybe Republicans watched the HBO miniseries *John Adams*, based upon David McCullough's best-selling book of the same name. In 2007 and 2008 John Adams, or at least McCullough's and HBO's rejuvenation of his image in the public mind, suddenly emerged at the confluence of contemporary political conservatism and popular culture (more about those in later chapters). John McCain tapped into these veins with his quotation of Adams's pithy axiom that "property is surely a right of mankind as real as liberty" in a speech about private property before the Cedar Rapids Rotary Club, one of several times McCain channeled that crusty founder. Former Massachusetts governor Mitt Romney mentioned Adams the most. Although Romney brought Adams up in a national context, most of those mentions identified Adams as author of the Massachusetts state constitution. Adams "would be surprised," Romney argued, to find the Massachusetts Supreme Court allow same-sex marriage, as it did in 2003. Whether Adams might have supported same-sex marriage as required by the equality clause of the Massachusetts constitution is neither here nor there. His disapproval of Benjamin Franklin's flirtations when they served together as diplomats to France might have signaled a conservative view of sexuality. Then again, Adams privately expressed strong opposition to slavery (although he did not lift a finger to combat it). The degree to which Adams's eighteenth-century conservatism might have

translated into early twenty-first-century conservatism is at best specu-
lation, but for some Republicans, Adams must have seemed a safer bet
than Jefferson, with his radical moments, or Washington, with his customary reluctance to comment.

In contrast to their essentialist competitors, Democrats tended to
express an organicist view of history and the Revolution. While they
looked for a past as usable as the one their political opposites had
found, they did not consult it for immutable truths. For them, the past
is darker, more ambiguous, more open to interpretation, and something
to improve upon. Yes, the framers were the architects of our political
system and conceived of a grand dwelling. But those architects did not
always agree on what they wanted and had to make further compro-
mises because what they knew they wanted was too expensive. Besides,
they were eighteenth-century men who built a house for their own
comfort. For Democrats, the people outside looking in—the enslaved,
women, Native Americans, and anyone else who wasn't a bigwig—were
just as important as the men inside, who could not have imagined that
those people might have a range of unanticipated requirements and
aesthetics. So, as more residents move in, and as their numbers and
needs change, they must continue to build additions and to renovate,
while keeping in mind the framers' vision of what the house could be
for those who chose to live in it. Furthermore, all these changes come
with a price to the people who toil to construct and maintain the building and to the very land upon which it sits.

Organicist politicians' task is to discern the broader promises of
the American Revolution and find ways to realize those promises for
Americans while minimizing their costs. Democratic primary candidate John Edwards voiced that vision, straight from the Declaration of
Independence, when he said that, "for America's part, I want the world
to see a country that works every day to live up to our founders' aspirations. That all people are created equal and that we're all endowed with
certain inalienable rights: life, liberty, and the pursuit of happiness."
Like a house, the United States is a living organism, continually growing and changing, but thriving best when it stays true to its most ideal-
istic principles: a dedication to equality, the belief in progress, and faith
in common purpose. For essentialists, the past sits in judgment of the
present; for organicists, the present sits in judgment of the past. Unlike

the essentialist vision of the Revolution as a golden moment and the United States in cultural decline, organicists tend to see history in terms of progress from a benighted world of slavery and patriarchy to a more egalitarian present and a still better future.

But moving toward an equality and appreciation of diversity that did not exist in Revolutionary America necessitates challenging the founders as much for their failure as lauding them for their achievements, a delicate balancing act. To have their cake and eat it, too, Democrats reclaimed the founders' dreams, rather than their deeds, and the founders' sense of the Revolution—and by extent, the republic—as a work in progress, rather than a completed act. They seized upon a resonant phrase from the Constitution: "in order to form a more perfect union." In its entirety or in shortened form, Democrats used the phrase thirty-five times, compared to only five by Republicans. The majority of those mentions came in the 2008 election. Not surprisingly, the candidates who least physically resembled "founding fathers," Hillary Clinton and Barack Obama, used this formulation the most. Clinton noted the nation's continuing economic and social gender inequities despite legal equality. "So long as there are gaps between our aspirations and our reality," Clinton told one audience, "that more perfect union still awaits." Clinton's oratory on gender was matched by Obama's memorable words on race. Obama's candidacy was both freighted with the burden and buoyed by the opportunities of his biracial background. He titled his March 18, 2008, address, entirely dedicated to the issue of race in contemporary America, "A More Perfect Union." Appearing at the National Constitution Center in Philadelphia and beginning with the opening words of the Constitution's preamble, "We the people, in order to form a more perfect union," Obama spoke of the Constitutional Convention's "unfinished" work: unfinished because it had not banished slavery. But "the answer to the slavery question was already embedded within our Constitution," he suggested, because it "had at its very core the ideal of equal citizenship . . . [and] promised its people liberty, and justice, and a union that could be and should be perfected over time." Constitutional law professor that Obama had been, he knew that the original document did not guarantee equality. Better as oratory than as history, Obama's speech offered an organicist interpretation consistent with his Democratic colleagues.

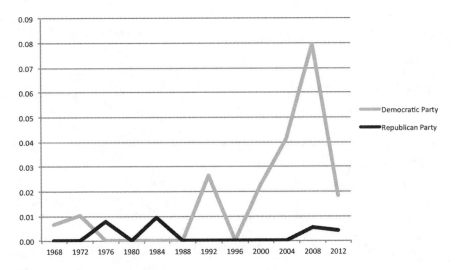

Figure 1.4. Mentions of "More Perfect Union" per Speech, by Presidential Election Cycle

While "founding fathers" sent a signal to Republican audiences about race and gender, Democratic candidates called on a phrase with diametrically opposed connotations, "created equal." Although politicians of both parties mentioned the Declaration of Independence in nearly equal measure, what they chose to emphasize of that document betrayed deepening ideological differences across the organicist-essentialist divide. In the text that Thomas Jefferson penned and that was approved by the Continental Congress, the second and most memorable paragraph begins with what became its most celebrated sentence, "We hold these truths to be self-evident, that all men are created equal, that they are endowed by their Creator with certain unalienable Rights, that among these are Life, Liberty and the pursuit of Happiness." What part of this sentence politicians chose to emphasize, and how they decided to use it, revealed their vision of the American Revolution most consistent with their vision of the American present. From 1968 to 2012, Democrats were six times more likely to mouth "created equal" than Republicans, but the disparity became the greatest from 1992 on. In 2008, the lone GOP candidate to utter those words was McCain, in his Republican Party nomination acceptance speech. He did so in reference to beliefs McCain claimed he and Obama had in common, to

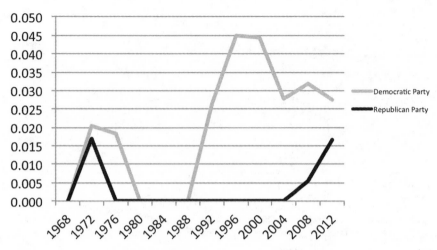

Figure 1.5. Mentions of "Created Equal" per Speech, by Presidential Election Cycle

appeal to the broader electorate, rather than to appeal more narrowly to Republicans. Four years later, Rick Santorum uttered these words on a half-dozen occasions, but only as part of the entire sentence, to empha- size not equality but a decidedly Christian "Creator." To GOP faithful for whom "equality" sounds like taxing the wealthy and—even increas- ingly, heaven forfend—"socialism," as conservative talk-show hosts have accused, the term "created equal" is anathema.

By contrast, Democrats, especially liberal ones, have treated the phrase "created equal" as central to their national ideal. The three Democratic candidates who mentioned "created equal" most often dur- ing the 2008 and 2012 campaigns were Edwards, Clinton, and Obama. That phrase's promise provided much of the subtext of their candida- cies. Edwards predicated his run on the premise of "two Americas," one graced with money and privilege and the other plagued by struggle and hard work. "Created equal" dovetailed with Edwards's major theme, even on speeches concerned with foreign policy. Obama once errone- ously quoted the phrase as part of "the first lines of the Declaration of Independence" but nevertheless spoke it several times. He did so to point out that the ideal of equality, though not fully realized, "applied to every American, black and white and brown alike," in a not-so-subtle allusion to his status as the first African American major party candidate. For Clinton, the phrase underlined her status as the first female candidate with a realistic chance of capturing the White House. Clinton remarked that she and Obama would not have been included in the nation's founders' original vision. In doing so, Clinton's history was closer to the mark than her rivals'; after all, South Carolina's political leaders were nothing if not consistent from the 1770s through 1865 that they wanted no part of any union that would curtail slavery. She used the phrase in the context of programs and policies designed to lessen social inequality and to welcome immigrants. Nonetheless, even as an aspiration that has been considerably broadened over the last two centuries, the hope for equality marked these Democrats as different from Republicans. If, as the historian Pauline Maier eloquently suggested, the Declaration of Independence is "American scripture," then its assertion of equality serves as a central tenet of twenty-first-century liberal political theology. The phrase "created equal" lies at the heart of organicist thinking in terms of its implications—and, given how little interest most founders had in true equality, it is organicism's most glaring blind spot.

More than the Republicans, the Democrats would seem to have easy purchase with one founder, Thomas Jefferson. Jefferson not only wrote the Revolution's most aspirational document, the Declaration that argues for equality—at least, rhetorically—but also is considered to be the founder of what later became the Democratic Party. Democratic president Franklin Delano Roosevelt championed the construction of Washington, D.C.'s Jefferson Memorial, backed by Democratic majorities in both houses of Congress (a dozen years after the completion of the Lincoln Memorial, commemorating the man the Republican Party claims as its founder). With only one exception—1972—Jefferson has been mentioned as much or more often by Democrats than by Republicans in every election from 1968 through 2012. That's excluding one kind of mention of Jefferson that I decided not to count: when candidates noted in passing that they were speaking at a Jefferson-Jackson Dinner. These are annual fund-raising events held by many state Democratic Party organizations, including the one ever-important to presidential hopefuls, in Iowa, usually the state that holds the first presidential primary. Numerous Democrats singled out Jefferson as one of their own. Bill Clinton called his compatriots the "Party of Jefferson" as opposed to the Republican "Party of Lincoln." Candidates sometimes evoked Jefferson as their party founder to stake a Revolutionary claim. In 2008, Barack Obama bragged to a Democratic audience that "we're the party of Jefferson, who wrote the words that we are still trying to heed—that all of us are created equal—and who sent us West to blaze new trails, to make new discoveries, and to realize the promise of our highest ideals." Here was organicism in two of its forms: that equality was central to the founding, and that the founding required further work.

As an indication of the Revolution's allure to candidates, they occasionally exhumed now-obscure Revolutionary-era figures to bond with specific audiences, make analogies, use particularly inspiring quotations, or buttress their contemporary policy choices with a Revolutionary foundation. Ronald Reagan quoted Dr. Joseph Warren, a prominent Bostonian killed in the Battle of Bunker Hill, during his 1980 campaign, "On you depend the fortunes of America. You are to decide the important questions on which rest the happiness and liberty of millions yet unborn." Reagan tied himself to the founders and cleverly included a catchword of the conservative religious right in debates concerning abortion, "unborn." Bill Clinton made a 1996 campaign jaunt to Robert Morris College. He later pointed out that Robert Morris "was one of the main financiers of the American Revolution, and he quit the Continental Congress in 1778 because he thought they were printing too much hot money." The story is dubious: Morris's term ended, and he was ineligible to serve again. To score points with his partisan audience, Clinton added, "I guess [Morris] would have quit the Congress in the twelve years the [Republicans] were making economic policy." In 2000, Republican New Hampshire senator Bob Smith channeled his inner Caesar Rodney, a Continental Congress delegate. According to Smith, Rodney "had cancer of the face, and he was scheduled to go to Britain to have surgery. Instead, he walked into that room, bandages on his face, and signed the Declaration, and sacrificed his life." Rodney did have cancer and did provide a crucial vote, but he didn't sign the Declaration until August, and he lived to 1784. Where Smith got the idea that Rodney planned surgery in Britain is anyone's guess. But the previously moderate Smith used the story to paint himself as an uncompromising conservative. Candidates of both parties brought up Thaddeus Koscuiszko and Casimir Pulaksi, two Poles who joined the Revolutionary cause, to audiences of Polish Americans. Other Revolutionary figures mentioned include Paul Revere and Nathan Hale, but not Patrick Henry, Sam Adams, or John Paul Jones. These eighteenth-century men still wait for their fifteen seconds of twenty-first-century political sound-bite fame.

For candidates of both parties, even obscure men merited inclusion more than any Revolutionary woman, in marked contrast to July 4 speeches by the nation's first generation of politicians, who often toasted women's contributions to the "glorious cause." Since 2000, there were barely more mentions of Revolutionary-era women than there were female primary candidates: Republican Elizabeth Dole in 2000 and Democrats Carol Moseley-Braun in 2004 and Hillary Clinton in 2008. No candidate invoked Betsy Ross—who has a higher name recognition as a historical figure than most U.S. presidents—much less more obscure figures such as Mary Ludwig Hays McCauly or Margaret Corbin (better known as the sources of the "Molly Pitcher" story), Mercy Otis Warren (one of the first historians of the Revolution), or Elizabeth de Berdt Reed (who penned the patriotic pamphlet *Sentiments of an American Woman*, inspiring the formation of an organization that raised money to support the Continental troops). In a short speech on the Virginia State Capital Grounds on October 23, 1976, Republican Gerald Ford alluded to Martha Washington in a list of prominent Virginians. The 2008 Republican primary candidate, Mitt Romney, named Abigail Adams, but only because he was talking about winners of the John and Abigail Adams Scholarships, which had been established during his tenure as governor of Massachusetts. Of all the candidates, two consciously considered women as founders. In 2004, Democrat Dennis Kucinich exhorted his audience to "call upon the Founding Mothers and their successors to temper us, to nurture us, to make us gentle, and to seek peace as a light within." Kucinich meant to honor Revolutionary women, but the kinds of qualities Kucinich ascribed to women both past and present are considered traditional Western feminine qualities. That's a far cry from calling upon women to defend the nation or make its laws. Hillary Clinton chose her own founding women, but not from the Revolution. Her female founders were those who signed the Declaration of Sentiments in Seneca Falls, New York, in 1848, calling for political and legal equality between the genders. Even the organicist vision had its limits on the campaign trail.

Surprisingly—at least, to me—there were limited references specifically to the Revolutionary War. Over the course of the dozen elections, I found fewer than a hundred references, combined, to the War of Independence, the Revolutionary War, the Continental Army, major battles, generals, and other military-related heroes, like John Paul Jones and Nathan Hale. These exhibit no discernible pattern, with mentions from Democrats and Republicans equally sparse. A notable exception occurred in 2012, when only Republicans Tim Pawlenty, Mitt Romney, and Rick Santorum mentioned the war, but even then, for a total of eight times, half of them by Santorum as he addressed a crowd in Mars, Pennsylvania, on April 3, 2012. The former Pennsylvania senator noted that his home state "has given a tremendous amount to our country," beginning with the Declaration of Independence and the Constitution, but also including the plans for Washington's leading the Continental Army across the frozen Delaware River to surprise British forces at Trenton and then Princeton (Santorum carefully left out that the battles occurred in New Jersey). He then pivoted to make the case for his candidacy, arguing that "we need someone who knows what liberty is all about." Santorum would have his supporters think that his cause was no less patriotic and crucial than that of Pennsylvanians' revolutionary forbears. Other references to the military tended to appear when candidates spoke in front of pro-military crowds. Addressing the National Guard Association on September 16, 2004, John Kerry praised his listeners' service. The Massachusetts senator intoned, "You can't live in the shadow of Bunker Hill, Lexington Green, the Bridge at Concord, and not know the meaning of Minutemen and citizen service to country." It was one of the very few invocations of the minutemen, perhaps to provide conscious distance between candidates and the ultra-conservative 1960s Minuteman movement, whose members stockpiled guns and plotted against what they perceived as Communist front groups—as Democratic candidate Hubert Humphrey took pains to do during a Knoxville, Tennessee, speech in October 1968. Given the opportunities for declaring a candidate's patriotism, the Revolutionary War remains comparatively unmined.

Candidates across the spectrum clothed their policy proposals with the Spirit of '76 by draping them in Revolutionary language, but organicists were more likely to propose creating new rights in the tradition of the founders. In 1972, Nixon called his revenue-sharing program a "Declaration of Independence" for state and local government because it also loosened restrictions on how the money could be spent. Both John McCain and Hillary Clinton called for a national energy Declaration of Independence, and Steve Forbes called for a health Declaration of Independence. Would-be presidents floated no fewer than eighteen new "bills of rights," which were actually proposed legislative programs rather than potential constitutional amendments. These are primarily a post-millennial phenomenon, with thirteen coming from 2000 on. Of those, all but one came from Democratic candidates. Candidates communicated their understanding of the original Bill of Rights in a way that contemporary audiences would recognize it as an bulwark of their rights as citizens, as well as, in organicist fashion, suggesting that the original did not go far enough. These included five "patients' Bill of Rights," a "credit card bill of rights," a "privacy Bill of Rights," two GI or veterans' bills of Rights (one from Mike Huckabee in 2008, the lone Republican in this group), a crime victims' Bill of Rights, and, for good measure, Richard Gephardt's 2004 Bill of Rights for Contract Farmers. Each of these proposals diverged widely from the actual Bill of Rights. The credit card, patients', and privacy bill of rights referred to individuals' rights in relation not to the national government but to third parties (credit card issuers, healthcare providers, and Internet companies, respectively). The various GI bills of rights would have created obligations on the part of the government rather than protected people from its possible predations. But the overall rhetorical point is clear in its combination of reverence for the original document and a sense that citizens desired an extension of fundamental rights appropriate to contemporary times. These new "bills of rights" reinforced the organicist tenet that the founders left work for future generations.

Because almost no one will actually check whether quotations are accurate, and any quotation of the founders seems better than none, candidates occasionally invoked the founders in ways that did them little credit. These gaffes include more than the factual blunders, like 1968 Democratic candidate Hubert Humphrey's claim that Thomas Jefferson was twenty-eight when he wrote the Declaration of Independence. Candidates have also showed a willingness to bend the stories themselves. Humphrey quoted Benjamin Franklin as saying, "We must all hang together or we will hang separately," which was close to what Franklin said in reference to the Revolution as an act of treason against Britain, a hanging offense. But Humphrey nonsensically placed Franklin mouthing it at the Constitutional Convention, when no one feared for his neck. In Michael Dukakis's eagerness to prove his military bona fides to his defense-spending-minded audience at an American Legion national convention in 1992, he related the story of "the congressional debate that took place almost 200 years ago during the Presidency of George Washington. Congress asked General Washington whether he could support an amendment to limit the size of American military forces to 3000. Washington said yes, provided that Congress would adopt another amendment limiting the size of invading armies to 2000." This exchange actually occurred in the Constitutional Convention between Elbridge Gerry, who wanted to limit the standing army, and Charles Cotesworth Pinkney. During George W. Bush's efforts to rouse the crowd at the 2000 Republican National Convention, he quoted Revolutionary Lewis Morris brushing aside his brother's sober objections to signing the Declaration of Independence: "Damn the consequences. Give me the pen!" According to Bush, "That is the eloquence of American action." Even if it did represent "American action"—it rather seems to represent American bluster, no less than Bush's later "Mission Accomplished" fiasco—there's absolutely no evidence that Morris said any such thing (the earliest any reference to it I can find is an unsubstantiated quotation from 1890). No less than in their claims and counterclaims concerning policies and each others' records, candidates' eagerness to refer to the Revolution sometimes outpaces their staff's willingness to check the facts.

Despite the many variables at play (who's in and who's out, the hot-button issues of a particular election, the particular audience to which a speech is delivered, what the speechwriter had for breakfast, and so on), one good proof of my analysis of the essentialist/organicist divide is its predictive power. If anyone didn't already know the ideological bent of the man who won the 2012 presidential election but had looked at the database that I compiled, all that person would have to do is listen to the first sentence of President-elect Barack Obama's victory speech: "Tonight, more than 200 years after a former colony won the right to determine its own destiny, the task of perfecting our union moves forward." Why "colony" rather than "colonies," only Obama and his speechwriters know (ask most schoolchildren, and they'll rightly tell you thirteen colonies rebelled), but the phrase "perfecting our union" was no accident. For organicist Obama and his exuberant audience, the founding era had begun something that needed continual refinement. The American Revolutionary past was something to learn from but not to return to. Conversely, the same evening, the defeated Republican essentialist Mitt Romney also hearkened back to the Revolutionary era in his concession speech. "I ran for office because I'm concerned about America," Romney told his disappointed listeners and then sought to draw a distinction between his ideology and Obama's. "This election is over, but our principles endure. I believe that the principles upon which this nation was founded are the only sure guide to a resurgent economy and to renewed greatness." Romney thereby implied that his principles (rather than Obama's) were the same, unchanging ones as those of the founding generation and that they were directly relevant to the challenges facing the nation. Speechwriters often rely on tried-and-true formulations, and their ideological references to the Revolution are no exception.

That references to the American Revolution have become political shorthand to politicians and voters indicates the degree to which contemporary Americans have internalized our collective memory's ideological divide. Because the American Revolution has become used in political speeches in ways predictably consistent with political ideology, its memory has become intertwined with what some political observers now call "dog-whistle politics." A literal dog whistle produces a high-pitched whine that canine ears—but not human ears—can detect. In politics, the phrase refers to the use of coded language that carries specific meaning to a particular, narrow audience that might be innocuous or unnoticeable to the broader public. Because liberals have accused conservative candidates of using ostensibly racially charged dog-whistle phrases, conservatives have complained that liberals are choosing to inject racial connotations where no such meaning is intended. That said, there's considerable research showing otherwise. Furthermore, although liberal observers have thrown the dog-whistle epithet at conservatives, liberal politicians have also used phrases for their audiences that all but the most astute conservatives might think innocuous. The term "workers' rights" seems fairly vague, as most Americans perceive themselves as working in one way or another, but to union members, it refers specifically to legal protections for collective bargaining. Political scientists Matthew Gentzkow and Jesse Shapiro found strong statistical evidence indicating that Republican and Democratic members of Congress tend to use different phrases. Today's successful politicians have refined the art of using coded language to appeal to narrow constituencies. In early-twenty-first-century America, when politicians praise a "culture of life," politically astute listeners know that candidates are not referring to issues such as access to health care or pacifism (or, for that matter, to petri dish experiments), all of which might sound to the unpracticed ear as relating to a "culture of life," but rather signaling opposition to legalized abortion. And so invoking the "founding fathers" has become coded political language, as has "perfecting the union." In American politics, the American Revolution is still being waged.

The politicized memory battles over events more recent than the Revolution, like the Vietnam War, have been characterized as being divided along lines of "official" and "vernacular" memory. The tensions between "official" and "vernacular" history, as scholars have defined them, are of at best limited use when thinking about our contemporary memory of the American Revolution compared to essentialism and organicism, just as the latter set of categories would be of limited explanatory power when considering the memory of World War II. "Official" history, on the one hand, refers to heroic, positive, nationalistic narratives that serve the state ("state" defined here in the generic sense), usually propagated by the government or its officers in official capacities. "Vernacular" refers to more local, particular, personal, and often painful memories, usually promoted by individuals, groups, and localities and tending to reflect their interests and priorities and to be much less celebratory. However, as we've seen from recent political speech, both essentialist and organicist interpretations of the Revolution are nationalistic, though in different ways. When competing presidential candidates, and indeed, alternating presidents, offer essentialist or organicist interpretations, to label one of those interpretations as "official" hollows out the specific meaning of the term. And at a distance of ten generations and with a tiny percentage of people having any family or local memory of the events of the American Revolution, "vernacular" memories of the Revolution are virtually non-existent in contemporary American memory. A significant exception to this distance is the oral history of African American families associated with particular founders, most notably the Hemings family. But those are balanced by the family traditions of the founding fathers' white descendants, whose memories are often are no less celebratory than coins, postage stamps, and statues—it's the stuff official memory is made of.

Nearly all scholars argue that when we study how an event is portrayed in contemporary life, we're not really looking at the past. Rather, we are looking at the present in which we recast history as a way of shaping the future. That's especially true, they would assert, in the case of politicians. Political candidates are most concerned with some combination of enacting policies about which they're passionate and getting elected (which of these two is more important varies by candidate and, perhaps, by the idealism or cynicism of the observer). They and their speechwriters are not trying to explore the past, to learn anything more about it, or to educate their audience; rather, they are trying to use bits of the past strategically to make their point and to motivate their listeners to vote for them. For politicians on the stump, the distant past can seem to be merely another treasure bin through which to rummage for useful rhetorical gambits, no less than popular culture, the relative merits of favorite regional dishes, their opponents' gaffes, the Bible, the comparative success of local sports teams, or yesterday's headlines. That's a far cry from a historian, having had many years of professional training, sifting through musty documents, analyzing and interpreting them, considering the writings of previous historians, and then offering a well-crafted interpretation that sheds new light on the past. Historians have a sense of responsibility toward their work and the past. We are trained to think in context, rather than to cherry-pick; to weigh evidence methodically; to wrestle with facts and interpretations that don't jibe with our own; and to produce interpretations that are nuanced, rather than dismissing life's complexities. No one in her right mind goes into history for the money. We do so out of a passion for the past. We choose the topics because they interest us, not because they're the subject of the next best seller. Speechwriters have no such call or obligation.

Even historians who perhaps ought to know better have sometimes claimed one founder or another as allied in some way with current political positions or parties. Historian Thomas Fleming, who has made a profitable career penning highly readable, well-researched accounts of the founding period and some of its most noted personages, has for some years written a wonderful intermittent online column called "Channelling George Washington," in which he conducts mock interviews with the first president's ghost. In January 2011, Fleming's Washington referred to the Federalists of the 1790s as the "forerunners of today's Republicans." Such claims are acts of selective recall, either inadvertently or perhaps willfully remembering some details and leaving out others. It's true that the Federalists tended to be more overtly nationalistic, to be more sympathetic to the wealthy, and to hate the French more than their opposite number, what were then called "Republicans" or "Democratic-Republicans"—just like today's Republicans compared to today's Democrats. But they also favored an active national government with a strong executive, burgeoning federal debts, and a powerful national bank (which in effect performed some of the same functions as the Federal Reserve Bank, the Treasury, and the Federal Deposit Insurance Corporation do today). Furthermore, many of them opposed the slave trade and even slavery and so could be said to be more forward thinking on race issues than the Democratic-Republicans. None of those characteristics describe the current Republican Party. For that matter, despite the current Democratic Party's being able to trace direct institutional lineage to those early republic Republicans, comparisons there are equally fraught. The party's first generations worked hard to keep slavery out of national politics—the better to protect the peculiar institution—and generally favored a weak national government and free trade, often at the expense of domestic manufacturing and workers.

Though this may be an uncomfortable thought, there's a little more commonality between political and academic practitioners than we professional historians, especially the academics among us—and I am one of them—might be willing to admit. No less than speechwriters and the politicians that employ them, historians have to make a living. When writing my first book, I was certainly motivated by a topic that, to me, was important and timely and that had contemporary relevance. What I had found was different than what previous historians had argued, and my conclusions were based upon years of archival research, close reading, statistical analyses, consideration of previous scholarship from various fields, and deep concentration. I was and am proud of the result, and the reviews in scholarly journals deemed the book a valuable contribution to how we think about the issues that the book addresses. But historians can't eat book reviews. Let's face it: had the book not been published, I would have lost my tenure-track position. Academic historians and self-employed authors must write to keep their jobs. Even for those historians with tenure, publishing is necessary for continued raises and professional advancement. While we like to think that the academic publishing peer-review system results in a pure meritocracy, the system is far from perfect, not always separating wheat from chaff. In addition, graduate students are either advised or get a sense of what sort of topics and interpretations are more likely to get published. It's not as bad as some conservatives have argued in terms of ideological litmus tests, but intellectual fashions do come and go. Most historians, certainly the historians of the American Revolution that I know, comprehend some connection between exploring the past and the present implications of their scholarship. The notion that we're transforming the world one footnote at a time is ultimately naive, but persists. At the same time, while I am perhaps jaded when thinking about political speech, I am also willing to credit most politicians with believing in the vision of the past that they're peddling.

Rather than a complete dichotomy between what historians write and what politicians say, or between history and politics, there exists a continuum of use and interpretation of the past. Historians may be at one end and politicians at the other, but we are all using it. We are all forwarding interpretations of the past. We have differing motivations and different standards. We rely in different proportions on what we think we know versus what we have to look up or investigate. Sometimes I wish speechwriters would be more responsible about that, but then again, I've also read many academic books and articles that could have benefited from some speech-writing punch. We all, or most of us, grew up in the United States, reading most of the same elementary-school textbooks, and for those of a certain age range, watching the same *Schoolhouse Rock* shorts on TV. We all have three visions of American society: how it was, how it is, and how it should be. And, to varying degrees, we try to bring that vision of how we want the nation to be into our professional work and our personal lives. The differences are ones of convention, that is, the cultural expectations of what it means to consider and use the past as a politician as opposed to a historian. One of those differing expectations between political rhetoric and formal historical writing—or at least, historical writing as it's practiced in the United States—is that politicians may send subtle cues about particular policies, but they are quite clear about their ideological worldview. By applying this chapter's charting of Revolutionary references against political ideology, we can see how the memory of the American Revolution itself has itself been politicized. We can then take this map and explore other phenomena like written history, public history, and films, where the practitioners are more cagey about their ideological predilections but where they and their audiences can nonetheless discern the consequences of their choices for how they interpret the American founding.

2

We Have Not Yet Begun to Write

Historians and Founders Chic

In January 2010, 2008, Republican vice presidential nominee and former Alaska governor Sarah Palin became a target of derision after a live television interview with conservative personality Glenn Beck because of her inability to name her "favorite founding father." Even Beck, a big Palin booster, found her indecision unsatisfying. Sarah Palin's choice mattered to Beck and, presumably, to his audience because it has become an ideological litmus test. Just as the ways that politicians invoke particular phrases from the Revolution tip their ideological hand, the choice of a favorite founder has also become a political tell. But perhaps more intriguing than Palin's answer ("all of them") was the question itself. Why such veneration of the founding generation, and why the necessity to pick favorites?

From the late 1990s, interest in the founding fathers has mushroomed. This fascination is rooted in more than the broad perception of contemporary politicians as unworthy of their predecessors, accurate or not, though that is certainly a factor. Other contributing elements include the essentialist appeal to the founders as a source of rhetorical authority and the rising stridency of an American conservatism looking to the past for heroes. But perhaps the key factor is the contrast between the Revolutionary era's powerful, decisive men and the perception, especially but not exclusively among today's politically conservative, of a United States whose cultural and political agenda seems increasingly focused on women, ethnic and racial minorities, and gay rights. For essentialists, the founding fathers' allure feeds nostalgia for white patriarchy. Organicist interpretations of the American Revolution challenge great men's greatness and sometimes forgo consideration of founding fathers entirely for stories about women and slaves. Notably, though, the great majority of recent best-selling books on the founding generation is about men, and most of their readers are men, too. David McCullough's best-selling, Pulitzer Prize–winning *John Adams* became the basis for the $100 million 2008 blockbuster HBO miniseries of the same name. Over the last decade, other best-selling books on the founding fathers include journalist Walter Isaacson's *Benjamin Franklin: An American Life* and academic Joseph Ellis's *His Excellency: George Washington* and *Founding Brothers: The Revolutionary Generation*. Cokie Roberts's best-selling *Founding Mothers*, which followed women through the American Revolution, is the prominent exception. *Newsweek* reporter Evan Thomas memorably labeled the renewed curiosity for the leaders of the Revolutionary generation "founders chic." But really, for the most part, it has been founding fathers chic. The use of founding "fathers" breaking away from a "mother" country is no coincidence.

This chapter considers founders chic, that phenomenon of high-profile books about the American Revolution. Authors are fighting their own subtle battle over the Revolution's contemporary meaning. Unlike politicians, who are clear about what they want (votes) but usually mention the Revolution in passing, biographers have all the room in the world for interpretation and nuance—but are much cagier about the political implications of their work. That doesn't mean that there aren't any implications or that authors don't consider them, only that sometimes we must look deeper to find them. Biographers have several ways that they throw an essentialist or organicist slant on their interpretations. They select whom to write about, they decide what to emphasize, they take sides with one interpretation or another, and, just as crucially, they choose what to leave out. In doing so, writers signal what they value and, in turn, what they believe their readers should value about their subjects, the American Revolution, and the nation itself.

There's a common misperception of a divide between conservative, highly positive biographies of founders intended for a popular audience and more critical ones written by academics, primarily for each other. But I found essentialist books written by academics, organicist books written by journalists and other independent authors, and vice versa. As historian Gregory Nobles has observed, academics writing about the American Revolution over the last two decades have tended to emphasize organicist topics: the enslaved, gender, Native Americans, the "lower sort." But that is not always the case, especially in professional historians' books intended for a popular audience. And several independent authors have written deeply organicist books for the general public. If there is a bright line between the books of academic and independent writers, it is that academic writers tend to think of the past as fundamentally different from today and past actors as being different from us. Independent writers, in contrast, are more likely to portray people in the past as thinking and behaving more or less like people in the present. But it's the divide between essentialists and organicists that elicits passion from writers on either side of the equation. What might seem like the most staid of conversations, one between reserved, tweedy academic authors, hides deep ideological animosity under a sheen of scholarly politesse. Changing interpretations of the founders and the adjudication of which founders were most consequential are part of a long conversation among historians, whether employed by universities or making a living by hawking their printed wares. Founders chic has become an ideological battleground, a proxy war waged by word processor.

Like anything that can be labeled "chic," founding fathers chic is a trend bound to a particular place and time, and dating its beginning is remarkably easy. *Newsweek* reporter Evan Thomas memorably labeled the renewed interest in the leaders of the Revolutionary generation. In an issue set to go on the newsstands in time for July 4, 2001, his article "Founders Chic: Live from Philadelphia" noted the appearance of McCullough's *John Adams* and Ellis's *Founding Brothers* on the bestseller lists and Congress's impending authorization of a national memorial to John Adams (a structure that remained little more than a gleam in the eyes of its supporters more than a decade later). Citing McCullough, who chalked up the founders' revival to "authenticity," Thomas suggested that, "in an age of media-obsessed, poll-driven politicians who cannot, it sometimes seems, make a speech or cast a vote without hiring a consultant, many Americans are nostalgic for an earlier era of genuine statesmen." (Thomas soon got into the act himself as the author of *John Paul Jones: Sailor, Hero, Father of the American Navy*, which briefly hit the best-seller lists in Fall 2003.) Much more than liberal politicians, conservative politicians have cultivated an air of "authenticity," of being, in George W. Bush's term, "deciders" who hold fast to principles rather than being buffeted by the winds of popular opinion and focus groups.

Many historians have mused on the reasons for the newfound founder fetish. Some have attributed the rise in interest in founding fathers to increased longing on the part of conservatives for an unambiguous, heroic past. That projection of a founders' true past becomes justification for policies and social positions that conservatives can associate with what they perceive as traditional values: the preservation of nuclear families consisting of a breadwinner husband, a stay-at-home mother, and god-fearing children who dress properly. That said, as historians Allan Kulikoff and Francis Cogliano have both observed, Americans across the political spectrum have always contested the merits of the founding generation. Current interest represents not only a resurgence of conservatism but also a rejoining of past battles on all sides.

There are other, more mundane factors, too. Famous founders may be among the most documented human beings on earth, making writing detailed biographies of them practical. They wrote prodigiously in dairies, to each other and for the public, and had a sense of history, wanting to keep copies of much of their correspondence, as did those to whom they wrote. The result is that some founders left literally tens of thousands of letters, diary entries, pamphlets, reports, and so forth. Over the last half century, those writings have been collected in massive, federally funded, multidecade projects, culminating in meticulously edited, published volumes of the major founders' writings. Many of these editorial projects were funded as essentialist projects to bolster nationalism during the Cold War, a development later decried by organicist historians like Jesse Lemisch, who astutely pointed out that much less had been done to preserve records shedding light on the rest of the population during the Revolutionary era. More recently, Ellis has suggested that the resulting research corpus represents "perhaps the fullest record of a political elite in world history." For example, *The Papers of Benjamin Franklin* began as a joint project of Yale University and the American Philosophical Society in 1954 and has published forty of an estimated forty-seven volumes encompassing the thirty-thousand some-odd Franklin-related documents that scholars have found. There's a reason we haven't enjoyed a flood of books on Patrick Henry, whose remaining papers number in the hundreds rather than the thousands. Although most of the books I looked at benefited from archival research, they all relied heavily on the published editions.

From the publishing side, biographies have provided tidy profits for the American publishing industry for at least a century. Popular authors like David McCullough, Walter Isaacson, Ron Chernow, and Joseph Ellis have become franchises, easily recognizable brands manufacturing a quality product. As historian H. W. Brands—who himself penned a Franklin biography—recognized, "The current revival reflects an appreciation of some brilliant writing. McCullough and Ellis are two of the finest nonfiction stylists now writing, and would attract readers whatever their subject." That these wordsmiths chose as their subjects men with nearly universal name recognition, like George Washington and John Adams, doesn't hurt. Founding fathers chic has been partly industrialized, from tax-dollar subsidized raw materials to the manufacturing process through distribution and marketing.

Nonetheless, founders chic may be more formidable for the heat generated rather than books sold. Noting that there hasn't been an explosion of Revolution-related movies and that attendance at Revolution-related historical sites like Colonial Williamsburg has declined over the 2000s, historian W. Fitzhugh Brundage has suggested that founders chic as a phenomenon appears mostly limited to trade publishing. Even in bookstores, Revolution-themed books form just one of many popular publishing trends. For my explorations of founders chic, I first looked for best sellers. Publishers guard their sales information like state secrets, and I couldn't afford to subscribe to Nielsen Bookscan, the least inaccurate measure of books sold in the United States. Unfortunately, the *New York Times* only counts relative sales in a given week, rather than absolute numbers, but it's the best I had access to. From 2000 through 2012, thirteen Revolution-themed books reached the *New York Times* hardcover, non-fiction best-seller list. A half-dozen books on the Revolution or about people from the founding generation were finalists or winners of the Pulitzer Prize for History or for Biography, and three tomes were winners or finalists for the National Book Award. I also considered at least another dozen books that didn't make either of these lists but were written by well-known historians and published by major commercial presses, especially those that made a splash in reviews and garnered other media attention. These sold less than a tenth of their better-grossing rivals (as of 2011, McCullough's *John Adams* had over three million copies sold). Professor Woody Holton's biography of Abigail Adams was fairly well publicized and moved around thirty thousand units, Professor David Waldstreicher's consideration of Benjamin Franklin less than a third of that. In retrospect, it doesn't seem like a huge number of books in a country of over three hundred million people. But their prominent placement in bookstores and the discussion of them in print, over the air, and online suggests that books on the founding generation have definitely struck a chord with the American public.

Long before a single copy is sold, the first choice any author makes is to choose a subject. The more academically oriented the author of a Revolutionary-era-themed work, the more likely that most or all of that writer's work concerns the founding period. That's a simple function of self-directed specialization and training. Career-long early American historians Joseph Ellis, Edmund Morgan, Woody Holton, and David Waldstreicher returned to the Revolution repeatedly, while independent writers like David McCullough, Ron Chernow, and Cokie Roberts have had Revolutionary phases to their careers come and go. What is more revealing than any purported divide between academics and non-academics is the particular figure or issue that authors tackle. For those whose books take on an essentialist slant, the choice usually comes down to a particular person. Several historians have observed that the founders who have gotten the most recent attention are the ones that have generally been claimed by conservatives as patron saints, among them George Washington and Alexander Hamilton. Founders chic has nearly passed by more radical founders like Samuel Adams, although the organicist historian Harvey Kaye took on the Revolution's most famous radical in *Thomas Paine and the Promise of America* (2006).

Of all the founders, Abigail and John Adams have received the most glorious rehabilitation, especially in relation to John's two-century-long reputation as brilliant but egotistical, dogged but obnoxious, and champion of independence but skeptical of common people. David McCullough's 2001 *John Adams* made the biggest splash of any founders-chic book. McCullough was no stranger to American audiences, having already written critically approved best sellers on topics ranging from the Brooklyn Bridge to the Panama Canal to Theodore Roosevelt, having hosted PBS's *American Experience* documentary series, and serving as narrator for many documentaries (most notably, Ken Burns's *The*

Civil War). The white-haired, avuncular McCullough seemed the very image of how many Americans imagine a historian: white, male, polite, baritone voiced, well preserved, and tweedy. After winning a Pulitzer Prize for his 1992 biography of President Harry Truman, he set to work on the original maligned one-term president. *John Adams* became an instant best seller and, indeed, may still be giant publishing house Simon & Schuster's biggest hit ever. In addition to flying off the shelves, it won the Pulitzer Prize for Biography, was made into an HBO miniseries (more on that in a later chapter), and even resulted in greater tourism for Quincy, Massachusetts, the town in which the Adamses' home is located. Regardless of John Adams's conflicted views on money, *John Adams* has been great for McCullough's pocketbook and serves as an examplar of the essentialist desire to find enduring rectitude in the founders.

As both its fans and detractors note, *John Adams* is first and foremost a celebration of Adams's character, one that finds him, above all else, a "good man." The book's first chapter introduces a John Adams "who cared deeply for his friends" and was "devoted to his wife." McCullough's Adams was "a great-hearted, persevering man of uncommon ability and force" and intellectually "brilliant . . . both a devout thinker and an independent thinker." Adams "was honest and everyone knew it." Which is not say that McCullough chiseled a marble statue in prose: Adams "could be high-spirited and affectionate, vain, cranky, impetuous, self-absorbed, and fiercely stubborn; passionate, quick to anger, and all-forgiving; generous and entertaining." He was "subject to spells of despair, and especially when separated from his family or during periods of prolonged inactivity." And of course, he was "ambitious to excel." Despite Adams's long political career and complex ideas, the book primarily considers his virtue. Even Adams's presidency, which impressed neither contemporaries nor historians, becomes ultimately measured not by its accomplishments (about which McCullough waxes nostalgic) or its failures (which McCullough glides past) as much as by how Adams weathered them. No matter the country's troubles: upon Adam's leaving office, his "bedrock integrity, his spirit of independence, his devotion to country, his marriage, his humor, and a great underlying love of life were all still very much intact." As with many admiring biographies, in *John Adams* Adams's achievements and laudable qualities—pushing for independence in the Continental Congress, negotiating loans from the Dutch during the Revolution, avoiding war as president, decrying slavery in his diary—were his own. His errors, like presiding over the 1798 Alien and Sedition Acts, the most repressive peacetime laws the nation has ever passed? Those were the fault of his times, which is how McCullough can paint Adams as a man for all times. And when something really wouldn't fit today's America, like Adams's nearly rabid distaste for democracy, McCullough doesn't mention it at all. As McCullough admits of his research and his thinking on Adams, "The man who emerges is truly heroic."

McCullough's writing process and the final product offer insight into the essentialist mind. Rather than political philosophy or acts of governance, integrity and doggedness separate McCullough's Adams from his more wanting peers. McCullough had at first set out to write a dual biography of Thomas Jefferson and John Adams. They seemed like opposite equals during the Revolutionary period, they carried on one of the most remarkable correspondences in American history as older men, and both died on the fiftieth anniversary of independence. But, as comes through clearly in *John Adams*, McCullough greatly admired the portly Massachusetts lawyer but not the willowy Virginia planter. So McCullough mostly wrote Jefferson out of the book, except to highlight how much of a spendthrift he was in comparison to the more miserly Adams, how many more letters Adams wrote to Jefferson than Jefferson wrote to Adams, and how Adams's virtuous views on slavery compared to Jefferson's perfidy. Having heroes rather than humans, as essentialism requires, necessitates villains rather than humans, too. Most essentialists find their villains in the organicists who, in their view, tear down the founders and thus critique essentialist values. McCullough, however, found in Jefferson a perfect foil for his admired Adams.

Essentialists find not only idols for the country but also personal heroes. Walter Isaacson's 2003 *Benjamin Franklin: An American Life* presents a judicious, if still complimentary, picture. Weighing in at 590 pages, it rang up over half a million copies in sales in its first year, second in founders-chic sales only to McCullough's *John Adams*. The book packed the kind of punch to be expected as a product of a writer and eventually national editor of *Time Magazine* and then CEO of CNN. Isaacson came to Franklin out of a sense of kinship—or perhaps "ambition" is the right word. Said Isaacson, "I was fascinated at how he had touched all aspects of my own career. I wanted to be more like Franklin. He retired at middle age from the world of media to become more involved in education and civic affairs," just as Isaacson left CNN a couple of years before the book was published. Isaacson saw in Franklin someone who, like him, had spent most of his career writing, editing, and managing media (for Franklin, newspapers and pamphlets; for Isaacson, a newsmagazine and cable news). Isaacson's adoration for Franklin comes through on the page. "Franklin is so lovable that I would spend the nights reading his letters," he fondly recalled about the ten-year period he worked on the biography at the same time he was running major media corporations. Isaacson wanted to rescue Franklin from the broad perception of him as "a penny-saving, penny-earning virtuecrat, when in fact he was a much more fun-loving and complex person who created his persona in the autobiography for PR purposes." Explained Isaacson, "You shouldn't confuse the maxim-spouting Ben Franklin with the wonderfully complex real person." Isaacson's Franklin, then, came across just as brilliant as the image Isaacson was trying to replace, only more canny about his public persona. For essentialist Isaacson, Franklin's timeless talent would transcend temporal boundaries between today and the past.

Essentialists also work to uphold their quarry's reputation. In *Alexander Hamilton*, author Ron Chernow plays not only the role of biographer but also that of defense attorney against the slander of Hamilton's foes, both those in Hamilton's own time and later historians, many of whom have judged him harshly. Chernow gushed that Hamilton was "charming and impetuous, romantic and witty, dashing and headstrong." One passage describes a former Treasury clerk's accusation that Hamilton, as secretary of the Treasury, had tried to manipulate securities markets for speculator William Duer. "It was testimony to the vile partisanship of the period," Chernow railed, "that a disgruntled former government clerk, tainted by a well-known history of drinking, could sustain such a public assault upon Hamilton's character." And yet the charge was plausible, surfacing mere months after Hamilton publicly admitted he had been engaged in a sordid extramarital affair. Duer and Hamilton were closely connected, and Duer's financial and real estate empire would soon collapse amid charges of wrongdoing. Time and time again, Chernow bats away the critiques of previous biographers.

As with McCullough's Adams, to Chernow, Hamilton's opposition to slavery trumps faults and elides misdeeds that might invite criticism. Among these were Hamilton's extremely antidemocratic views, his scheming to encourage a military coup near the end of the Revolution, his adventurism commanding an army to establish martial law in western Pennsylvania during Washington's presidency, his efforts to increase the federal debt so as to enrich wealthy speculators, his manipulation of Adams's cabinet, and his fermenting public desire for war against France in the 1790s (the same war that McCullough praised Adams for avoiding). Chernow excoriated "the slaveholding populists . . . celebrated by posterity as tribunes of the common people," in contrast to "the self-made Hamilton, a fervent abolitionist and a staunch believer in meritocracy," who has been "villainized in American history textbooks as an apologist of privilege and wealth." Chernow's next admiring biography was of one of those slaveholders, George Washington. For an essentialist, opposition to slavery means character, but as long as one has character, slaveholding is but a sign of past times.

Before criticizing Chernow too sharply for being seduced by Hamilton's personality and genius, we should remember that Chernow was not alone. On the Caribbean island of Nevis, Hamilton was an illegitimate son, orphaned at age twelve, but he impressed a local merchant enough for the man to sponsor the boy's passage to New York. Hamilton arrived with nothing but letters of introduction and enough money to partially support his college education (it took him a decade to pay off his debts—something that today's college students might find familiar). During the Revolutionary War, Washington relied on young Hamilton, who became a lieutenant colonel at twenty, often more than anyone else, entrusting him with tasks far beyond that of an adjutant. Hamilton partnered with James Madison and John Jay to pen the collection of essays that we now refer to as the Federalist Papers, influential in the debate over the Constitution's ratification and enshrined in the canon of political philosophy concerning representative government. As the first secretary of the Treasury, he was incredibly innovative. To say that he single-handedly invented modern finance or modern markets is a stretch, but a credible case could be made. And he was the prime strategist and intellectual light of the Federalists, one of the nation's two major political parties from the 1790s through the 1810s. I don't count myself among the advocates of Hamilton's ideas or policies, but to have done all this so quickly, and all on the power of his own personality, work, and intellect, should be enough to impress anyone. Chernow's biography exemplifies a signal challenge to how we think of the founding generation, especially its most gifted men. For all their faults, it is should be possible to note the achievements and qualities of men such as Washington, Franklin, Adams, Hamilton, Madison, and Jefferson without papering over their failings or merely repackaging the fiction that they single-handedly created what actually took millions of people to build—namely, a new country.

Most biographers' measured encomiums toward the founders read like backhanded compliments compared to conservative TV host Glenn Beck's ur-essentialist evaluation of the nation's first president. *Being George Washington: The Indispensable Man, as You've Never Known Him* graced best-seller lists in 2011. By "being" Washington, Beck meant that he (Beck, that is) and his readers should try their best to follow Washington's examples in their private and public lives. In doing so, Beck followed a long tradition. Among the best-sellers of the nineteenth century was Mason Weems's biography of Washington, the source of the chopping-down-the-cherry-tree story that Weems almost surely invented, meant to instruct young Americans on how to emulate the heroic founder. Beck began with a wink. "Contrary to popular belief, George Washington was not born as a 555-foot, 5-inch monument." But Beck did not cut Washington down much, calling him "a human, capeless superhero." Washington learned to be virtuous, disciplined, honorable, self-sacrificing, and god-fearing, and, just as Beck was trying to be, all Americans can attempt to be more like the nation's first president.

Passages in the present tense, or that relate undocumented conversations or the thoughts of historical figures (even, at one point, one of Washington's horses), signal that Beck's book had no pretensions of offering a traditional biography. Beck intended *Being George Washington* to be more immediate, exciting, and inspiring than conventional history. The book offered a chatty, accessible account of crucial moments in Washington's life, replete with Beck's habitual references to Star Wars, sideswipes at career politicians and government in general, and regular invocation of Washington's religiosity. Sidebars tell of

the peripatetic national government, which met in eight different locations before settling in the District of Columbia; the faithful support
of Glenn's wife compared to Peggy Shippen's leading Benedict Arnold
astray; and Washington's humility compared to today's politicians.
Among the book's appendices is a carefully curated list of Washington
quotations, intended to demonstrate Washington's virtuosity, opposition to government spending, commitment to national defense, distaste
for party politics, and warning against changing the form of government. *Being George Washington* presents a pure founder, whose timeless
political positions concord with Beck's own. It's essentialism distilled.

Some academic authors, too, write essentialist books about the
founders, even historians with a liberal bent. From 1996 through 2013,
no fewer than five of Joseph Ellis's volumes hit the best-seller lists:
American Sphinx: The Character of Thomas Jefferson (1996), *Founding
Brothers: The Revolutionary Generation* (2000), *His Excellency: George
Washington* (2004), *American Creation: Triumphs and Tragedies at the
Founding of the Republic* (2007), and *Revolutionary Summer: The Birth
of American Independence* (2013). Ellis's National Book Award–winning
Jefferson study inaugurated founders chic. Ellis came to the conclusion that the sage of Monticello was able to compartmentalize the many
aspects of his life to avoid confronting their contradictions. Much like
Isaacson's identification with Franklin, Ellis felt a kinship with the sage
of Monticello—both bookish, red-haired Virginians who attended the
College of William & Mary—an affinity strengthened when Ellis ventured north to graduate school in the 1960s. But his later books reaffirmed that his goal was in contending with the matchless men of the
founding. In the introduction to his Pulitzer Prize–winning *Founding
Brothers*, Ellis referred to the recent newfound reverence toward the
cohort that fought the Second World War. "Despite recent efforts to
locate the title in the twentieth century," Ellis argued, the small group of
men at the center of politics during the Revolution "comprised, by any
informed and fair-minded standard, the greatest generation of political talent in American history." Ellis has stayed loyal to his revolutionary subjects and the guiding principle underlying his interest in them.
Describing the thought process behind *American Creation*, he wrote
that "I come away from it still believing that the gathering of political
talent at this historical moment is unlikely ever to be surpassed." Though

informed also by his ability to be critical of his biographical subjects, Ellis's writing nonetheless betrays some essentialist admiration.

Perhaps unique among those who write primarily essentialist histories, Ellis's esteem for the founders' accomplishments has remained tempered by his critical eye toward the men themselves. In *American Sphinx*, Ellis tried "to steer an honorable course between idolatry and evisceration" of Jefferson who, Ellis acknowledged, "symbolized the most cherished and most contested values in modern American culture." For Ellis, Jefferson "was one of those dead white males who still mattered." Nonetheless, Ellis worked on the book with his eyes wide open to the moral and cultural morass biographers face when sizing up this most central and controversial of American Revolutionary icons. Ellis did not shy away from Jefferson's most notable contradiction. In describing the Virginian's arrival in Philadelphia, Ellis wrote that "the man who, precisely a year later, was to draft the most famous and eloquent statement of human rights in American—and perhaps world—history entered national affairs as a conspicuously aristocratic slaveowner." But Ellis also had a question to ask beyond simply what made Jefferson tick. He wanted to know how a man could juggle in his head contradictions like slavery and the equal creation of all men and how Jefferson could square his philosophical opposition to executive power and government spending with his unilateral, expensive Louisiana Purchase while president. Ellis concluded that Jefferson idealized the past and the future, but when it came to present paradoxes, Jefferson erected "capsules or compartments inside his own mind or soul . . . to keep certain incompatible thoughts from encountering one another." In other words, Jefferson was able to avoid putting two disparate thoughts into his mind at once when doing so might have been difficult or inconvenient. Ellis drew a Jefferson whose accomplishments stood beside grievous faults, among them a great failure to confront those shortcomings. As Ellis's biography demonstrates, because of the opportunities of nuance and texture that the hundreds of pages of a book allow, essentialist work can be highly sophisticated.

If contemporary writing about the American Revolution reflects anxieties and debates in contemporary American life, perhaps no arena is more fraught than that of the roles of women and men. "The old adage applies: Men make history," wrote Ellis in *Founding Brothers*. He meant to emphasize that events happen because of people's decisions, but his use of the male gender reveals more than he intended. Of the seventeen *New York Times* non-fiction Revolution-related best sellers from 1997 to 2012, all save one have been about men. Founder's biographers tend not to be shy in their treatment of their leading men. The "father of our country" has been the greatest object of authorial bromance. In *His Excellency*, Ellis described George Washington as "the epitome of a man's man: physically strong, mentally enigmatic, emotionally restrained." Ellis suggests that Washington's contemporaries thought of him as "physically majestic" and that "Washington's sheer physicality made his reserve and customary silence into a sign of strength and sagacity." Even Washington's prose, although "awkward," was at least "muscular" (perhaps Jefferson's more elegant prose seems flabby by comparison). I'm not accusing authors of making this up. Chernow, in his *Washington: A Life*, took pains to point out Washington's contemporaries' impression of his masculinity: four of the nine times the word "manly" appears in Chernow's book describing Washington, he's quoting Washington's admirers. That said, Chernow's detailing of Washington's body would not completely be out of place in a book published by Harlequin rather than Penguin. Chernow's Washington "was powerfully rough-hewn and endowed with matchless strength," so chiseled that "when he clenched his jaw, his cheek and jaw muscles seemed to ripple right through his skin." As a young man, Washington "possessed strong but narrow shoulders and wide, flaring hips with muscular thighs that made him a superb horseman. It was the long limbs and big bones, not the pinched torso, that hinted at superhuman strength, and his hands were so gigantic that he had to wear custom-made gloves." In addition to Washington's "massive physique," his "features were strong, blunt, and handsome." Excuse me; I'm blushing. To elevate the men, essentialists emphasize their masculinity.

If founder biographies serve as celebratory odes to founding fathers, their theme song for women would be "Stand by Your Man." *John Adams* was written nearly like a dual biography of John and Abigail, but not only did John get top billing, Abigail didn't even appear on the marquee. According to McCullough, John's pungent writing indicates that he could have been a novelist, but, despite Abigail's expert management of the couple's farm and finances for a quarter century while

John was off saving the world, McCullough never suggests that Abigail could have been an entrepreneur. Rather, she was only John's anchor, his helpmeet. Chernow praised Eliza Hamilton's forbearance during and after her husband Alexander's public admission of an extramarital affair. Isaacson at least criticized Franklin's brusque treatment of the long-suffering Deborah Read, Franklin's common-law wife, although not as strongly as Franklin's incredibly callous behavior deserves. Like nearly all historians, Isaacson stoutly denied that Franklin had sexual relationships with any other woman after he and Read were married, despite the many on-paper flirtations we know of. Maybe he did, and maybe he didn't. But for someone with such a reputation as a ladies' man, and as the acknowledged father of at least one son out of wedlock (William Franklin, the last royal governor of New Jersey), Franklin has gotten the benefit of the doubt for no reason other than he was a founding father, just as Jefferson used to. Big essentialist biographies tend to sell best before Father's Day and the holidays, and their prime purchasing demographic is white, middle-aged, older men. It's no stretch to think that contemporary angst concerning gender makes these biographies comforting to their readers. Regardless of either women's or men's behavior in them, the men remain admirable patriarchs in essentialist biographies, secure in their manhood as fathers of nation and family.

What makes these books essentialist is their searching for men who are not only men of their time but men for all time. "All my books are about courage and what makes civilization," said McCullough. "I'm interested in the creators" like the men who designed the Brooklyn Bridge, or John Adams, who had a hand in creating the nation. These biographers unabashedly emphasize that their subjects were crucial or, as historian James T. Flexner called Washington in 1974, "indispensable." For McCullough, as for Ellis and Chernow, the central question at issue is one of character outside of time. To Chernow, "One falls back on timeless truths about human nature. Think William Shakespeare instead of Sigmund Freud." But William Shakespeare was no less a product of his time and place than was Freud and no less or more universal. The turn-of-the-seventeenth-century English playwright's insights into human nature were for the most part about emotions (ambition, jealousy, love, revenge) and the exposure of his character's intentional inner lives. By contrast, the twentieth-century Austrian Jewish psychologist wrote of roiling inner lives (of the unconscious, of urges, of sex), suggesting that people are willful on their own as well as being organisms sometimes willful beyond control or knowledge. Freudian thought embodies a modern sensibility dangerous to conservatism in its implication that human beings may not have free will and that people are sexual beings. Perhaps it's no coincidence that author Fawn Brodie's Freudian rather than literary portrait of Thomas Jefferson was the first major book to argue openly that Thomas Jefferson had a sexual relationship with a slave, a quarter century before the DNA evidence came out (more on that later). The asserted timelessness of what essentialist authors choose to emphasize, such as leadership, vision, ambition, and honor, hides other parts of human nature that would place their subjects in a less-flattering light. Because these authors and their readers want the founders to serve as exemplars for us, to throw shadows on their subjects would cast doubt on our worthiness, as well.

Even those essentialist works that focus on women ultimately reinforce the idea of a male-dominated revolution and the timeless qualities, in this case, of their female contemporaries. Cokie Roberts's 2004 *Founding Mothers: The Women Who Raised Our Nation* spent eleven weeks on the best-seller lists. Roberts is a longtime broadcast journalist, primarily with National Public Radio (NPR); the daughter of two members of Congress; and the author of several best-selling books. She and her husband, Steve Roberts, write a nationally syndicated newspaper column. After Cokie penned a column praising Abigail Adams and Martha Washington, Steve told her, "This is your next book," and she agreed. Roberts's book presents what would appear to be an organicist subject, women, with an essentialist twist: it is explicitly "a book of stories—stories of the women who influenced the Founding Fathers." Roberts mostly sticks to those women who mothered or married the founding fathers we all know, although she does leave room for such women as Elizabeth Freeman (the enslaved woman whose suit for freedom resulted in abolition in Massachusetts) and Prudence Wright, who organized a group of women to protect their town near Lexington. Ultimately, though, rather than being women of their time, Roberts decided that "that there's nothing unique about them. They did—with great hardship, courage, pluck, prayerfulness, sadness, joy, energy, and humor—what women do." Roberts's founding mothers were no shrinking violets, and yet, ultimately, Roberts's book reinforces a world in which no matter how well or badly men behave, women forbear.

While essentialists find timeless traits, the practice of founders chic exemplifies changes in the politics of personality from the early 1990s on. American electoral politics has always revolved around a gloss of personalities and candidates' personal stories as much as the substance of policy and governance. In 2000, Democrats looked on incredulously as George W. Bush, the son of a president and grandson of a senator, and who favored tax policies largely slanted toward the rich, successfully portrayed himself as a political outsider and champion of the common (white) man. Such political positioning wasn't so very different from William Henry Harrison's campaign in 1840, when that scion of one of Virginia's first families won on the basis of a campaign emphasizing Harrison's invented (and false) cider-swilling and log-cabin-living lifestyle. The 2004 barbs accusing John Kerry of being an effete elitist were tame compared to the dirt hurled at the first Massachusetts-bred presidential candidate, that overambitious and obnoxious monarchist John Adams, or, for that matter, what Adams's supporters said about his two-time opponent, that Francophile atheist slave-lover Thomas Jefferson. Mitt Romney is a member of the Church of Jesus Christ of Latter Day Saints (that is, the Mormon Church), meaning to some voters that he was not worthy of being president—but not nearly as dangerous as Al Smith in 1928 and John Kennedy in 1960, both of whom, as Catholics, were sure to hand the pope keys to the White House. John McCain is the maverick, bucking party leaders—like the Great Engineer Herbert Hoover, who would use logic rather than party loyalty to untangle Washington's political knots. One might argue that electoral politics and questions of character and personality have always been joined at the hip in American culture.

But there is something qualitatively different in the age of the twenty-four-hour news cycle on cable TV news, talk radio, and the Internet. Political figures have become both increasingly exposed to the public and more isolated from everyday lives. We know their foibles, like celebrities (and they appear on the talk shows, blog, and twitter), but they are also enclosed in a bubble of staff, lobbyists, campaigners, consultants, donors, journalists, bloggers, and handlers. We are treated to an endless stream of each candidate's glories, while we bemoan their personal and policy failures: too many taxes and not enough services, too many regulations and not enough consumer protection, too much mollycoddling the poor and too much being soft on the rich, too much war and not enough security. Founders chic fits perfectly into the trend over the last twenty years toward the politics of personality. Rather than consider the policies that people stand for or the movements of which they are a part, American politics has increasingly emphasized personality. Comparing himself implicitly to Bill Clinton, George W. Bush ran on the strength of his character, on restoring honor to the White House. Subsequent Republican candidates have touted their own authenticity compared to liberals. Founders chic functions as an extension of personality politics. John Adams's incorruptibility made him a conservative model in the 2000s, no less than George Washington's virtue made him into Glenn Beck, or vice versa.

The recent canonization of Ronald Reagan by American conservatives provides an interesting parallel to their essentialized treatment of American Revolutionaries. In both cases, conservatives have characterized their heroes as hewing to unwavering and clear principles and then invested those idols with an authority to be broached at our peril. Even before the nation's fortieth president died in 2004, movement conservatives had begun to lionize him unconditionally. In 1997, Grover Norquist formed the Ronald Reagan Legacy Project, aiming to place a Reagan memorial in every U.S. county. The project connects politics with commemoration: it is a subsidiary of the lobbying group Americans for Tax Reform. The group wields politicians' pledges never to raise taxes as a cudgel against any measure that could be construed as a tax increase, regardless of current taxation levels, fiscal constraints, or how the revenue would be used. Despite Reagan's ideological opposition to bigger government, he was far more flexible and practical than Norquist would have his followers be. Although the Economic Recovery Tax Act of 1981 significantly cut federal income taxes, Reagan signed eleven bills during his presidency raising federal taxes of some sort or another, clawing back nearly half the revenue that the 1981 measure had lopped off. Conservatives have brandished Reagan's memory against nuclear disarmament, even though he initiated nuclear weapons limitation talks with the Soviet Union and later publicly advocated the end of atomic weapons. Reagan worship among Republicans became so thorough that, in

2008, Republican presidential primary candidates Fred Thompson and Mike Huckabee sparred over who had supported Reagan longer, with Huckabee making the astonishing case that backing Gerald Ford rather than Reagan for the Republican presidential nomination in 1976—as a majority of Republicans did at the time—was tantamount to apostasy. The ideological purification of Reagan's memory has come hand in hand with the demand among conservatives to purge moderates from the Republican Party, just as the sanctification of the founding generation represents essentialists' attempt to claim an American present free from what they perceive as divergent views of American politics and culture.

Founders chic also mirrors interest in another seminal American event. In the first years of the 2010s, as we're now deep in the grip of the many events commemorating the Civil War's sesquicentennial, the parallels between a revived love for the Lost Cause over the last couple of decades and founders chic have become ever more pronounced. Both were touched off by surprising hits. The mania for the Civil War predates that of founders chic by nearly a decade and can be pinpointed to September 21, 1990, the first night of Ken Burns's *The Civil War* on PBS. No one at PBS could have reasonably expected that a nine-part documentary featuring academic talking heads and camera pans of century-old photos would be its largest-ever blockbuster, exceeding the audiences of the commercial networks that week—inciting such mania that there was a run on blank videocassettes to tape subsequent episodes—and launching a whole new fascination with that conflict, just as few people could have foreseen that a cinderblock-weight biography of cranky, tubby John Adams would have topped best-seller charts and inspired an HBO miniseries (the connection between the two: David McCullough narrated *The Civil War* and wrote *John Adams*). Each harkens back to a purer, whiter, romanticized past, when men were men and did manly things while their women stood by them, when officeholders were statesmen rather than politicians, and when political causes were noble rather than tawdry. To be sure, marked differences abound. For founders chic, there are no hopes for the South to rise again and no sepia photographs of earnest young men soon to die. There's no magnolia—moonlit or otherwise—and no Rhett and no Scarlett. There are no fights over state flags, school mascots, or statues in town squares. There's a more ambiguous connection to slavery. And there's no equivalent to big Stars and Bars decals on pickup trucks. But those last differences are crucial and very revealing of founders chic.

The founders-chic best-seller phenomenon at times presents a gentrified, politically correct neoconfederate America. If you're into founders chic, you can be from anywhere in the country, you can show off that you're interested in history, you can have heavy books in your bookcase or uploaded onto your iPad, you can listen to audiobooks at your health club (and not be wearing a Stars and Bars T-shirt) or in your Acura (that might sport a sticker from your or your child's selective private alma mater), you can browse shelves in bookstores that serve lattes, you can talk about your reading at cocktail parties (for those people who still go to cocktail parties), you can show that you've joined the 2010s (or, at least, the 2000s). Many of the themes of today's Lost Cause percolate through founders chic, though in far more subtle undertones. There's still the gender bias in that the majority of the books are about men and few question their patriarchal mores. There's still an interest in slaveholders, made more palatable for elite audiences by noting how "conflicted" men like Washington, Jefferson, and Franklin were about slavery while mostly eliding their continued racism and, worse, the actual suffering of the slaves themselves—sometimes the tone of these books gives the impression that founding fathers were forcibly bound to their slaves rather than the other way around. And, like the Lost Cause, there's still the admiration for heroic figures of the past in contrast to those of today. The difference is one of class and region, in that the middle- and upper-class white men who are the primary audience of founders-chic books can, consciously or not, distance themselves from what they rightly perceive as the social stigma of Confederacy worship while still finding a comfortingly white, patriarchal, heroic American past.

In contrast to essentialist writers seeking to elevate the founders, organicist-leaning authors are more likely to be animated by particular issues or historical questions about the Revolutionaries and their times. In asking their questions, organicist writers evince a different sense of the past and its uses from their essentialist colleagues. It's more than organicists' holding a dimmer view of the famous founders' motives and actions than their essentialist competitors; it's breaking the hold founding fathers have on America's collective imagination. "I do not see myself as debunking individuals for its own sake, to redress some balance, though sometimes that is needed," says historian David Wald-streicher. "The obsession with their reputations," he suggests, "is itself the problem." Organicists want us to understand rather than emulate, comprehension that can only come if we are not walking on eggshells for fear of offending the past or present. Organicists want to shift our gaze elsewhere, broadening Americans' perception of who the found-ers were, by writing about more people than the handful of men who appear on stamps and money. Historian Gary Nash has asserted that "we have not appreciated the lives and labors, the sacrifices and strug-gles, the glorious messiness, the hopes and fears of diverse groups that fought in the longest and most disruptive war in our history with visions of launching a new age filling their heads." And finally, organicists argue that this broader Revolution had a more radical spirit than the famous founding fathers, the Constitution they wrote, and the Revolution as popularly remembered.

Today's organicist authors carry on a long tradition of historians plumbing the Revolution for progressive or liberal causes. For more than a century and a half, writers have been debunking the hoary leg-ends of an infallible founding or broadening our concept of who the Revolutionaries were and what the Revolution meant. Elizabeth Ellet's 1849, two-volume work *The Women of the American Revolution* profiled rich, celebrated women like Martha Washington and little-known ones like Esther Skinner, a widowed mother in central Pennsylvania who shepherded her children to safety after a battle. To show African Amer-ican contributions to the nation, and thus undercut racism, abolitionist William C. Nell compiled *Services of Colored American, in the Wars of 1776 and 1812* (1852) and *The Colored Patriots of the American Revolu-tion* (1855). Charles Beard's 1913 *An Economic Interpretation of the Con-stitution of the United States* contended that the Constitution did not represent the noble product of fifty-five eighteenth-century Solons but, rather, was the product of men whose main concern was the propping up of their speculative investments. The book set off a national furor. Appalled editors of the *Marion (Ohio) Star* raged, "scavengers, hyena-like, desecrate the graves of the dead patriots we revere." Not coinciden-tally, given the *Star*'s worship of the nation's framers, the paper's owner, future president Warren G. Harding, later coined the term "founding fathers." In recent decades, organicist historians have again examined the struggles of more obscure men and women. For historian Alfred F. Young, Deborah Sampson—a woman who dressed as a man to join the Continental Army—could serve as an example to "countless other Americans who seek to cross boundaries, and who will not be alone, thanks to the efforts of their forerunners." The implication is that everyone can participate in today's politics and society and that working for a more egalitarian, accepting society is no less American than cutting down cherry trees (or the confession thereof).

Not all authors writing about white, founding fathers are seeking what they perceive as eternal truths or a past peopled by better men. Academic historian David Waldstreicher has written two well-regarded books examining topics with a seemingly essentialist bent: Benjamin Franklin and the Constitutional Convention. Waldstreicher says, "I see myself as trying to stake out a postheroic position that tries to explain things the way they really happened, not just the sunny side that makes us believe how great America was and is." *Runaway America: Benjamin Franklin, Slavery, and the American Revolution* (2004) dedicates little rumination to Franklin's character or what we can learn from him that we can apply to current politics or, for that matter, to ourselves. Franklin has come off easy recently, especially among biographers like Isaacson, for his very late-life conversion to antislavery. But as Waldstreicher notes, just like Franklin's ostentatious wearing of a beaver-fur cap in France, Franklin's seeming championship of freedom was image building rather than game changing. *Runaway America* recounts the stories of eighteenth-century runaways along with Franklin's many encounters with freedom and unfreedom in his own life. For Waldstreicher, the book didn't even begin with Franklin. He was teaching a class on early America, and among the readings for the semester were Franklin's autobiography and a published collection of eighteenth-century newspaper ads (many in Franklin's own paper) describing runaway slaves and servants, offering rewards for their return. Waldstreicher began writing a book based on the ads but realized that their stories and Franklin's were intertwined. His next book was no less about great men than *Runaway America* and equally less about men's greatness. *Slavery's Constitution: From Revolution to Ratification* chronicles the founding generation's thoughts and actions concerning slavery from the 1760s through the drafting of the Constitution. Slavery, its implications, and how to reinforce it, Waldstreicher contends, weren't just incidental parts of the Constitution but in fact suffused the nation's central governing document. That accusation is no less harsh than Beard's.

In what was usually a very conscious decision to counter the story of a male Revolution, several authors of high-profile books chose women as their subjects. The most prominent scholarly biography of a well-to-do Revolutionary-era woman published over the last decade is history professor Woody Holton's *Abigail Adams: A Life*. Working on a scholarly article about Revolutionary-era speculators, he wanted to find one major holder of securities to represent the group. To his amazement, one of the names that jumped out at him was Abigail Adams. Although Holton's choice of an Adams involved a certain degree of serendipity, his writing about Abigail, and how he chose to write about her, is indicative of an intentional ideological mind. Holton hails from one of Virginia's most notable political clans. His father, Linwood Holton, was governor of Virginia in the early 1970s, and his sister Anne is married to Tim Kaine, a former governor of Virginia now serving as a senator. Before his academic career, Holton was a creative, increasingly liberal political operator (his cheekiest stunt was to print a full-deck "Pack of Lies," each card countering one of Oliver North's claims in North's ill-fated 1994 Virginia Senate run). His first book argued that planters like Washington and Jefferson were pushed toward revolution in order to maintain their position atop Virginia's political and cultural heap. Holton's second book detailed how the Constitutional Convention, and the document it produced, resulted largely from the fears of wealthy creditors and reflected their concerns. The goal of Holton's writing has been to elevate the contributions of everyone besides the great men—slaves, Indians, poor farmers, women. "My focus on ordinary people helps me justify the fact that I didn't go into politics," Holton has said. Holton's inclusive Revolutionary grunge work depicts and therefore promotes a far more inclusive society than the founders-chic books just down the shelf.

Other authors sought women from what early Americans called "the lower sort." In *Masquerade: The Life and Times of Deborah Sampson, Continental Soldier* (2004), Alfred F. Young doggedly revealed the life of a woman who dressed as a man in order to join the Revolutionary cause. Young dedicated his long career to recovering the lives of common people in the American Revolution, although he chafed at the idea

that any person was "common." He edited books on Revolutionary-
era radicalism, designed museum exhibits, and informally mentored
scores of scholars. By the 2000s, Young had achieved a status somewhere between patron saint and pied piper of organicist historians. After
having finished a book on Boston shoemaker George Robert Twelves
Hewes, he was asked, "Where are the women?," and Sampson seemed a
worthy topic. Young didn't paint Sampson as a feminist in the sense of
working to better the lot of women. But he noted that Sampson inspired
other women, both contemporaries and in later feminist movements,
just as she became a target of scorn for those in her time who abhorred
her transgressions. Of all Revolutionary-era women, the least rich one to
became most famous was Betsy Ross (beating out the composite historical figure known as "Molly Pitcher"). Historian Marla Miller gave Ross
the full-star treatment in *Betsy Ross and the Making of America*. Miller
wanted to dispel the haze that surrounds the legend of a poor seamstress,
consulted by a Washington-headed committee of the Continental Congress, devising and sewing the nation's first Stars and Stripes. The book
recounts the life of Elizabeth Griscom, as Ross was known for most of
her adult life, because, for Miller, Griscom's story "reminds us that the
Revolution . . . hinged not just on eloquent political rhetoric or character displayed in combat, but also on Betsy Ross and thousands of people
just like her—women and men who went to work every day and took
pride in a job well done." These organicist historians celebrate the labor
of everyday Americans, rather than the words of more prominent ones.

Historian and law professor Annette Gordon-Reed's path to her
organicist academic blockbuster emerged from a lifelong fascination
with Thomas Jefferson and race in America. As a third grader, she
read about the bookish Virginian and became captivated by his having written the Declaration of Independence yet being a slaveholder.
As a teenager she was already reading a published edition of Jefferson's
farm account book. In 1997—a year before DNA evidence emerged—
her *Thomas Jefferson and Sally Hemings: An American Controversy* was
published, marshaling a strongly documented and meticulously argued
assault on the flimsy evidence that had been used to deny Jefferson's
decades-long relationship with Hemings, whom he owned (and who
was his dead wife's half-sister). Gordon-Reed's 2008 *The Hemingses of
Monticello* follows Hemings's entire nuclear family, but Sally remains

the best-known figure. That book won just about every major award for which it was eligible, including the Pulitzer Prize, the National Book Award, and over a dozen academic prizes. Rather than praise the relationship between Thomas and Sally as a love match or decrying it as serial rape, Gordon-Reed at every juncture considered their potential motives, given what they knew and what the consequences might be. She offers readers informed speculations, for which she proposes conjectures that might be more likely than others based upon copious evidence. Perhaps the most interesting chapter is the one dealing with Thomas and Sally's time in Paris. Gordon-Reed asserts that Sally surely knew slavery was no longer legal in France. She could have walked away. That Sally didn't, Gordon-Reed argues, lends credence to the Hemings family's oral history of a bargain between Sally and Thomas: that he would set her children free. Gordon-Reed managed to write a moving story of the lives of slaves, and yet Thomas comes off as human, too. It's organicist history at its best.

What was left out of books is at least as telling as what was left in. Every writer must pick and choose what goes on the page. Otherwise, we'd be trying to relate the history of everything from the Big Bang (or, if you prefer, the book of Genesis) forward every time we touch the keyboard. Nonetheless, historians are taught that within the scope of what we've chosen to investigate, we must deal with all the evidence, no matter how unpleasant, complex, or contrary to what we'd like to believe. Perhaps because I'm a trained historian, I find McCullough's omissions far more egregious than Holton's. They both opted to leave out important figures. In contrast to McCullough's dropping Jefferson from *John Adams*, Holton wrote a biography of Abigail, rather than a joint biography of John and Abigail. The reasons for those choices are telling: for Holton, an intellectual choice to emphasize the underemphasized, for McCullough, a desire to bury what he did not like.

Unfortunately, as is often the case in essentialist histories, that urge to submerge the unpleasant, rather than deal with it, became necessary for McCullough to be able to paint John Adams as a hero for all times, including ours. McCullough perhaps intentionally ignored copious evidence that John abhorred common people and, by extension, democracy. For example, in passages concerning John's reaction to *Common Sense* and John's response, *Thoughts on Government*, McCullough notes

Adams's dissatisfaction with Paine's picture of self-government. But McCullough doesn't mention the real reason, one that John made no bones about in a letter to Abigail, that Paine was "too democratical." McCullough knew about the letter: he quoted other passages from it. But he wouldn't or couldn't admit that Adams hated democracy. For their part, organicist takes on the past often emphasize the lives of people who in some way challenged the gendered, racial, or class structures of their time. In doing so, they sometimes let us forget that most common people were not radicals, most slaves did not rebel, and most women accepted their subsidiary legal status. In fact, none of the people depicted in these books were people of our times, and to make them so is a disservice to them and to us.

Founders-chic biographies also tend to beatify the founders by leaving something out: in addition to being statesmen and generals, the founders were also very much politicians, and often narrow ones at that. To be fair, part of the challenge here for biographers—and readers—is that eighteenth-century American politics were very different from contemporary politics. Today, candidates run for election; then, they stood for office. The difference between the active metaphor of "running" and the passive metaphor of "standing" is very apt. Today's candidates must tirelessly press the flesh, boldly ask for political donations, and shamelessly explain in ads, speeches, and debates why they are better suited than their opponents. A candidate who attempts to stand by the wayside would nonetheless be political roadkill. Today's campaigning would have appeared scandalous in eighteenth-century America, especially among the elite men most likely to be candidates. At least as they described their own actions, candidates would let it be known that they were amenable to holding office. Their friends, relations, and allies would talk up the candidate by the quill in private letters and by the pint in taverns. As with any political claims, these suggestions of gentlemanly repose should not be taken at face value because, privately, candidates almost invariably accused their opponents of unseemly pandering. Yet they still found ways to campaign. In the South, candidates were expected to "treat" all voters, regardless of their political predilections, by paying for drinks at militia musters and county court days, which one Virginian witheringly described as "swilling the planters with bumbo," a popular rum-based punch. There's little in the biographies of Jefferson's or Adams's electioneering, much less of Washington's land acquisitions in the context of Virginia and federal policy (the relocating of the capital made him big money). Excepting Holton's significant discussion in *Abigail Adams*, no biographer notes that securities issued by the Continental Congress and then Congress, voted for by John and invested in by Abigail, were the sources of the Adamses' nest egg in old age. We're left with evaluations of politicians without their politics, especially actions that would make them look more like ordinary men on the make than extraordinary statesmen.

The unspoken lament in much of founders-chic literature is that today's politicians don't live up to the standards of their eighteenth-century predecessors. Those founding men didn't read polls; they consulted their Plutarch for political wisdom. In terms of the prominent use of allusions to ancient Roman senators, today's biographers are right. But few of the men who were among our foremost founders would stand a chance in today's politics, either. Washington was stiff and forbidding. Jefferson was a poor public speaker. Adams was notoriously undisciplined in his remarks. Today we rail against politicians whose entire career is in government, but John Adams was in office (elected or appointed) nearly all his adult life and didn't make a dime on his own from 1777 until his retirement in 1801. Thomas Jefferson alone has been the subject of a best seller focusing on politics. Confessing that "one of my many character flaws is that I actually like politicians," journalist Jon Meacham took on the project specifically because "I thought that Jefferson as a political figure had not been fully examined." Meacham's admiring essentialist biography, *Thomas Jefferson: The Art of Power*, treats the Declaration's author as a canny moderate fashioning compromise with his foes for the nation's sake. It's a strange take. Like *Time Magazine* (or, for Meacham's sake, *Newsweek*), Jefferson can be quoted to support just about any position along the American political spectrum: he wrote thousands of letters to hundreds of people over a period of six decades, and was particularly adept at offering vague bromides that allowed his correspondents to hear what they wanted to hear. But that's different from compromising. Jefferson resigned from Washington's cabinet rather than find a way to work with the admittedly headstrong Hamilton. Other authors discuss positions but rarely the men directly as politicians. That might shatter the illusion.

Although one might think that professors refrain from political battles, their writings on the Revolution suggests otherwise. In academic circles, the most prominent essentialist historian of the American Revolution remains Gordon S. Wood. Wood's first major book, *The Creation of the American Republic* (1969) won the Bancroft Prize (an annual award for the best book in American history); his second major book, *The Radicalism of the American Revolution* (1992) won the Pulitzer Prize; and his third major book, *Empire of Liberty: A History of the Early Republic* (2010), was a Pulitzer Prize finalist. They are expertly researched, elegantly written, and powerfully argued. The first book of his grand trilogy details what elite Revolutionaries thought they were doing, and the last two relate how elite Revolutionaries bemoaned what everyone else was doing. He has defined the Revolution as "constitutional and conservative" in its intent but radical in its results of universal white male suffrage and the rise of an abolitionist movement, although he was only able to stake those claims by stretching the Revolution to the 1830s. As early as 1989, historian Colin Gordon noted the conservative strain in Wood's scholarship. For his part, Wood disdains organicist critiques of the Revolution. In no fewer than three of his books in the 2000s, Wood dredged up the same quotation straw man, of which he does not identify the source (it's actually from a 1991 book on Native Americans), that the Revolution "failed to free the slaves, failed to offer full political equality to women, and failed to offer citizenship to Indians." Rightly noting that these were unrealistic expectations, Wood tars all organicist interpretations with the same brush, suggesting that such takes "tell us more about the political attitudes of the historians who make such statements than they do about the American Revolution."

For Wood, what he perceives as the politicization of history constitutes a cardinal professional sin. Asked for advice about what topics potential historians should study, Wood offered only two pieces of wisdom: first that students should follow their passions, and second that, "above all, they should not treat their history writing or history teaching as conducting politics by other means." Perhaps Wood perceives himself as above or beyond the world of politics. One of the central messages of Wood's scholarship is that the elite founding fathers deluded themselves, wanting to establish a republican form of government by men like themselves but instead getting a democracy. Wood believes he exposes eternal truths about the men who matter, while organicists merely play politics. In the greatest of ironies, Wood has never admitted publicly, or perhaps even to himself, that his choice of topics and his interpretation of them are no less political acts than those of the organicist historians that he deplores. To be fair, his professional historian colleagues have not always treated him kindly, either. During my first year in graduate school, among the proceedings at the annual conference of the Organization of American Historians—the primary professional organization dedicated to the study of American history—was a forum on *The Radicalism of the American Revolution*, released the previous year. Given the announcement that the book had won the Pulitzer Prize just days before, Wood expected at least some praise, which is customary at such events. Rather, a few of the panelists took a verbal machete to what Wood perceived as his masterpiece, the result of two decades' research, thought, and writing. Wood was so shaken that my dissertation advisor took him out for a consolatory drink. But, then again, Wood is far from blameless, having made a habit of harping on other historians for being "political" rather than extending them the good faith that he would like his own readers to extend to him.

Gary Nash ably plays the role of Wood's organicist nemesis. Although both are products of traditional, conservative universities, Wood remained ensconced in the Ivy League at Brown University, while Nash ventured west to UCLA. Wood has won more popular kudos, but Nash has been no less influential on the academic profession, having trained a veritable army of historians, written or edited close to two dozen books, served as president or on the board of a range of professional organizations, and been a point man in the culture wars over public history and history education. He shaped his career around recovering and retelling the stories of everyone during the Revolutionary period other than the great white men. Up to the 2000s his most well known books included *Red, White, and Black* (1974), one of the first multicultural history textbooks; *The Urban Crucible* (1979), an analysis of the role of economics and class in the third quarter of the eighteenth century; and *Forging Freedom* (1988), which chronicles Philadelphia's African American community from the 1720s to the 1840s. No stranger to politicized history dustups, Nash was one of the co-directors of the writing of the National History Standards in the early 1990s, an effort initiated by Lynne Cheney, George H. W. Bush's appointment for the National Endowment for the Humanities. However, once the standards were published, Cheney and others attacked them, and they were eventually scrapped. Although Nash's tone in his academic writing is no less authoritative than Wood's, his choice of topics and interpretation are worlds away from his East Coast rival.

Nash's *The Unknown American Revolution: The Unruly Birth of Democracy and the Struggle to Create America* (2005) serves as a capstone to his scholarly career. Nash wanted to tell the story of the "ordinary people who did most of the protesting, most of the fighting, most of the dying, and most of the dreaming." They did so, according to Nash, in search of "a redistribution of political, social, and religious power; . . . the overthrowing of ingrained patterns of conservative, elitist thought; the leveling of society so that top and bottom were not widely separated; the end of the nightmare of slavery and the genocidal intentions of land-crazed frontiersmen; [and] the hope of women of achieving a public voice." Nash illuminated the struggles of people like the black patriot Lemuel Haynes, the Cherokee warrior Dragging Canoe, the tenant farmer champion William Prendergast, and the poet Phillis Wheatley. Nash thereby demonstrates that national independence and the establishment of a capitalist order were far from the only Revolutionary aspirations, and in fact they often came in conflict with many people's desire for a more equitable society in the form of freedom and full citizenship for African Americans and a more broadly democratic economy and government. In doing so, Nash's book provides a rich riposte to the essentialist fawning over the founding fathers as having created a virtuous republic all on their own. Just as Wood's scholarship mostly ignores common people, Nash mostly ignores their faults. No less than their richer neighbors, Revolutionary-era common white men, too, generally aspired to own slaves, take Indian lands on the cheap, and lord it over their wives (who otherwise wanted much the same things) and believed themselves to be better than French Catholics, blacks, and Indians—as their actions indicate. Essentialist scholarship often romanticizes the famous founding fathers, while organicist scholarship risks romanticizing everyone else.

As avatars for their respective academic camps, Wood and Nash have no love lost between them. In a 1987 journal forum dedicated to considering *Creation of the American Republic*'s enduring scholarly influence, Nash blasted Wood for ignoring Revolutionary-era newspapers and manuscripts that might have broadened his view. For Nash, *Creation of the American Republic* was "incomplete, too homogeneous, too static, and too shallowly rooted in the soil of social experience." Nash accurately pointed out that Wood's book brushes aside "the thought of social groups separated by barriers of race, class, and gender from the white male elite with which Wood is primarily concerned," thereby blinding Wood even to the implications of the elite men's words he wrote about. For academic historians, them's fightin' words. In turn, Wood has bared his contempt through a series of nasty reviews in proper places, like the highbrow *New York Review of Books* and the *New Republic*. To some extent, Wood's critiques of Nash, and by extension much of organicist history, hit the mark and, in other ways, goes over the top. Wood's review of *The Unknown American Revolution* begins with the obligatory acknowledgment of Nash's early contributions before tearing apart the book and its author. "Nash is so bound up in the modern Marxian categories of class warfare," Wood fumed, "that he can make little sense of what happened." Although *The Unknown American Revolution* follows many of the issues that it raises through to the early nineteenth century, the book ostensibly ends at 1786. Nash thereby avoided the conundrum of considering the Constitution, which, despite its undeniable pro-slavery and anti-democratic bent, was nonetheless celebrated by many common people upon its adoption. Wood and Nash have grown even more uncivil to each other in their own scholarship. For historians, the only thing worse than being cited negatively is not being cited at all. Neither man even bothers to refer to the other's work in his own research, no matter how important, useful, or relevant—as if celebrated physicists Stephen Hawking and Richard Feynman somehow managed to write papers about the same topic while ignoring each other's discoveries. It's gotten personal because it's political.

The feud between Nash and Wood should dispel any vestigial illusion that the ivory tower rises above politics' din. We academic historians of the American Revolution have long denied the idea, even to ourselves, that we are engaged in a form of civic debate. This was not always the case. The nation's first historians were very clear in their understanding that the history of the Revolution should not and, indeed, could not be separated from contemporary civic concerns. The roots of historian's disavowal of politics in their work grew over the last century with the professionalization of academic history in the United States. Professionalization has been a marvelous development, resulting in rigorous standards for training, broadly agreed upon criteria for the evaluation of historical writing, and venues in which to debate historical interpretations. But even with the postmodern realization, now nearly universally accepted, that historians cannot possibly be objective automatons, most professionally trained historians have internalized the idea that the discipline of history remains an intellectual exercise from which present social, political, and civic concerns must be banished. We otherwise risk the dreaded charge of "presentism"—that is, looking at the past through the lens of the present. Few historians have had the courage and self-awareness to point out what Jesse Lemisch did in 1971, when he wrote that "American historians—left, right, and center—are welcome to their politics, but there is no denying that they *have* politics."

This withdrawal has accelerated over the last forty years. With the 1960s explosion of educational opportunity in the United States, the professoriate has become increasingly diverse and liberal at the same time that a more politically powerful and strident conservative movement has sought to marginalize liberal voices from public debate. One of the major scholarly journals of early American history has at times discouraged authors from openly considering the contemporary implications of their conclusions in its pages. Academic historians live between the accusation of lacking professionalism and the conservative charge that liberal academics are foisting their views on students. We are left with what sometimes seems like an insurmountable combination of professional, personal, and political constraints on admitting that we are engaging in civic conversation with our scholarship. That's not to say that such obstacles can't be overcome, only that historians have become reluctant to try.

The continuing battle over Thomas Jefferson's relationship to slavery, and with Sally Hemings, reveals how tangled the politics of founder history has become. Jefferson's reputation among historians has been the most volatile of any of the founders, but on one subject they had long spoke in unison: that he was not the father of Hemings's children. They took Jefferson at his word when he refused to engage an

1802 accusation that he was sleeping with "dusky Sally," a charge that echoed through newspapers at the time. And academic historians discounted the Hemings family oral history, especially because Jefferson family oral history offered the convenient if flimsy alibi that Thomas's nephew Peter Carr fathered Sally's children, thus accounting for physical resemblances. Then Fawn Brodie's 1974, best-selling psychological portrait *Thomas Jefferson: An Intimate History* extrapolated from little evidence that Jefferson and Hemings were lovers. Still, because no written records directly indicated that Thomas had feelings for Sally, historians could continue to tell themselves and their readers that the great (white) man could not have had a relationship with an enslaved (black) woman. Ellis's *American Sphinx* (1997), which climbed the bestseller lists within months of when Gordon-Reed's book-long brief was published, denied any sexual connection. But that same year, Ellis was contacted by a reviewer from a scientific journal, asking him to weigh in on the meaning of DNA evidence collected from Hemings descendants and compared to the Jefferson line. In response to "What does it mean?," Ellis replied, "He did it." In 1998, Ellis co-authored an article about the DNA. Putting the DNA results alongside the early 1970s discovery that Jefferson had been at Monticello nine months before each of Sally's births, Ellis changed his mind and even *American Sphinx*, for which he re-wrote various sections, stating that the sexual liaison "is now proven beyond a reasonable doubt." Essentialist Ellis had only been one in a long string of historians to suspend disbelief concerning Thomas and Sally. Now, as a responsible historian, he had given organicists their greatest ammunition.

Many Jefferson admirers denied and decried the new developments. After the DNA evidence was released, the Thomas Jefferson Memorial Foundation, which runs Monticello, immediately modified how it interpreted the plantation's designer, and in 2000 it released an exhaustive review of all research to that point, concluding that a preponderance of evidence indicated "a high probability that Thomas Jefferson fathered Eston Hemings, and that he most likely was the father of all six of Sally Hemings's children appearing in Jefferson's records." But a minority of the members of the foundation commission that wrote the report issued its own rebuttal. They relied almost entirely on Jefferson's sole, oblique denial of the affair in a letter to a political supporter, the misdirections of a few of his white descendants, and the observation that the statistically high probabilities of Thomas's paternity as determined by the timing of Sally's pregnancies and the DNA evidence still was not 100% (exactly the kind of evidence Gordon-Reed had found so thin). They perceived the great man to be besmirched with charges of tawdry interracial sex, about as far from essentialist heroism as one could fall. The God and Country Foundation, dedicated to protecting the nation's proud essentialist heritage, held a declamatory press conference, featuring Jefferson genealogist Harold Barger to "correct a great injustice to a great Founding Father." Some members of the organization of Jefferson's white descendants, the Monticello Association, balked at allowing Hemings family members to attend their annual gathering; protested one, "We're not racists. We're snobs." That barrier, too, eventually fell, although not without resistance. For a few years, the Jefferson field lay fallow, but enterprising writers and their publishers could not long resist the Sage of Monticello's siren call. Essayist, journalist, and intellectual Christopher Hitchens penned the short biography *Thomas Jefferson: Author of America* (2005), and Jon Meacham produced *Thomas Jefferson: The Art of Power* (2012), both admiring portraits little concerned with slavery. But Jefferson's image as a man only of ideas, rather than one of the flesh, had taken an irreparable hit.

In what seemed like a role reversal, organicist Annette Gordon-Reed eventually rode to Jefferson's rescue concerning his relationships to slaves and slavery. Independent scholar Henry Wiencek's *An Imperfect God: George Washington, His Slaves, and the Creation of America* (2003) earned kudos from essentialist historians John Ferling and Gordon Wood, as well as from organicist historians, as a model of how to deal with the founders and slavery. It chronicled Washington's halting transformation from a typical Virginia plantation owner to the only major founder who freed all his slaves (although only in his will, revealed upon his death). Wiencek's sequel, *Master of the Mountain: Thomas Jefferson and His Slaves* (2012), was far less forgiving of its subject. Wiencek attributed Jefferson's public about-face concerning slavery, from denunciations in the 1770s to silence in the 1790s and beyond, to what he identified as Jefferson's "4 percent theorem," a 1792 estimation that slaveholding netted Monticello's master "a 4 percent profit every year on the birth of black children." Wiencek further charged that this "Henry

Ford of slavery" practiced a slavery "crueler than we have been lead to believe." The debate over Wiencek's assertions played out in the reviews, reporting, and op-ed pages of a slew of national print and online publications. Unlike in previous controversies, this time organicist historians took Wiencek to task for flaying a famous founder. Their beef was that he wrote with what retired Monticello historian Lucia Stanton characterized as "a breathtaking disrespect for the historical record and for the historians who preceded him." Worse, "rather than tell[ing] us anything new about Thomas Jefferson and slavery," Gordon-Reed charged, "it is, instead, a book about Henry Wiencek," who was attempting to "become the *true* protector of the enslaved people of Monticello." According to his critics, he was even tougher on Jefferson than the sources warranted. Here we have Gordon-Reed, a scholar whose works have been among organicists' most celebrated, taking another organicist to task for injecting his own political agenda for history. An essentialist could not have done it any better. Maybe, just maybe, we're all playing politics.

This chapter began with my wondering why it should be asked who someone's favorite founder is. Just as Glenn Beck meant the founder fave question to be a litmus test for Sarah Palin, perhaps I once took it the same way. As a kid, I read a lot, especially about the past—not exactly a surprising revelation coming from someone with a Ph.D. in history. Growing up, I had a weak spot for Thomas Jefferson, he of the lofty language and eclectic accomplishments. I empathized with his temperament and his politics: his use of seemingly democratic and sometimes even radical language, his championing of the division between church and state, and his status as Democratic Party icon. Having a fondness for technology and architecture, I also appreciated his being an inventor and designing his beloved Monticello. He was even tall and gangly, as I've always been. Everyone pays homage to that other tall Revolutionary, George Washington, but Washington has always been a conservative hero, even more than Hamilton (evangelicals and small-government folk don't have much positive to say about Hamilton, that little-churched father of the national debt). Washington was even more remote from me than he was to his contemporaries, who found him to be stiffly reserved. I knew enough about Adams's self-admitted obnoxious disposition—maybe from having seen the movie 1776?—not to hold him in too worshipful a regard, plus he was a lousy president and quite disdainful of common people. As an adult, I grew ambivalent. By my time in graduate school in the mid-1990s, enough evidence had surfaced for me to believe that Jefferson had indeed engaged in some kind of long-term sexual relationship with a person he could have beaten, bought, or sold, and for all his soaring prose, Jefferson freed no slaves except his own offspring. I had gained critical maturity but lost a sense of admiration for truly remarkable achievement.

By the time I began my work on this book, if you were to ask me who my favorite founder was, I would have said, "None of them." I'm not sure my opinion has changed over the course of my writing, but now at least I have a better idea of what choosing a favorite founder—father or not—would mean. As philosophers of history and of memory have observed, history has always been ideological, inherently political. Just like moviemaking and public history and even politics, history writing has its standards and ethics, but it will remain a healthy component of Americans' debates concerning our past and, by proxy, what we want for ourselves as citizens and as a nation. Essentialist histories continue to emphasize the outsized accomplishments of a few white men establishing a nation but retaining order. In doing so, wittingly or no, they make the political and cultural argument that the United States is a tidy, white, conservative, patriarchal nation. For their part, organicist writers picture a multicultural, forward-thinking and sometimes even radical past, potentially inspiring a more progressive present. In a casual interview, Annette Gordon-Reed was asked, "Who are your favorite historians?" Perhaps remembering the flap over Sarah Palin, Gordon-Reed replied, "All of them." I'm either a bit less charitable than Gordon-Reed or a bit less diplomatic; maybe it's because I know and read so many historians. We are, after all, people. And as people, we are inherently political animals. That's doubly so when writing about the American Revolution from whatever viewpoint.

3

We the Tourists

The Revolution at Museums and Historical Sites

In the summer of 2011, I traveled to the pasts. I say "pasts" because I mean more than one: the various contested notions of our nation's past, as well as my own. In mid-June, I packed up a suitcase, my computer, and some books, and started up my time machine, ingeniously camouflaged to look exactly like a well-cared-for 2001 Ford Focus. I headed east from my current home in northwest Ohio. Over the following month, in addition to attending a challenging seminar that met three days a week in Philadelphia, I drove nearly 3,200 miles in my personal quest to see the Revolution represented. I visited forty-three buildings and sites and observed sixty-four different talks, tours, films, and programs, many of them multiple times. I traipsed around three of the nation's largest cities and several smaller ones. I talked to scores of interpreters, tour guides, curators, park rangers, storytellers, and administrators. I took 1,374 pictures, admittedly a bit excessive, but with a digital camera, they're only pixels. Counting my temporary home base—a spartan dorm room at Philadelphia's Drexel University—I spent the night in ten different locations (none of them places where Washington had slept, at least to my knowledge). I ate several eighteenth-century-style meals and drank more than several eighteenth-century-style beers. In all these experiences, I tried to look through the eyes of tourists and museum professionals, of laymen and historians, of white folk and black folk, of women and men, and in any other way that I could. Focusing mostly on Philadelphia, as the de facto capital of Revolutionary America, I also considered a few other places central to Revolutionary remembrance, including Mount Vernon, Monticello, and Colonial Williamsburg (CW).

Most Revolution-related historical sites and museums that I visited presented variations on one seemingly innocuous theme, liberty. At the same time, they offered elements of essentialist and organicist interpretations that varied according to a range of constituents including not only audiences but also their staffs, their donors, and their parent institutions. The various historical sites, museums, and attractions that I visited are engaged in the same ideological discussions concerning the American Revolution as politicians and writers but in different and more subtle ways. Politicians are free to appeal to a small, energized, ideological slice of the electorate, with the knowledge that their words are ephemeral. They reach for the Revolution precisely because they can use familiar tropes that resonate with audiences who will not question their veracity. Book authors can count on having the space to make an extended argument with more nuance but lacking the punch of political speech. Neither holds true for museums and historical sites, which have the time, motivation, resources, and desire to portray history responsibly (I don't write "accurately": they're not always right on verifiable details, and they often disagree on what's important). Most sites and museums hone particular exhibits over years of development, often in consultation with on-staff and external advisors. They have an eye toward broad potential audiences, wanting to draw in as many visitors as possible across the nation's political spectrum while offending no one. But they have a fickle audience with a short attention span. Furthermore, most of these are non-profit and must be mindful of their sponsors, whether public or private or, in many cases, both. American Revolution sites, museums, and attractions provide an accessible and nuanced but nonetheless ideological presentation of the American Revolution, and with critical issues at stake: not only how we think of the Revolution itself but also its implications for contemporary American society.

The nation's most sacred Revolutionary pilgrimage site is presented in a distinctly essentialist frame. The National Park Service (NPS) administers Independence Hall and its attendant structures as well as various nearby sites as part of Independence National Historical Park (INHP). Half-hour, eighty-four-person tours run through Independence Hall every fifteen minutes all day, every day but July 4 (when throngs of people are quickly herded through) and Christmas (when it's closed). Led by NPS rangers, Independence Hall tours begin in a side room with the usual disclaimers and rules for big tours in old buildings—photographs but no cell phones, videos, smoking, food, or drinks, and so on—and

Figure 3.1. Independence Hall, Revolutionary Philadelphia's grandest building, now dwarfed by the ordinary office buildings behind it. The tower is covered by netting painted to look like the tower, camouflaging the scaffolding necessary for restoration work.

Figure 3.2. Ceremonial Reading of the Declaration behind Independence Hall. A local news camera captures the action.

an explanation of the large painting in the room. Completed in 1987, it portrays the signing of the federal Constitution in 1787, affording the ranger the opportunity to point out a familiar figure, George Washington, and to explain that Independence Hall hosted both the Continental Congress and the Constitutional Convention. The tour progresses through the two main ground-floor rooms in Independence Hall: first the courtroom, then the room that tourists have really come to see, the Assembly Room, in which the Declaration of Independence was signed. Both rooms have a railing, limiting camera angles and preventing contact with the furnishings. Shepherding a group takes up more time than one might think. The ranger's challenge is to explain American national independence, the Constitution, colonial jurisprudence (in the courtroom), and something about the building and its various artifacts in under twenty minutes' talking time to an audience that cannot be assumed to know anything. I know something of that challenge, having faced a similarly daunting task when I worked as an interpreter at

CW's Capitol Building. Perhaps a provocative rethinking of the American Revolution and of its relation to the contemporary United States would be too much to ask. The essentialist tour celebrates essentialist documents in the structure in which they were written. The building is at once full of the rangers' loud tones and tourists' shuffling and clicking and murmuring but devoid of eighteenth-century life.

By contrast, the square behind Independence Hall teems with vibrancy for the INHP's annual showcase spectacle, an event embodying the essentialist mindset. Every July 8 the NPS stages a reenactment of the Declaration's first public reading. Many sites present an annual reading—for example, Exeter, New Hampshire, which hosts a festival around the anniversary of when the Declaration was first read there, on July 16, 1776. Some sites do that on a regular basis, like CW and, for that matter, INHP, though not on such a grand scale. When I visited, local radio and TV crews converged on the small, crowded square for audio and visuals that play well on broadcast media. A costumed man playing Colonel John Nixon standing on a raised platform read the Declaration with pomp and brio. A dozen INHP costumed interpreters handed out copies of the document printed on the replica press in Benjamin Franklin's print shop (several blocks east, also administered by the park). They led the crowd in huzzahs and hisses at the appropriate moments; in the eighteenth century, public readings were participatory events. Occurring at midday, the event attracted tourists, local parents walking their babies and toddlers, and office workers on lunch break. The crowd booed the king and taxes and cheered liberty and the signers. Regardless of the Declaration's content, the ritual of its reading sets it apart as a holy document. For most Americans, the only other context in which they habitually experience a canonical text being read aloud ceremonially is in their house of worship. Combining the relic and the ritual makes for a powerful catechism reinforcing the Declaration of Independence as holy writ and the Revolution as a completed event.

Just a few blocks away from Independence Hall is one of the most conflicted examples of the exaltation of independence. Every July, Philadelphia's Christ Church displays its most valued possession, its eighteenth-century edition of the Book of Common Prayer. A big volume—ten inches by twenty, and close to four inches thick—the tome is displayed under lucite, opened to the page on which, in July 1776,

Reverend Jacob Duché crossed out the sections that direct the congregation to pray for the safety of the king, nobles, and magistrates. Because George III as king of England was head of the Anglican Church (now the Episcopal Church in the United States), Duché's careful strike-throughs represented a profound civil and religious rebellion. His defacing the Book of Common Prayer was an act of apostasy. But here it sits, in an ancient church, or at least, what passes for ancient in U.S. cities, displayed near William Penn's baptismal font, more congregational heirloom than a symbol of daring courage and speaking truth to power. The church has always been a pillar of Philadelphia's power structure. Its churchyard hosts the graves of Robert Morris (signer of the Declaration, Revolutionary financier, and Constitution framer) and other prominent American Revolutionaries, and its nearby cemetery boasts the remains of movers and shakers, most notably Benjamin Franklin. If you want rebels of another kind, you must walk down the street to the Quaker meeting house, the current home of a congregation that in 1754 rejected slavery. In Christ Church, the Book of Common Prayer's setting limits its interpretation to that of relic rather than inspiration. Admittedly, displaying it otherwise would be hard. Christ Church continues to be used for worship and cannot be substantially rearranged. But the Old South Meeting House in Boston, too, is still used and manages to squeeze in interpretive exhibits designed to challenge visitors to consider more fully the historical context of the Revolution as well as recent parallels of actions that took place there. In Christ Church as in Independence Hall, Revolutionary acts of conscience with great potential for examination have been transformed into essentialist religious acts to be venerated.

Just north of the Revolution's most iconic building sits the building that houses the Revolution's most enduring symbol, the Liberty Bell. In 2003, the NPS opened its new home, part of the process of reconfiguring Independence Mall that included the construction of a new visitors center and the placement of the National Constitution Center (NCC). Tourists entering the building walk through its exhibit, which details the Bell's evolution from a local, mediocre-sounding, utilitarian instrument to national symbol. Visitors wend through a series of pictures and photographs depicting more than the Bell in its various homes and on display at different times. The first panel that visitors see tips them off that this is no essentialist, chest-thumping carnival of freedom. Under a large excerpt of the Bell's inscription, "Proclaim Liberty throughout all the Land unto all the Inhabitants Thereof," and next to an enlarged photograph of the Bell, the caption notes that it "is a symbol of liberties gained and a reminder of liberties denied." The exhibit efficiently relates how the Bell was made, how it came to Philadelphia, its crack, and how the Bell gained iconic status. The exhibit constantly reminds visitors that, throughout most of the nineteenth century, the twentieth century, and now into the 2000s, while some people have perceived the Bell as a symbol of freedom achieved, others—especially the enslaved— have seen it as a reminder of unfulfilled promises. Beyond the winding exhibit, tourists can approach the Bell, ingeniously placed so that they see Independence Hall beyond, framed against the sky instead of the drab office towers directly behind it. Visitors who arrive when the exhibit hall is closed or don't want to wait in line can view it from outside the window. The building itself fits with the built environment in such a way that it doesn't attract attention to itself or, for that matter, the Bell either. In contrast to how the Bell's original home (Independence Hall) is interpreted, the Bell's interpretation offers an organicist bent.

To enter the Liberty Bell Center, tourists must walk by the most compelling addition to Independence Mall, what seems like a house for which the builders somehow forgot to build walls and a roof. The first president's house, now also known as the "first white house" site, is placed where George Washington and then John Adams lived during their presidential terms in Philadelphia. The site combines physical recreations of the original building's front-door frame, first-floor window frames, and first-floor fireplaces. White lines slashing across the dark slate paving stones denote the location of the first floor and exterior walls and an area beyond the house with a window in the ground to view a preserved corner of the below-ground excavation. Wall-mounted flat screens offer film loop vignettes portraying the stories of slaves who lived and worked there. The site is open and the films run twenty-four hours a day. Of the various Revolution-related Philadelphia sites, this one has provoked the most controversy, having first been ignored, then planned as a minimal, essentialist celebration of the founding fathers, and then eventually implemented as the most organicist of any national site dedicated to the American Revolution. When

Figure 3.3. The First White House, viewed from the north. Note Independence Hall's tower above it in the distance.

tourist buses disgorge their charges across the street, white American groups stride briskly through the first white house installation, stopping to look for a moment or two, having been distracted by the audio or video, and move on to get in line to see the Liberty Bell. Black people of all ages linger, raptly watching, often standing through the entire loop in front of one screen and before strolling to another. Sometimes they absorb silently, sometimes families discuss what they see. This is the nation's first official site dedicated to acknowledging and exploring the experience of the 20 percent of the entire population of Revolutionary America whose work and suffering made the nation's freedom possible. Less than one hundred yards away from the essentialist Independence Hall, the first white house is a model of organicist interpretation.

The first white house and the Liberty Bell Center provide visitors with a distinct narrative, from slavery to the promise (if not always the reality) of freedom. However, these structures were not first imagined as a cohesive whole. They were the subject of intense, public, and sometimes rancorous debate. Because of the Bell's many meanings, the significance of slavery to the site, and its location in a city that is over 40 percent African American, the matter of interpreting the Liberty Bell and the first white house became an issue that erupted into a political brouhaha. The debate played out in NPS conference rooms and memos, in the press, in public forums, and even in Congress. In the late 1990s, the NPS began to plan a makeover for Independence Mall, including replacing the building that had exhibited the Liberty Bell since the Bicentennial with one that would allow for better flow of people and, after September 11, 2001, that could be more easily secured. The interpretive plan that the INHP originally scripted for the new exhibit leading to the Bell offered an unabashedly celebratory story of freedom, with little consideration of slavery. As for the first white house, the INHP had budgeted for nothing more than a plaque marking the location where Washington and Adams had lived as presidents in Philadelphia. One NPS employee later excused this glaring omission by claiming that, "if there was ever a conspiracy of silence about slavery in the executive mansion, it was an unspoken conspiracy shared by the Park Service, the academy, independent historians, and special interest organizations." Still, she admitted that "the [initial] public meetings failed to bring members of the African American community to the conversation." In Fall 2001, while the NPS was preparing to build the Liberty Bell Center, the historian Edward Lawler settled a long-simmering debate by publishing an article about the house that placed it on a plot just north of where the new Liberty Bell pavilion was to be built. Academics, community activists, and the town's newspapers (both the *Philadelphia Inquirer*, which is the city's big daily, and the *Philadelphia Tribune*, a community-oriented paper) pounced.

Less than a decade after the Smithsonian Institution caved in to conservative complaints concerning its proposed display of the *Enola Gay* (the World War II plane that dropped the atomic bomb), the furor over the Liberty Bell Center and first white house showed that public history is a matter of passion at both ends of the political spectrum. In the previous dustup, veterans' groups and members of Congress had decried what they perceived as an exhibit critical of the United States's decision to use an atomic weapon, rather than celebrating the veterans who flew the plane. Gary Nash, much of whose scholarship focuses on

Philadelphia, gave an interview in early 2002 on WHYY (the Philadelphia NPR station) lamenting that the INHP did not consider the presidents' house worth interpreting. Nash later helped rally local historians. Philadelphia mayor John F. Street and U.S. Representative Bob Brady took up the cause, as did *Inquirer* columnist Acel Moore. A community group spearheaded by the Philadelphia activist, lawyer, and radio host Michael Coard formed Avenging the Ancestors Coalition (ATAC) specifically to promote the building of a memorial at the site. With pressure coming from multiple angles, NPS officials began to tread more cautiously. An area that the NPS had planned to pave over and serve as a place for visitors to stand in line as they waited to see the Liberty Bell had become a planning and public relations headache. The park's superintendent, Martha B. Aikens, was willing to meet with outsiders but limited discussion to the lone panel regarding slavery in the Liberty Bell's new building and declared that the presidents' house site would not be addressed at all. She had drawn the battle lines between an essentialist celebration and those who wanted a more organicist interpretation.

This time, unlike the *Enola Gay* episode, when no one could serve as a broker between protesters and insiders, NPS Chief Historian Dwight Pitcaithley rode to the rescue. After a particularly intense moment at a May 2002 high-stakes meeting among INHP personnel, historians, and staff members from a local congressman's office, INHP could have circled its wagons, and its critics could have given up on the process. But Pitcaithley had the standing and presence of mind to call for a break, talk to each group separately, and then bring the parties together. The NPS then impaneled prominent historians to come up with new interpretive materials for the Liberty Bell building, but they soon found out that doing so was not enough. Negotiations commenced between the NPS and the Ad Hoc Historians, a group consisting of scholars and activists pushing for a more inclusive interpretation. To keep costs down—imperative given that the process had already been budgeted for—they decided to use the initially-contracted-for images but rewrote all of the panels and captions to portray the Liberty Bell's story in terms of its complexity. The new developments did not please everyone. Conservatives lamented what they perceived as the hijacking of what should have been a celebration of George Washington. One lambasted the push to change the interpretation as "attempts to reopen old racial wounds and retell the past [that] are little more than dated cultural Marxist ploys." The transition from a mostly essentialist memorialization to one incorporating organicist themes was not an easy one.

While the Liberty Bell Center project continued to move on a fast track, opening in 2003, the first white house took considerably longer. Archaeologists found the site richer than anticipated. They discovered artifacts relating to the actual work of the home, mostly performed by slaves when Washington—but not Adams—lived there. Adams owned no slaves and found slavery distasteful enough not to engage in it. Because of the cramped NPS budget, supporters of the project had to raise money for the design and construction of the installation. Eventually, they cobbled together $11 million from corporate donations, private donors, a federal grant, the City of Philadelphia, and—with the prodding of Pennsylvania governor and former Philadelphia mayor Ed Rendell—a grant from the Delaware River Port Authority. The installations for the first white house, including the vertical outlines of the house, the video screens, and an area under glass where visitors could peer down to the original foundation, were officially opened in December 2010. There have been some hiccups. The window to the archaeological remains kept fogging up, and five of the video screens went kaput because of leaks and ventilation problems. Those issues have since been addressed.

A very different animal from the original plan, these interpretations emerged from the new collaborations among the NPS, the INHP, historians, and local activists. It reflects an organicist aesthetic while still providing some essentialist quotations, especially for the Liberty Bell. The site is now primarily dedicated to the contradictions between freedom and slavery, with only a small section devoted to the political substance of Washington's presidency and even less to Adams's (Adams continues to spin in his grave, propelled by his jealous ego). The INHP embraced the new process and new interpretation. In its new long-range plan, published in 2007, the park pledged that "interpretive programming will encourage visitors to consider what was so revolutionary about the American Revolution, contemplate the promise and paradox of liberty, recognize the dynamic tension inherent in our heritage as expressed in E Pluribus Unum, and appreciate the extraordinary life and legacy of Benjamin Franklin." That the federal historical park in Philadelphia should celebrate Franklin, its most famous son, is no surprise. But the other goals denote a transformation, compared to its previous reluctance, in the words of former INHP superintendent Martha Aikens, to "create dissonance for visitors," which can lead to complaints not only from tourists but often from members of Congress wanting a more robust celebration of what they perceive as the triumphant American Revolution. While doing research for this book, I heard some off-the-record grousing about the installation in professional public history circles: some rue that it barely commemorates Washington's and Adams's presidencies, others its failure to tell a coherent narrative. Such bitterness may be more than a little ironic, as the new installations challenge visitors in ways that public history professionals themselves hope to do, if they felt they could be less risk averse. More than that, they know that the process behind the ultimate result set an expectation that public history professionals and institutions may have to be more responsive to a messy political process than they would like.

But to Philadelphia's African American community, the president's house/slave memorial site has delivered a nearly unalloyed success. With the exception of some of the African American programming at Colonial Williamsburg, it is the only founding-era site anywhere I observed that fully captivates the attention of African Americans. The Avenging the Ancestors Coalition hosted an enthusiastic public celebration of the installation's first anniversary, with Coard proudly proclaiming that the first white house "has become our Mount Rushmore, our Liberty Bell, our Statute of Liberty." The consensus among public historians, and among the academics who analyze public history sites, is that Americans don't want to be challenged to be reminded of traumatic events in their past. But maybe that conventional wisdom requires revising when we consider the African American past. It's not that blacks don't want to confront "the tough stuff of American history," as the historians James Oliver Horton and Lois Horton put it. It's that they want to have a hand in presenting their own history. Having one installation designed partly by the African American community, and specifically for the interpretation of slavery during the American Revolution, surely is not too much to ask. If having one corner of a Center City Philadelphia block emphasize slavery makes some whites unhappy, they are free to shed their tears at Independence Hall, which dominates the mall along which the first white house sits, or perhaps in the National Mall in Washington, D.C., under the shadow of the Washington Monument or Jefferson Memorial. Those essentialist shrines are no less white than the stone from which they were cut.

Both the site and the process reflect the ways that the NPS and those who work with it are trying to transform the organization, from one that provides essentialist, flat views of the past to one that offers Americans a more nuanced interpretation of the nation's past. These issues have been the subject of much scholarly and water-cooler discussion among those who work in public history, who are tugged in various directions, and who have scant resources. The history professionals who work at historical sites are aware of some of the limitations of the interpretations visitors encounter, as my observations and my conversations with them made clear. Many of the organizations overseeing sites have gone through what for them were traumatic experiences when they did venture interpretations that might be more controversial—as those who lived through the *Enola Gay* and Liberty Bell Center controversies can attest. But as the contentious history of the first president's house site indicates, trying to pass off bland exhibits doesn't work either. A 2011 report completed by a committee of historians and undertaken at the NPS's request surveys the challenges that the NPS faces. The authors of *Imperiled Promise: The State of History in the National Park Service* observed that historical interpretation often takes a back seat to preservation, staff historians don't have the resources or time to engage in meaningful dialog with academic historians, history is usually presented as being objective and finished rather than as a process to be reinterpreted, and, while individual sites are sometimes more adventurous in their presentation of the past, overall the NPS has a risk-averse culture when it comes to presenting the nation's past. To be fair to the NPS, it navigates an ideological minefield, especially in a political environment in which it can be materially punished for falling on the wrong side of a powerful member of Congress.

The complexity that *Imperiled Promise* asked for is hard, maybe unrealistically so. Academic scholars tend to be quick to pounce on the simplification we encounter at historical sites, but sometimes too harshly. When I was a graduate student at the College of William & Mary—which is in Williamsburg, Virginia—my advisor half-seriously remarked that every book and article on the multipage reading list of his graduate-level syllabus was "absolutely essential to understanding the American Revolution." (I can still hear him saying it.) I had worked the previous summer at Colonial Williamsburg and was still occasionally doing tours on nights and weekends. At CW's Capitol Building, my fellow costumed, third-person interpreters and I had to cram the Revolution into about forty minutes, much of which was taken up simply by explaining the building and moving people through it. Tourist parents are hot and bothered, as are their kids. Interpreters must assume that visitors have little prior knowledge of the Revolutionary period and that even much of what they think they know may be demonstrably wrong (for example, that slavery was reserved to the southern states or that the vast majority of Americans supported the Revolution). Year-over-year attendance figures have plummeted over the last couple decades at most American historical sites, and no one wants to turn off potential repeat customers. The virtue of interpreting an essentialist Revolution at sites like Independence Hall is that doing so does not upset expectations or contradict visitors' assumptions, it is simple, and the few people who would complain about such an interpretation are likely to be random customers, rather than big-time donors or political powerhouses.

The arrangement of buildings on Independence Mall indicates one of the primary reasons for the reluctance to offend or challenge visitors to American Revolution sites: for Philadelphia and other cities, history tourism brings in big bucks. At least there are no billboards on Independence Hall, yet, or on the other buildings on Independence Mall. That said, crossing Market Street from the first white house site, one encounters the Independence Visitor Center, a football-field-long building intended to serve as the gateway to all the historic sites in Philadelphia. The Independence Visitors Center represents a partnership between the NPS, the City of Philadelphia, and local and state tourism boards, and it is run by a non-profit that increasingly must fund itself in its quest to sell historical tourism, which Philadelphians hope can be a growing industry. The $38 million building opened in 2001 and is the most visited site in Philadelphia, outpacing the Liberty Bell Center. In addition to hosting perhaps the largest-grossing souvenir shop in Philadelphia in its south end, where most tourists enter the building, much of the structure is dedicated to concierge desks that offer information, sell tickets to tours and historical sites in the city and region, and help with hotel reservations. The building's north end houses a small café and smaller additional gift shop, mostly dedicated to impulse buys.

There is nothing nefarious about promoting history tourism, especially in a city so hard-hit by manufacturing's decline over the last half century. The number of leisure visitors to the greater Philadelphia region increased from twenty-three million in 1997 to thirty-four million in 2012, and they support an estimated eighty-four thousand jobs—many of them due to Philadelphia's history attractions. Indeed, the desire to exploit history tourism unites the white, Italian American former business executive James Cuorato, the president and CEO of the Independence Visitor Center, and the African American activist Coard, not exactly the political bedfellows one might expect, given Philadelphia's historic and persistent ethnic and racial divides. Essentialist or organicist, nobody wants to rock the boat too much if it would mean endangering cash flow.

As the consideration of these buildings suggests, Philadelphia hosts a range of disparate sites and buildings with some relation to the American Revolution. While the visitor center is bland—intentionally so—the non-profit amalgam Historic Philadelphia straddles the essentialist-organicist divide, pursuing a split-personality strategy. In 2005 Philadelphia mayor John F. Street established Once Upon a Nation, since renamed Historic Philadelphia, to help coordinate history tourism. Historic Philadelphia and its big-money sponsors wanted a grand, state-of-the-art spectacle to celebrate Philadelphia and its role in the national founding. The result was *Liberty 360*, touted as the first 3D film in the round, displayed in a custom-designed small theater that allowed people to stand so they could turn and see the action all around them. Technologically impressive when it opened, it's a colossal failure by any other measure. The 3D and theater-in-the-round elements are superfluous eye candy that dramatically increased costs while adding little in terms of cinematic wonder. *Liberty 360* draws poorly. Even at the height of the July 4 weekend I spent in Philadelphia, the film did not attract big crowds. The movie's script resulted from many hands and many iterations. This is film-by-committee at its worst, a mishmash of patriotic pastiche and historical kitsch. Featuring the actor Charles Hall portraying Benjamin Franklin, the film's organizing principle is a mystery concerning the contents of a box that Franklin holds, that contains the key to the American Revolution and the United States. At the end, the box is revealed to hold "liberty." In a box? Historic Philadelphia spent millions on this and won't get another chance at it for decades. But the film's sponsors got what they wanted: a prominent acknowledgment, a tax deduction, and a self-congratulatory essentialist extravaganza displaying the Revolution as an innocuous event celebrating a contemporary, flawless society.

In contrast, Historic Philadelphia's other major public history initiative is ingenious, mostly well executed, and engages tourists like few other such efforts. The "Once Upon a Nation" storytelling program, launched in 2005, consists of a series of thirteen semicircular benches, each one beside a major historical building or landmark in downtown Philadelphia. From 11 a.m. to 3 p.m. daily during the summer, by each bench stands a yellow-shirted actor who tells historical, non-fiction stories associated with the site. Families can walk from site to site, bench to bench, where the actors give children paper Betsy Ross flags and, after every story, a star sticker to put on the flag—thus the thirteen stations. The stories range from the dawn of the seventeenth century to the present, from a humorous incident between Benjamin Franklin and John Adams to the story of escaped slave Henry "Box" Brown, who earned his nickname by mailing himself in a crate from slavery in Baltimore to Philadelphia freedom. All of the fifteen to twenty stories I watched were well performed. They were not all necessarily less celebratory than *Liberty 360*, but they express an entirely different sensibility: rather than the inevitable glory of America, they tended to portray ordinary men and women and highlight more obscure anecdotes. This is the low-tech opposite of the grand *Liberty 360*: human scale, human stories, told by humans. Families gravitated to these benches, and some lone adults, too. The younger children did not always understand the stories, but they enjoyed the storytellers' theatricality and attention and collecting the gold stars. The stories helped children and adults make a more visceral connection with buildings that are otherwise sacred national shrines. Storytellers still presented only one side of history—that of the person whose story they were relating—and did not suggest that our reconstruction of the past is open to interpretation. The stories, then, had organicist content without an organicist sensibility. But they did make the history more human.

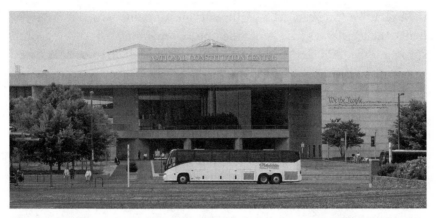

Figure 3.4. The National Constitution Center, poised to swallow another bus-full of tourists.

One of those benches sits in front of the National Constitution Center, which makes a splash entirely with private funds. The NCC's massive, angled, concrete-and-glass building sits on the northern end of a long, grassy mall facing the comparatively modest Independence Hall, as if the two buildings were mismatched bookends for a giant empty green shelf. Through its name and location, the NCC retains the cachet that comes with the perception of being a public organization without the obligation to make its curatorial process a matter of public discussion. Though privately run, it sits on public land, lending the erroneous impression that the NCC is the official keeper of the Constitution's legacy (when I mentioned the NCC to an official at the National Archives, the federal agency that keeps the physical document, she testily pointed out to me that "the Constitution is ours"). The signature part of the NCC visitor experience is "Freedom Rising," a multimedia extravaganza viewed in a steeply banked, circular theater with a stage at the bottom. Narrated by a live person introduced as an "actor," it chronicles the settling of the English American colonies, the Revolution, the Constitutional Convention and celebrates seminal events in constitutional history. The center's permanent exhibit rings the theater. It is organized in sections that correspond to the phrases of the preamble of the Constitution: "We the People," "in Order to form a more perfect Union," "establish Justice," "insure domestic Tranquillity," and so on. It also features installations dedicated to the three branches of government established under the Constitution:

the executive (one can get a picture of oneself being sworn in as president), the legislature (depicting the impeachment trial of Andrew Johnson), and the judiciary (one can sit in one of nine chairs and hear cases, just like the Supreme Court). Nearly all parts of the exhibit consider a wide swath of Americans—soldiers and peace protestors, cops and rioters, immigrants and nativists, capitalists and unionizers—all participants in what is portrayed as the inevitable march of progress.

Both "Freedom Rising" and the exhibit emphasize one theme straddling organicism and essentialism: the Constitution and the country that it serves are constantly and inevitably expanding freedom. That freedom is both national, in the sense of the United States being an independent nation, and personal, increasingly for women, African Americans, and Native Americans (notwithstanding that the last three hundred years could be more accurately written as a reduction in Native Americans' freedom). Political scientist Mariah Zeisberg has noted that the NCC presents inclusiveness in terms of people but blandness in terms of ideas. As with many institutions that aim to attract the widest possible audience, its designers' and consultants' major victory is having produced something that challenges nobody. Here's a major museum about the Constitution that neither somewhat liberal former Supreme Court Justice Stephen Breyer nor staunchly conservative Supreme Court Justice Antonin Scalia could find a bone to pick with— and if that big a comment on the Constitution provoked neither of those men, chances are it won't ruffle the average person off the street, either. Making an exhibit that offends no one is a deeply conservative project, "conservative" in the sense that it reinforces the status quo. We are all free, but only the people and corporations that gave a ton of money get their names on the wall and perhaps a say in how the museum was designed. We are all free, except to question the underlying structure of the Constitution or its possible alternatives. We are all free, as long as we let everyone keep what they have and let governors govern. We are all free, so any attempt to address contemporary inequality becomes framed as trampling on someone's freedom. The NCC presents a multicultural veneer on a deeply essentialist product.

We would expect Philadelphia's hodgepodge to present history tourists with a range of messages. Surprisingly enough, Colonial Williamsburg—the living history museum in tidewater Virginia run by a single non-profit foundation with the sole purpose of educating visitors about the American Revolution—delivers a message no less conflicted concerning the nature of the Revolution. It thereby reveals that, as an institution, CW has various internal and external constituencies contesting what the Revolution was about and how it should be portrayed. Compared to Philadelphia, a city trying to promote a scattered network of sites managed by different organizations, CW's interpretive challenges would appear to be easy. Actually, it's just a different set of puzzles with no perfect solution.

The City of Williamsburg was founded in 1632 and served as Virginia's capital from 1699 to 1780. For the next century and a half, it settled into comfort as a small, sleepy Southern town, home to the College of William & Mary and not much else. The non-profit Colonial Williamsburg Foundation was established in 1926, backed by John D. Rockefeller, Jr., one of the country's richest men. Rockefeller secretly bought up most of the downtown, razing nearly every structure except for eighty-eight buildings that remained from the 1770s; those still standing had to be gutted to be restored to eighteenth-century appearance and layout. Today, CW has a visitors center with a football stadium's worth of parking and hundreds of new and restored colonial-style buildings spread across 301 acres. Despite the many millions that Rockefeller, the Wallace family (of *Reader's Digest* fame), and other big donors have poured into CW, it still depends upon income for operating revenue from tickets, its restaurants and hotels, and its gift shops. Over the last quarter century, CW's paid visitation has declined, from a peak of over 1.1 million paying visitors in the late 1980s to a mere 670,500 general admission tickets in 2011, although it estimates that about 1.7 million people strode through the historic area that year, which one may do without buying a ticket to enter the buildings. Colonial Williamsburg's essentialist DNA sometimes contrasts with its more recent, occasionally organicist tendencies.

For many visitors, the Colonial Williamsburg visitor experience begins online at its split-personality web presence: www.colonialwilliamsburg.com, primarily a marketing site, and history.org, primarily an education site. The physical introduction to CW is not much different, starting with CW's modern, glass-and-steel visitors center. First up, gift store, book store, and eatery, then tickets, then a chance to see *The Story of a Patriot*. In the historic area, trade shops, taverns, and houses—some open to the public, others that are support buildings, still others that are private residences rented to employees—line CW's back-ward-L-shaped heart, with the fortress-like Capitol Building at the top of the L and the elegant Governor's Palace at the other end. Although the streets are closed to motor traffic during the day, people tend to walk on the tree-lined, shaded sidewalks, leaving the hot, broad road to horse-drawn carriages giving pleasure rides. Perhaps most striking is how quiet it is compared to the big cities that host most of the other sites I visited: no cars rushing by, no beeping of trucks backing up, no music piped out of stores, no construction machinery, only the sound of people on the sidewalks and the clopping of horses down the pave-ment. Everything looks as authentic as can be made, but of course it's still an artificial town in which the vast majority of the people one sees are tourists, with a smaller number of costumed interpreters and actors (most of them white) and a yet smaller number of uniformed service workers (most of them black). In that way, it's not far from how it was when I worked there, when I was a graduate student at the College of William & Mary. Upon my return more than a dozen years later, I saw with all fondness that, with its meticulously reconstructed buildings and real horse-drawn carriages, CW still looks a little like Disneyland and still smells a bit like road apples.

Colonial Williamsburg's interpretations are an amalgamation between organicist and essentialist ones because the institution itself has many internal and external constituents, all with somewhat differ-ent demands and views. Rockefeller envisioned CW as an essentialist project: a way to restore and celebrate a more pure, more traditional, more homogenous, more heroic America than the one he perceived around him in the 1930s (the great irony being that, as an oil scion, he owed his Midas-sized fortune to the industrial, modern, corporatized nation that his family had helped United States become). Colonial Wil-liamsburg's flagship buildings continue to be the Governor's Palace, the symbol of royal authority in Virginia, and the Capitol Building, where the elected legislature met and thus was the symbol of the people— or at least, the symbol of the elected government of propertied white men. For more than half a century after its opening, CW presented an image of a United States founded by great and virtuous men, from the moment tourists viewed *The Story of the Patriot* through their building tours with the white, proper "hostesses" who emphasized their grand Virginia forbears. Colin G. Campbell, CW's president since 2000, had previously served as president of the Rockefeller Foundation and so is keen to further the benefactor family's essentialist vision. Colonial Williamsburg still depends on donations from corporations and the rich, and in the face of declining overall ticket sales, it has placed its revenue bets on catering to the wealthy through its expensive Williamsburg Inn, several fancy golf courses, and the recent construction of a luxurious spa. Many of its visitors still want the fife-and-drums celebration of American heritage. In his 2011 annual report, Campbell pledged that CW would undertake further efforts to "explore the role of course and the rule of law," to "examine the military and the role of religion in society," and to "examine the democratic efforts of other nations and link them to our own." Although none of these individual goals are inherently essentialist, taken as a piece they jibe with the kind of orderly Revolution that most interests essentialists.

However, over the last three decades or so, CW has slowly complicated its interpretations, pushed by its academic-oriented research department and the tourists themselves. When I worked at CW in the mid-1990s, the shift had already begun. The trade shops were interpreting the lives of artisans, white and black, male and female. Colonial Williamsburg initiated programs to interpret the 50 percent of eighteenth-century Williamsburg's population it had previously ignored: the enslaved. This included reconstructed slave dwellings at Carter's Grove, an eighteenth-century plantation site seven miles from the main CW grounds (it has since been sold to cut costs). Colonial Williamsburg's best-known attempt to interpret slavery was its onetime 1994 reenactment of an estate auction, including slaves. Drawing national media attention, the National Association for the Advancement of Colored People (NAACP) protested that Colonial Williamsburg was making a tourist spectacle out of slavery's misery. After seeing the program, Jack Gravely, the NAACP's Virginia political action chairman, changed his mind, praising it as "passionate, moving and education." The reenactment represented a triumph of research and performance. Nonetheless, the experience understandably made CW skittish about future projects.

In 1999, CW launched "Enslaving Virginia," a provocative suite of programs depicting slave life. It not only showed the enslaved as

individuals who had to make difficult choices but also included whites
as owners and even as part of slave patrols—prompting some onlook-
ing tourists to try to revolt forcibly against them (CW interpreters had
to step out of character to calm down the angry customers). Colonial
Williamsburg has since quietly invested more in its African American
and slavery programming, doing so partly because of the increased
influence of the academically trained leaders who supervise its interpretations but also because, against the wisdom prevailing when I was
an employee, visitors actually asked for more. If half the population of
Williamsburg was enslaved, they asked, what did slaves do here? Who
were they? What work did they do? The interpretive staff fielding these
questions on a daily basis pushed for more on slavery and the enslaved.
Rather than slavery scaring off visitors, especially those with children, it
had become a subject of interest.

Another recent initiative at CW indicates that, like other Revolution-
related sites, it is trying to thread the needle by celebrating freedom.
In 2006, after years of development, CW launched its "Revolutionary
City" programs. These are two-hour-long suites of street theater pieces
performed by costumed actors in the heart of the historic area, dra-
matizing particular moments from 1774 through 1781, all based upon
historical documentation (some too much: the lone chronological
outlier, George Washington's 1797 presidential farewell address, would
have benefited from more editing in this context). The museum already
knew what the NCC, Historic Philadelphia, Mount Vernon, and other
sites have since discovered: that what most engages people is *people*,
and while statues are better than nothing, live people are even better.
Furthermore, as Rex Ellis, then vice president of CW's Historic Area
bragged, with some justification, "We have the best three-dimensional
theater in the country." If a family stays at CW for three days, it will see
programming from each of the three themes, "The Collapse of Royal
Government," "Citizens at War," and "Building a Nation." Each theme
has numerous variations, but on a given day, the performance consists of three or four set pieces featuring different historic personages
ranging from slaves to famed founding fathers. When I visited, large
crowds of visitors remained transfixed on the drama and, a sure sign
of engagement, walked determinedly as the storyline shifted between
venues. Each scene was passionately acted, and—making me happy as

Figure 3.5. Colonial Williamsburg's Revolutionary City. Tourists look on, riveted, as actors portraying enslaved men debate the cruel stability of staying in slavery against the dangerous and risky prospects of escaping to the British lines.

a historian—nearly all of them involved some degree of tension. There are limits. While some showed the agonizing decisions to be made for or against loyalty to the British Crown, none of them featured an otherwise sympathetic white embracing a pro-slavery position, a necessary portrayal for Americans to comprehend and confront that slavery was far more complex than we acknowledge. Still, CW is humanizing Revolutionary-era Americans and their decisions, and that is a big change for the better. Colonial Williamsburg's street theater offers the most successful amalgam of organicism and essentialism that I saw in terms of history and tourist engagement.

Colonial Williamsburg has made considerable strides, but just as with Philadelphia and the rest of the nation, CW does not fully confront race in either past or present. In November 2011, CW sent out an email titled "75 Years of Unparalleled Hospitality," promoting the Williamsburg Inn. The Inn, its famed golf course, and a new salon and sauna facility make

CW a resort location. But, as many African Americans are still no doubt aware, no CW-owned hotel ever appeared in the Green Book, the directory of African American friendly travel establishments that was published annually from 1936 until 1964, when the federal Civil Rights Act forbade racial discrimination in hotels and restaurants. Black drivers wanting a place to stay had to continue east to Newport News or west to Richmond. To be fair, this is marketing. But just as CW sells itself as recreating an authentic past, its own institutional past is still part of the place and people's perceptions of it. In addition, marketing emails CW sent out in 2011 and 2012 featured pictures of African American couples or families, not in a montage of mostly white faces but as the principal images. That's a big change. The museum is trying much harder than it used to, though with little success. Both in absolute numbers and compared to the overall visitor population, the number of African American visitors has dropped, from about forty thousand in the late 1990s to fewer than twenty thousand in 2012. Admittedly, recruiting African Americans to portray enslaved people has always been a difficult task, given the understandable reluctance to interpret a life of being shamed and degraded. But it's still the case that Williamsburg's half-enslaved Revolutionary-era past is now bizarrely recreated by an institution in which the vast majority of the employees in twenty-first-century suits and eighteenth-century costumes are white and the majority of employees in uniforms (maintenance and groundskeeping crews and housekeeping in the various CW-owned hotel properties) are people of color. Though reinterpreting the past, CW has not yet escaped it.

Whereas CW, in its many sites and programs, offers the whole range from ultrapatriotic essentialism (including an evening program that climaxes with tourists singing "God Bless America") to strong organicism (some of the edgier programming concerning slavery), Mount Vernon and Monticello have taken sides and provide an interesting set of contrasts. These founder's homes bear great similarities in what they are and how they are run. Both were saved by individuals and fostered by private organizations in the nineteenth century, when Virginia and the federal government rebuffed the owners' attempts to sell the sites to make them public shrines, and they continue to be privately run. Both are major tourist attractions that draw primarily because of their owner's fame. Both continue to woo successfully large donors and small, both individual and corporate. Both not only have significant houses to show but also the surrounding grounds, offering many interpretive opportunities concerning all the economic and social elements of a working eighteenth-century Virginia plantation. Mount Vernon is near the banks of the Potomac River, less than a half hour's drive from Washington, D.C., and thus an easy side trip for tourists and school groups, attracting about a million visitors annually. That's more than double the numbers through the turnstiles at Monticello, perched on a hilltop outside Charlottesville, Virginia, and remote from other major tourist destinations. Mount Vernon faces the greater challenge of managing the steady flood of visitors rather than Monticello's varying stream, though it also commands considerably deeper financial resources to do so. Beyond these comparisons, what stands out most is the difference between Mount Vernon's unabashed celebration of Washington as both person and icon, compared to Monticello's more ambivalent consideration of Jefferson, his times, and his legacy. Just as Washington was indomitable and Jefferson eloquent, and their houses are quite different, how their homes and plantations are currently interpreted offers a study in contrasts. Monticello today delivers a primarily organicistic counterpoint to the mostly essentialist vision offered at Mount Vernon.

Mount Vernon has embraced essentialist interpretations in a twenty-first-century, high budget, sophisticated package. As much as the house itself, what dominates visitors' experience in the eighty-five minutes they average there, according to internal surveys, is their time spent in its expansive, state-of-the-art orientation center and museum. In terms of architecture, landscape design, use of space and materials, multimedia installations, traffic flow, and the challenge of integrating seventy-one thousand square feet of new buildings into an eighteenth-century landscape, the facilities serve as an impressive example of what can be achieved when money is little object, having been finished in 2006 at the cost of $116 million. Tourists enter through a low-slung, half-submerged, wood-and-glass building. Their first encounters inside send a mixed message. Upon entry, tourists unavoidably encounter a life-size set of bronze statues of George and Martha Washington hand in hand with her grandchildren, Nelly and Washy. It instantly humanizes George, although his pose is still somewhat stiff (this is bronze, after all) and his face rather formal. Rounding the statues and heading toward

Figure 3.6. George Washington in Bronze and Glass in Mount Vernon's Ford Orientation Center.

the theater and entry into the garden, visitors see a small-scale model of the house and a then panel of stained-glass windows depicting scenes from Washington's life, including the completely mythical story of his cutting down a cherry tree. Within twenty yards of a creative, conscious attempt to humanize Washington, he's apotheosized in a medium that most Americans are used to seeing portraying Jesus, as if the first president were moving through his own stations of the cross. Washington was a larger-than-life, heroic figure even to his contemporaries, though few worshiped him in this way.

Mount Vernon visitors watch an introductory film, *We Fight to Be Free*. Such films are standard in history tourism: they run from the genre's granddaddy, Colonial Williamsburg's *The Story of a Patriot*, shown daily since 1957 in theaters specifically designed for it, to the short documentary in Pennsylvania's Washington Crossing State Park, viewed on a twenty-seven-inch tube television set held on a rolling cart in a trailer's side room with half a dozen rolling chairs. Films provide a transition from tourists being all hot and bothered and getting out of a bus or a car after a long ride, put them in a more pensive frame of mind, and provide the necessary broader context to understand the site. Entry films offer opportunities for donors to be prominently acknowledged in the credits, more ego boosting than contributing to everyday operations or restorations that corporate logos can't be plastered on. They are also expensive, must last for many years, and must not offend visitors. Introductory films tend to be conservative in content and storyline. Mount Vernon's entry, *We Fight to Be Free*, is this generation's greatest contribution to the breed. Starring veteran screen actor Sebastian Roché as Washington, it is an all-Hollywood, multimillion-dollar production in terms of writing, sets, editing, and sound and dramatizes several incidents in Washington's life: leading troops during the outbreak of the French and Indian War, the first time he and Martha met, his decision to cross the Delaware River, and his relinquishing his command at the end of the Revolutionary War. Mount Vernon Executive Director James Rees described it as an attempt to portray "Washington as America's first action hero," and it does not disappoint on that score, with much attention being lavished upon the battle scene and its violence. Like much of the Mount Vernon experience, it challenges the stiff image of Washington on the dollar bill, only to replace it with a 3D character whose relation to his own time or ours is no more apparent—except that he is no less heroic, indispensible, or distant. All essentialist celebration, no organicist reflection.

By contrast, Monticello's visitors' experience begins with an introductory fifteen-minute film at the modern but comparatively modest (compared to Mount Vernon, that is) wood-and-glass Monticello visitors center. Unlike the Hollywood heroic *We Fight to Be Free*, *Thomas Jefferson's World* was almost entirely filmed at Monticello, following Jefferson's life, interests, and accomplishments. Whereas the former film merely mentions slaves in passing, the latter prominently notes that the Monticello plantation community included 140 enslaved people, who not only did the main work of building, planting, and sowing but also had lives of their own beyond that of their owner—in other words, the story of Monticello comprises both that of Jefferson and that of the African Americans who lived there, together and separately. Immediately, then, the great man is off his pedestal and at least sharing the stage with other humans, as the film eventually discusses the contradictions between Jefferson's words and his slaveholding. It even coyly addresses the Hemings revelations, though carefully avoids any definitive statement: "Many historians now believe that years after his wife's death, Thomas Jefferson was the father of the children of the slave Sally Hemings." By the time this film was made—2009—one would be hardpressed to find many reputable historians, especially specialists in that period, who believe otherwise, but it's still a brave statement to make from an institution that considers keeping Jefferson's reputation as part of its charge. Finally, the film points out that despite the grand rights articulated in Declaration of Independence that Jefferson drafted and their use in many contexts at home (women's suffrage, the civil rights movement) and abroad (Haiti, India), "These rights have not been fully achieved." Such organicist statements put the film in strong relief contrasted to *We Fight to Be Free*'s suggestion that we will only see another person like Washington "if we remain true to his memory."

The house tours at these two destinations are fairly standard for the genre, reminding me of the 1990s ones I led at Colonial Williamsburg's Governor's Palace. They are fairly quick, about twenty minutes tops, a compromise between trying to give visitors a sense of the house and maximizing the structure's capacity; the buildings were designed as

Figure 3.7. Monticello. Visitors await entry on the front steps. Note the scaffolding to the right: then as now, Monticello was an eternal construction site.

plantation homes, not mass tourist attractions. As with most historic house tours, these relate a history of the acquisition of the site and its construction, a gloss on some of the more prominent artifacts, how the different spaces were used, and anecdotes about important visitors and concerning its main residents. Mount Vernon's covered George and Martha Washington together, and then Martha in mourning, reflecting that the house is furnished as close as possible to how it was at George's death in 1799, when the house was inventoried. Monticello's addresses Jefferson and the many ingenious design elements that he incorporated into the building.

Tourists usually spend more time out of the houses than in them. For both sites, that means a lot of time looking at the outbuildings, gardens, and tomb. At Mount Vernon tourists can see a plethora of plantation facilities: grain mill, distillery, stables, and gardens. Although acknowledging slaves' work, these facilities' labels also suggest that they were the brainchild of the great man. Monticello has invested more interpretive effort in its kitchens and slave quarters, emphasizing that Monticello was a community rather than a reflection of one man's will. Perhaps the most interesting contrast lies in the two men's gravesites. Jefferson's tomb, marked by a ten-foot-tall marker, sits modestly behind bars in the Jefferson family graveyard, where descendants can still be buried. Washington's grave is in a crypt flanked by flags, and an attendant cautions all visitors to remove their hats and to be quiet even outside. Over two centuries later, he's still lying in state. The house of "the father of our country" offers an essentialist past, while that of the author of the Declaration of Independence offers an organicist one.

My last encounter with the Revolution on my 2011 grand tour was by the Lexington Green, a dozen miles outside Boston. The Lexington tourist office sits across the street from one corner of the green, in a two-story, white clapboard house, and is run by the local chamber of commerce, another example of the intersection between history tourism and local boosterism. A book for sale there caught my eye: the glossy paperback biography of Prince Estabrook, an enslaved local man who was among the wounded on the nearby field on April 19, 1775. Estabrook later served in the Continental Army and by 1790 was a free man—exactly how he got his freedom we may never know—and living in the household of Benjamin Estabrook, his former owner. The volume was a true labor of love, written by the local journalist Alice Hinkle and featuring an interview with Charles Price, who has been playing the role of Estabrook in the Lexington Militia (a local reenacting regiment) since the 1970s. Outside the building is a small rock with a plaque in honor of Estabrook, placed there in 2008. Lexington may seem to be an easy place to talk about freedom, both in the eighteenth-century and in the twenty-first-century sense. Massachusetts was the first state to fully free the few slaves within its borders. Despite all the talk over the last few years about a "post-racial" America, contemporary Lexington, an expensive bedroom community, is still nearly free of African Americans: as of the 2010 census, only 473 of its 31,395 residents were black. One can chalk up the current dearth of Lexington African Americans to many long-term trends. Nonetheless, save for the original white house in Philadelphia, whites far outnumbered blacks at every historical site I visited. The talk of "liberty" at these many sites serves as a congratulatory bromide for whites, but it's no surprise that blacks find them less

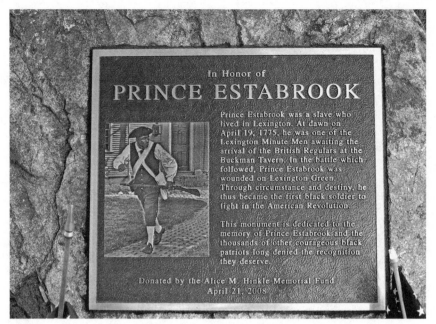

Figure 3.8. Prince Estabrook Memorial Marker. The engraved photograph is of the reenactor Charles Price.

attractive places to visit. The American Revolution may have begun in Lexington. But in this affluent, comfortable community, despite its milking of Revolution tourism, the revolution ended a long time ago.

A year later, I went to one last site. On June 26, 2012, after a hiatus of eleven years, a tourist attraction reopened in Boston: the Boston Tea Party Ships & Museum. The previous tea party museum had burned down. Efforts to build anew required money (a total of $28 million, a good chunk from public coffers) and, seemingly even harder to come by, the stack of permits necessary for its reincarnation as a floating structure accessible from a bridge across Fort Point Channel. The tea party museum is a venture of Historic Tours of America, a privately owned corporation billing itself as "America's Storyteller" that operates tours and other history-themed attractions in a half-dozen American cities. The key to understanding the Boston Tea Party Ships & Museum is that it features neither of the two characteristics usually associated with museums: artifacts and a primary mission to educate. Its lone

Figure 3.9. The Boston Tea Party Ships & Museum. Flanked by replicas of eighteenth-century ships, the structure floats attached to a bridge in the heart of the commercial and industrial city.

object, the Robinson tea chest—allegedly one of two surviving crates from the original Tea Party—is displayed as piece of the true Revolutionary cross rather than as an object of instruction. Director Shawn Ford says that the facility makes no claim to be a museum, but when the word "museum" is printed on the tickets, appears on the building, and graces every official tchotchke in the cavernous gift shop, we shouldn't blame tourists for expecting one. Historic Tours of America unabashedly exploits the idea of a museum to provide cover for an experience designed to stir emotion, combining live actors, reconstructed ships, the opportunity for customers to toss hollow "crates" overboard, holographic talking figures, talking portraits of George III and Samuel Adams reminiscent of the paintings in Harry Potter, a large-screen movie with surround sound, and a free cup of tea (cookies, though, will cost you extra). Considering it on those terms, the facility is a smashing success.

The Tea Party Ships & Museum takes the rising interest in the American Revolution to its logical, profitable conclusion: promoting a comforting freedom experience for $25 a head. Like most Revolution-related historical sites, books, and movies, it does not purport to promote any political position. Ford has adamantly denied any affiliation with the political tea party, and for their part, tea partiers have sought no ties to the Revolution-themed attraction. Rather, Historic Tours of America wants to cash in, but also with a desire to do so in a responsible way, given what it sees as the constraints and the standards of its line of work (in this case, the growing for-profit history tourism industry). Like many other contemporary depictions described in this book, Historic Tours's Tea Party experience offers some organicists details by delving into women's experiences and noting that the original Tea Party was part of a mass movement. But ultimately there's nothing to challenge the facility's triumphal Revolutionary tone, especially after watching the movie at the end, *Let It Begin Here*, which closes with a prompt for the customers to sing "My Country 'Tis of Thee," a ritual that Ford admits inspires some visitors to tears as others roll their eyes. Even though the planning for the museum was completed well before today's political tea party appeared, they feed off each other in a synergy of campaigning and commercialism. There's not much new to learn here about the American Revolution, but it speaks volumes about how we continue to use it for a variety of pecuniary and political purposes.

At the Boston Tea Party & Ships Museum, as at other sites I visited, "freedom" muddies the central divisions in the contemporary memory of the American Revolution. Public history sites and tours emphasize freedom because it can be portrayed as an anodyne, unanimously approved American value. Who is against freedom? Accordingly, "freedom" constituted the common thread than ran through just about every exhibit, every tour, every introductory film, every reenactment that I saw. Everyone in eighteenth-century America, it seems, wanted "freedom," whether from Britain or slavery. As the historian Alon Confino has observed, national memories can be composed of "common denominators" between competing visions of the past. By latching onto "freedom," institutions can appeal to organicists who value racial and gender equality. There may be no better example than Colonial Williamsburg's tony Spa, which in March 2013 hosted a weekend dedicated to women and African American freedom. But freedom is also a fundamentally essentialist value in contemporary American culture and politics. "Freedom" as portrayed in Revolutionary public sites and tours is nearly always framed as national freedom, personal freedom, or economic freedom. The celebration of freedom as portrayed at most sites recognizes individuals rather than the mutual obligations between individuals or between individuals and the community (whether by "community" we mean society in a general sense or the community as embodied by the government). Some interpretations, no matter their intent, can be read by tourists to have either meaning. For example, one panel in the Liberty Bell Center notes that, "like liberty, as strong and durable as [the Bell] appears, it is fragile and easily damaged." To African Americans, that could be read as an indictment of recent efforts to curtail voting rights, while tea partiers could see the statement as referring to the Affordable Care Act.

Such interpretations thus ignore the deep responsibilities that come with freedom and the understanding that freedom only happens within a structure that supports it. American Revolution sites reinforce a strain of libertarianism that represents the agenda of America's most privileged and affluent residents, who want to be bound by no rules and to minimize their public responsibilities. Public history sites reflect another conservative undercurrent in American culture by always finding individuals to celebrate rather than the much broader movements of which they were a part. Finally, by offering a narrative that suggests the inevitability of the march of freedom, they silently excuse or ignore past wrongs. Of course, none of these is more glaring than the issue of slavery. In addition, besides Colonial Williamsburg's trade shops and a few of its Revolutionary City sketches, there is near silence on class. We hear about the bewigged men in Independence Hall but not about the people who elected them; at least we learn about slavery at Monticello, but nothing concerning Jefferson's relationship with the less well-to-do whites or free blacks in Albemarle County. The National Constitution Center mentions the abolition of slavery but offers little on how the peculiar institution was the warp and woof of the original document, and completely ignores the ways that its writing and, historically, its interpretation have favored the well-off compared to their less-propertied neighbors, customers, and employees. American Revolution sites thereby short-circuit discussion of past inequalities or concern for present ones: after all, the story implies, injustices come out in the wash eventually, so no need to rectify them—especially in ways that would require broader inconvenience or sacrifice.

Through the portrayal of this narrowed sense of "freedom," the American Revolution has been made safe for public agencies and for corporate and individual sponsors, co-opted as an endorsement of current social and economic conditions. The celebration of freedom is deeply American and politically correct in its emphasis on racial diversity, a seemingly race-neutral mode of rhetoric that belies the more ugly reality of racial, gender, and class inequality by many objective measures. Publicly funded sites like those run by the NPS need not fear that a senator will hold hearings on a particular exhibit and threaten to withhold funds from the Department of the Interior, the agency that supervises the National Park Service. Corporate sponsors of privately funded sites and programs like Mount Vernon, the National Constitution Center, and Colonial Williamsburg can represent themselves as upstanding corporate citizens and have their logos displayed prominently to the millions of tourists who go to these sites. Those sponsors hope that visitors make the implicit association that these corporations are eternal, integral, and salutary elements of the nation, rather than historically contingent institutions that, in the American context, were founded as anti-democratic institutions (read my first book for proof of American corporations' long anti-democratic bent). Rich individuals receive the ego boost of seeing their names associated with the essential American institutions, get to hob-nob at receptions, and gain the admiration of their peers. Employees get the pleasure and prestige of working at some of the nation's most hallowed sites as long as their interpretations fit with parameters that won't offend financial and political sponsors. Tourists encounter a result that offends no one and challenges no one, thereby rendering American Revolution sites closed to politics and open for business.

I don't question the motives of the people involved. Individuals and corporations generously donate their money and often considerable time. Nobody's getting rich working at any of these sites: employees and volunteers flock there motivated by deep passion and dedication for the American Revolution, particular sites, and educating the public. Many of the interpretive staff that I talked to yearn to offer more challenging interpretations. But corporate names displayed prominently on the donor walls function no differently than corporate logos plastered on racing cars, both in the perception of the public and in the hallways of the institutions themselves. They provide an avenue for corporations to be associated with heroes and for the heroes to be enlisted in public relations. In 2010, Chrysler broadcast cheeky TV commercials depicting George Washington driving a Dodge Charger. Ford has done Chrysler one better. By being a major sponsor of Mount Vernon, Ford has the first president himself as one of their pitchmen. In other words, the bland emphasis on freedom does not result from a conspiracy, right-wing, left-wing, or otherwise: rather, for public history, it's the path of least resistance.

The ideological uniformity of American Revolution sites and interpretations becomes strikingly apparent in contrast with outliers that do not fit the mold. Unlike sites administered by public agencies or funded through the generosity of large corporations and cultivation of rich donors, the National Liberty Museum in Philadelphia is the brainchild of one man, the printing and publishing magnate Irvin Borowsky. Accordingly, it doesn't face the ideological constraints that management of other sites do. Nestled in a narrow, three-story structure amid taller buildings, across slender Chestnut Street from Carpenters Hall, this idiosyncratic museum dares to tell a much more critical story of "liberty" than do slicker, more-visited sites. Permanent exhibits include a gallery of presidential portraits in a room with a huge replica of Howard Chandler Christy's *Scene of the Signing of the Constitution of the United States* (the original of which hangs in the Capitol Building in Washington) and various works of modern art from Borowsky's personal collection. Unlike any of the other museums or any of the tours that I took, this museum notes freedom's costs. By this I do not mean the blood price so often uncritically cited on bumpers stickers and from the floors of Congress ("freedom isn't free"): all nations, from the most libertarian democracies to the most totalitarian regimes, have required the death of its soldiers or those of its allies to retain sovereignty. Rather, the National Liberty Museum also exposes the price of the abuse of liberty. Other museums sidestep debates concerning the Second Amendment or cite it and move on, their sponsors and curators unwilling to stir

Figure 3.10.
National Liberty
Museum. It is
tucked away on a
narrow street, with
no parking of its
own, and enjoys
little fanfare.

either gun-rights proponents or gun-control advocates. By contrast, a National Liberty Museum second-floor gallery features multiple installations enumerating and interpreting the death and destruction caused through gun violence. Freedom of expression is presented nearly everywhere else as an unalloyed good. The National Liberty Museum challenges this public history orthodoxy head-on: near a gallery celebrating religious freedom, another one includes several installations noting the number of incidents resulting from bullying and hateful speech. Admittedly, it's a one-sided point of view. But it's one more side than those many institutions offering nothing but liberty.

Meanwhile, the explorations of African Americans at the first white house, Monticello, Colonial Williamsburg, and other sites placate both essentialist and organicist sensibilities while sidestepping much of the necessary moral work to be done if we want to come to grips with race. Showing the humanity of the enslaved is absolutely necessary, but, sadly, it is not sufficient to addressing the problem of race either in Revolutionary America or, by implication, today. We must show the founders both signing heroic documents and signing bills of sale for human children, beating the British army on the field of battle as well as beating human beings on their own plantations, as unpleasant as that may sound. By focusing only on the humanity of the enslaved but avoiding the slavers' inhumanity, we absolve the Revolutionary generation of its greatest collective failure, one that many of that generation recognized was wrong, even if most whites (North and South) were too economically and socially attached to slavery to get rid of it. If racial inequality is not the founding generation's fault, the logic flows, then surely it couldn't be our fault, either. By giving the founding generation a pass, we do not have to acknowledge that our generation actively perpetuates conditions in which race continues to be a major dividing line between whites and blacks in terms of divorce rates, median salaries, life expectancy, incarceration rates, education levels, residential location, infant mortality, and political representation. We abdicate our own responsibilities to deal with these problems—doing that would require energy and dipping into our own pockets to help others. The genius and the flaw of just about all the sites that I visited is that they inspire a connection to an inevitable American project, rather than to one that we continue to shape. There were some exceptions, of course: the National Constitution Center permanent exhibit includes an installation prompting feedback from visitors on constitutional issues. But on the whole, they are all essentialist sites in that they present the past as finished and the process of democracy as completed, rather than as a work in progress.

We as individuals are also works in progress. It was one thing to read books or watch movies about a subject, even one about which I'm passionate and knowledgeable. It was another to be in the actual setting and the actual buildings and on the real ground where the events that I've studied and written about and thought about took place. As a professional academic, I had preferred to believe that I was above the sentimentality that Revolutionary sites work to inspire. I had convinced myself that I had traipsed up and down the Eastern Seaboard on my academic charge to conduct a clinical, dispassionate study of how the American Revolution is interpreted. But, in a finding that would surprise neither my family nor my physician, it turned out that I was no less human than the other people milling through Independence Hall or shifting a few steps to the left to gain a better vantage point of a costumed interpreter at Colonial Williamsburg's Capitol Building. Philadelphia held additional resonance for me because I had lived there, and Colonial Williamsburg because I had worked there. Yet on my odyssey to American Revolution sites, what moved me was less the places or structures themselves than the people working in them and, at least as much, the individuals, couples, and families who made pilgrimages and spent their precious money and vacation time to see those same sites that I had come to see. They had come out of a deep sense of connection, a deep sense of wanting to tread on the same ground as the nation's founders, to understand themselves, and to feel a connection with their fellow citizens and their nation.

The stirring of visceral connections among the sense of place, the love of country, and either essentialism or organicism holds significant ramifications for how Americans perceive the nation, who belongs to it, and how it should be governed. That emotional draw is something special that binds people together in the imagined community that we call the United States. As many historians and theorists of memory have observed, associating past events with a particular sense of place can provoke a gut response, even when people are visiting a site where they have never been to consider happenings in which neither they nor anyone they knew took part. Such sites provide a common bond among citizens and between citizens and their governments, creating a sense of common past, a store of memories central to people's sense of identity. But if even the most dispassionate of observers is not immune to the tug of Monticello's entry hall or Philadelphia's Graff House (where Jefferson drafted the Declaration of Independence), then there may be little hope that the great majority of visitors would be able to experience such sites with a critical eye. When the buildings that are preserved are the sites of great achievements or are associated with the men who are central to their accomplishment, there lies the challenge for nuanced interpretation that necessarily calls for an acknowledgment of both

Revolutionary successes and failures. Perhaps that is why I found Colonial Williamsburg's Revolutionary City theater and the first white house site so compelling: they open us to the possibility of qualified reverence, one that allows for both the admiration of Revolutionary achievements and the questioning of Revolutionary failures. Among all the possibilities for experiencing history, historical sites hold the greatest potential to stir the soul and challenge the mind, and among all American historical events, none holds our fascination more than the Revolution. The more we make these experiences human, the better the conversation we can have.

4

Give Me *Liberty's Kids*

How the Revolution Has Been Televised and Filmed

A lone violin plays a mournful tune while the panicked young redcoat runs through wintry woods. He looks back before clearing the trees to a high mountain plain. The camera pans back, showing him sprinting toward three mounted officers alongside a small regiment of smartly marching British soldiers. A close-up shows the soldier pointing back at the woods, talking, although the only sound is the fiddle's whine. Quick close shots show the British flags, the officers shouting, the men shouldering their muskets as one to fire. The frame shifts to a pan shot of the woods from which the first soldier ran, then a close-up showing guns at the ready. A soldier gazes expectantly. Back to the woods: with a roar, three black, 425-horsepower 2010 Dodge Challenger SRT8 coupes race into the plain. The middle one boasts a flagpole sticking vertically out its passenger-side window, bearing a large Stars and Stripes. Fear hits the bewigged British officer's face, and he turns his horse. The British line breaks. Close-up of George Washington at the steering wheel, black seatbelt diagonally bisecting his blue-and-buff Continental uniform. A wildly shaking handheld camera captures the chaos of the terrorized British in flight, one officer falling off his horse, a soldier tripping to the ground. As the cars rip through the British, a male voice-over intones, "Here's a couple of things America got right"—pause for cut to Washington, standing beside his vehicle among the three—"Cars, and freedom." Then a waving Dodge flag fills the screen, with "Dodge Challenger" superimposed in white letters, before transition to black and the violin's last note.

That car commercial first aired on July 10, 2010, during a men's World Cup soccer match between the United States and England (unlike the sixty-second, pre-staged advertising rout, the game was a tie). "America's full of awesome folk tales, from Paul Bunyan to Davy Crockett," said the commercial's art director, Jimm Lasser. "There's something kind of funny about a magical Dodge Challenger that helps win freedom for America." Observers debated the commercial's content, its timing, and its politics. The business journalist Jim Henry noted the irony of such flag-waving on the part of Chrysler, which had been part of the German auto giant Daimler-Benz's portfolio until 2007 and in 2009 was bought out by Italy's Fiat. Plus the car was actually manufactured at the company's Canadian plant in Brampton, Ontario. Given the commercial's touting of a Detroit muscle car and conspicuous use of the red, white, and blue, advertising watchers speculated that the spot intentionally appealed to members of the tea party (more about them in the next chapter): they embodied the middle-aged, white male demographic most likely to buy a retro-looking muscle car and most angry about the recent federal bailout of the auto companies, including Chrysler. Such commentary signals that, when the American Revolution hits the screen, whether on TV or the movies, people quickly interpret what they see in political terms. If a whimsical, sixty-second car commercial can carry such ideological freight, then longer depictions, too, can be loaded with political meanings.

This chapter analyzes the ways that producers, directors, and screenwriters have portrayed the American Revolution. Although filmmakers often seek to make their work into seamless narratives, films and shows—along with the debates within their creative teams—reveal essentialist and organicist faultlines. Industry conventions for historical movies and, especially, television constrain Hollywood creative teams' organicist attempts to highlight diversity and the humanity of all people (both hallmarks of multicultural history) during a time when "all men are created equal" proved to be an aspiration at best and empty slogan at worst. Rather than play "historian cop," citing films for historical inaccuracies, we should consider the inherent difficulties of trying to apply a multicultural sensibility to portrayals of the American Revolution in formats that emphasize immediacy and emotional power over extended and nuanced consideration, and we should acknowledge that historical films are exercises in ideological narratives rather than pure windows into the past. This chapter notes the tension between the multicultural ethic broadly accepted by many (but far from all) of the creative workers in the film industry, on the one hand, and on the other, the more traditional historical narrative of the Revolution focused on the political and military elites that they rely on, that their corporate parents are comfortable with, and that they ultimately offer to audiences. Such presentations do more than flatten the complexities of the Revolution: they provide the appearance of near-unanimity by representing a chorus of differing voices that in the end agree. In these varied treatments, the Revolution and its shorthand symbols become fodder for shaping patriotism and citizenship and provide further evidence of their broad recognition and continued symbolic power in American popular culture.

Whether designed to be box-office hits, produced for an upscale cable television audience, or made as educational vehicles for children, recent major screen portrayals of the American Revolution have presented an essentialist interpretation with organicist trappings. That is at least a mild a departure from how the Revolution appeared on-screen during the twentieth century, in which, for example, slavery was occasionally mentioned but actual enslaved people weren't characters unto themselves. As I found in watching many hours of movies and television shows, writers and directors have more recently shown increased sensitivity to racial diversity, to female characters, and to the differences of opinion among Americans, as opposed to the more white, male, flat treatments of previous Hollywood productions. This new sensibility appears in a variety of ways, ranging from the casting of women and African Americans as major characters to the subtle, silent inclusion of visual details in passing. It reflects the American consensus built over the 1970s and 1980s toward greater inclusion as well as the changing political proclivities of screenwriters, directors, producers, and especially, movie executives, as the industry has shifted from quite conservative to much more liberal, although not uniformly so. But even when the creative teams behind various film projects hold political views or educational agendas that might seem to suggest an organicist view toward the Revolution, the final products continue to manifest signs of essentialism. They do so both in their view of history as a single truth and in their investment in the portrayal of the moral superiority of the American cause and its nearly unambiguous success. The people behind these films work according to cultural industry conventions in which TV and movies have modes of storytelling that necessarily emphasize the personal over the structural, character over content, and the visually dramatic over slower or internal transformations. In doing so, they naturally focus on founding heroes over messy complexities.

People interested in the American Revolution complain that it has not been the subject of many movies or television series or, for that matter, especially good ones. Since *The Declaration of Independence* graced the silver screen in 1911, there have been no more than a couple score of movies and major TV series about the Revolution, although it has attracted its share of stars, among them Henry Fonda, Claudette Colbert, Kirk Douglas, Burt Lancaster, Laurence Olivier, Al Pacino, Lloyd Bridges, Billy Crystal, Annette Bening, Jeff Daniels, and Paul Giamatti, many of them no doubt personally drawn to the topic. Among the most memorable are *The Howards of Virginia* (1940), starring Cary Grant as a Revolutionary Cary Grant (that is, more or less playing his debonair self); the Disney series *Swamp Fox*, based loosely on the derring-do of Continental officer Francis Marion; and the musical *1776* (1972), which melded quotations of the signers of the Declaration of Independence with early 1970s camp. None of them have been big hits, including the flop *Revolution* (1985), in which Al Pacino demonstrated that he should stick to movies with a twentieth-century timeframe. As if to prove the point that making the Revolution profitable theater fare is a nearly impossible task, *Sweet Liberty* (1986) starred Alan Alda as a history professor whose book on the Revolution gets mangled by the scriptwriter and director charged with turning it into a box-office winner.

As with most questions academics consider, historians disagree on why the Revolution on-screen record is so meager and of little quality. Unlike more recent events, we don't have any film footage of Revolutionary figures, and in the paintings we do have they're wearing funny clothes and holding feathers for pens. As film historian Mark Glancy has pointed out, for many decades British capital and potential profits helped bankroll the big Hollywood studios, which led them to be reluctant to cast Brits as villains. Studios want sympathetic protagonists, so for filmmakers over the last few decades, it certainly hasn't helped that many prominent founders were slaveholders. Some historians have pointed out that the founders are so different from us that they're hard for contemporary moviemakers and audiences to grasp. But the idea that we might find characters in a film alien to us hasn't stopped many

filmmakers from making movies about all sorts of people from different places and cultures (and, for that matter, about aliens, too), portraying them behaving suspiciously like contemporary Americans. None of
these theories are totally wrong, but almost all of them could be applied
to the film treatments of any number of historical events.

We might be placing the bar too high: there aren't many good major
films about any period in American history because movie industry logic works against the complexity such movies would require. To
fund a project in Hollywood, its champions—a screenwriter, director,
producer, or star—have to convince a major studio of the film's profit
potential. That's not an easy task, as major motion pictures are notoriously hit-and-miss. Knowing whether a movie will break even based
upon little more than a script and a few casting ideas can be devil-
ishly hard to predict. Studios want some assurance that the film can be
quickly described and that viewers can latch onto it. Movie executives
look for a conventional story, setting, or both. That's why the big studios
love movie franchises, big stars, and genres, because they are known
quantities to the ticket-buying public. Hollywood has made billions of
dollars churning out comedies, romances, musicals, and costume dramas featuring the boy-meets-girl, boy-loses-girl, boy-gets-girl-back-
again plotline. Conventional settings include the sleek offices and high-
rises of contemporary American cities as well as the seemingly placeless
and timeless American suburbs. To be made into the kind of pitch that
movie executives are likely to green-light, scripts usually have to fit
within the confines of what movie people call a "genre," that is, movies
that fall within a set of viewer expectations concerning their characters, plot, and setting that are easily recognized, like "superhero action
movie," "spy thriller," or "teen comedy." Genre movies are good bets
because they can be easily promoted to audiences in the United States
and abroad that already have expectations of what they will see, unlike
movies that are completely unknown quantities, but genre movies don't
lend themselves well to history.

There are only a few historical movie genres, and they have less to
do with history than with more contemporary issues. World War II and
Vietnam War movie genres are now historical, but they both began as
contemporary genres rather than historical ones. American war movies are about fighting the good fight (or sometimes the bad fight, in the

latter case), and they continue to be. Westerns have never been about history: they rarely pretend to portray real events, real characters, or even real places. Costume dramas are all about character development and nothing about history, which is why so many of the same plots get adapted to contemporary settings (for example, the eighteenth-century French drama *Dangerous Liaisons* later made into *Cruel Intentions*, taking place in today's Upper East Side of Manhattan). That's it. Otherwise, there aren't many movies about any one American event or historical process. The Civil War has been the subject of a few more movies than the American Revolution, but merely four of them were particularly notable: D. W. Griffith's *Birth of A Nation* (1915), *Gone with the Wind* (1939), *Glory* (1989), and *Lincoln* (2012). Only the latter two are still considered plausible historical interpretations in addition to their qualities as movies. Beyond the dearth of productions, also working against what historians perceive as historical accuracy is that genre films tend to have straightforward plots. Historians envision history as complex, nuanced, and multicausal, with events having multiple possible beginnings and inconclusive or ambiguous endings. Conversely, screenwriters are taught to give films a simple structure: movies should have three acts—a clear beginning, a confrontation, and a satisfying resolution—separated by plot points on which the action pivots. In sum, there aren't good movies about the Revolution, not necessarily because of some inherent flaw in the subject matter or a cultural industry blind spot, but because there are so few good historical Hollywood movies at all.

The post-millennium pair of films that offer the interpretation of the American Revolution seen by the most people were not really about the Revolution: *National Treasure* (2004) and its sequel, *National Treasure: Book of Secrets* (2007). Although the idea for the first movie dated five years before Dan Brown's 2003 international super-selling novel *The Da Vinci Code*, these modern-day scavenger hunts in the tradition of 1950s B movie serials benefited from the renewed interest in historical mysteries, treasure, and conspiracies that the book stirred. The making of the *National Treasure* movies fulfilled the characteristics that one observer has called essential to the manufacturing of movie profit, as "calculated blockbuster[s] designed with the multimedia marketplace and franchise status in mind." Starring big-name actor Nicholas Cage, directed by the seasoned Jon Turteltaub, and shepherded by megahit

action-film producer Jerry Bruckheimer, the first of the two films cost
$100 million to make and raked in $173 million in the United States; the
second grossed $220 million domestically. Disney Studios bankrolled
the movies as part of its 2000s foray into wholesome action movies,
with lots of running and occasional explosions, but with heroes who
don't tout guns and with no sex or cuss words. Studio executives hoped
to attract preteens to adults and cash in on brand-building synergies.
National Treasure showcases Visa cards and Urban Outfitters, and was
launched with commercial tie-ins to McDonalds, Kodak, Verizon, Visa,
and Dodge. While neither of the *National Treasure* films is about the
American Revolution per se, each of them invokes founding fathers
as nearly oracular figures, portrays founding documents as relics, and
presents the past as a something that can be known definitively, containing an absolute truth, if only we uncover the full set of facts. In
doing so, the *National Treasure* franchise delivers an unambiguously
essentialist interpretation of the American Revolution. Perhaps that
is to be expected: because purely commercial entertainment ventures
depend upon cultural industry interconnections with other major corporations, *National Treasure* and its sequel delivered a safe product for
its sponsors and its audience.

National Treasure and *National Treasure: Book of Secrets* each string
together entertaining and often witty scenes beginning with clues and
conversation and escalating into chases and stunts. Both movies feature
Benjamin Franklin "Ben" Gates (Nicholas Cage), Abigail Chase (Diane
Kruger) as his love interest, and Riley Poole (Justin Bartha) as his side-
kick. In the first film, treasure-hunter Gates—he prefers "treasure protector"—seeks a trove of ancient booty gathered by the Knights Templar and then transferred to America via the Freemasons, including
founders such as George Washington and Gates's namesake. Ben and
Riley discover clues indicating that they need the Declaration of Independence to solve the puzzle, and so Ben encounters Abigail, a curator
at the National Archives, where the Declaration is stored. Knowing a
ruthless rival will try to steal the Declaration, Ben decides the best way
to protect the nation's birth certificate is to steal it himself. A message
written in invisible ink on the back of the Declaration points them to a
clue in Philadelphia's Independence Hall and eventually on to the climactic scene under New York City. The opening of *National Treasure:*

Figure 4.1. Stealing a National Treasure. Ben Gates (Nicholas Cage) steals the Declaration of Independence, protective case and all, from the National Archives, in Jon Turteltaub, dir., *National Treasure* (DVD; Buena Vista Home Entertainment / Touchstone, 2007).

Book of Secrets finds Ben giving a lecture on Lincoln assassin John Wilkes Booth, only to be confronted by Mitch Wilkinson (Ed Harris), who has found a document indicating that Ben's great-great-grandfather, Thomas Gates, was the assassination's mastermind. But as Ben works to clear his name, enlisting Riley, Abigail, and his parents (Jon Voight and Helen Mirren), and scrambling through Paris streets, Mount Vernon (George Washington's plantation house), London's Buckingham Palace, the White House, and the Library of Congress, he finds that Wilkinson is really after a lost city of gold and willing to kill for it.

Two elements of the *National Treasure* movies establish their essentialist ideology. The first is that both films treat the objects that the founders made as unspeakably sacred. What the Declaration of Independence meant in 1776, or today, is irrelevant in *National Treasure*. Rather, its existence as something to be protected and venerated as a relic, unchanging and unexamined, obliterates any consideration of its earthbound context or ramifications. Similarly, the *National Treasure: Book of Secrets* sequence at Mount Vernon doesn't address what actually happened there, much less why. Instead, the script emphasizes that this was George Washington's house—*his house*—and so holds a clue to the next treasure. The films' emphasis on clues rather than content is best illustrated in contrast to the prototypical movie that Turteltaub envisioned when he first cooked up the idea for *National Treasure* in the mold of a 1980s big-money movie franchise: *Raiders of the Lost Ark* and its two

Figure 4.2. Mount Vernon as Stage Prop. The president (Bruce Greenwood) and Ben Gates discuss a map during a party at Mount Vernon. Jon Turteltaub, dir., *National Treasure 2: Book of Secrets* (DVD; Buena Vista Home Entertainment/Touchstone, 2008).

sequels. The hero of those movies, Indiana Jones (Harrison Ford) was also a treasure hunter of sorts seeking objects with unambiguous religious value, most notably the lost ark of the covenant, from the Hebrew Bible, and the holy grail, from the New Testament. But there's a crucial difference between the Indiana Jones and *National Treasure* movies. In the *Raider* films, understanding what the relics represent, that is, what they mean, becomes the difference between success and failure. True belief in forces beyond human ken distinguishes Indiana Jones from his Nazi opponents in the first Indiana Jones movie; in the third, Jones's survival hinges on his understanding that the quest for the holy grail is a test of mettle rather than a race for personal glory. By contrast, although in the second *National Treasure* Ben does begin with a less potentially enriching motive—restoring his family's honor—the artifacts created by the founding generation are prized primarily for their talismanic value rather than for what they may have originally meant. They are set in time, not to be examined or questioned, but only venerated.

The other way that the *National Treasure* movies enforce essentialism is by portraying an understanding of the past as a train of knowable, indisputable facts rather than as a matter of multiple possible interpretations. There are plenty of arguments among professional historians about some matters that in theory can be dated or counted, such as how many people were forcibly shipped from Africa to the Americas during the transatlantic slave trade (although even that debate not only involves counting people listed on extant ship manifests but also considering the thornier question of how many people came across for whom documentation no longer exists or never did). But the *National Treasure* movies treat history as a knowable series of clear-cut facts, rather than as a complex matter of nuanced interpretation. In fairness to the movies' creative team, they did their best to adhere to those facts. Turteltaub was very scrupulous in his handling of the kind of historical references that should appear on-screen. Despite a chaotic creative process in which writers, actors, and the director were improvising dialog right up until the moment scenes were shot, Turteltaub noted that "the only thing we had to be very careful about was keeping our historical facts straight. That was something we couldn't fake." Both movies peddle the premise that history is a series of clues, part and parcel of essentialist thinking. There are facts, and all we have to do is find them, and the only new history is from newly found or rediscovered documents, not from new interpretations—because there can only be one true interpretation. What sets *National Treasure: Book of Secrets* in motion could be seen as a matter of interpretation, the question of whether the fictional Thomas Gates contributed to Lincoln's assassination. Ben's desire to clear his ancestor's name is not an act of analysis, but one of detective work, to find the irrefutable documentary evidence clearing Thomas. That's still essentialism: there are facts, and if we can reveal them all, we know the truth.

Despite the popularity of the *National Treasure* franchise, when people find out that I teach the American Revolution, they tend to ask me about two things. One is the tea party movement. The other is *The Patriot*, even more than a decade after it came out in the theaters. Reviled by reenactors and hated by historians, *The Patriot* crops up as a favorite historical movie among students and casual history fans and is by far the most commercially successful movie ever made specifically about the American Revolution. From start to finish, it was designed as a manufactured vehicle for profit, replete with "a large budget, enhanced production values, star presence, large-scale story material, and display of technical virtuosity," as the film observer Michael Allen has written about blockbusters. Critics gave *The Patriot* measured kudos for its look, the quality of its acting, and being primarily driven by characters rather than battles, though they were less complimentary about its verisimilitude. As *Toledo Blade* movie reviewer Nanciann Cherry put it, "*The Patriot* breaks no new ground, and its history isn't always accurate, but as rousing entertainment, it delivers the goods." *The Patriot* stars Mel Gibson, one of the world's biggest box-office attractions at the time, commanding $25 million for his role in the film. Columbia Pictures poured $110 million into production and added $29.2 million for marketing, signing on big-budget director Roland Emmerich and noted film composer John Williams. Released in late June 2000—a week ahead of July 4 weekend—the movie spent close to sixteen weeks in theaters, grossing $113 million domestically and another $101 million outside the United States. That the movie made proportionately less of its gross abroad compared to other big-budget, blockbuster-style films was no big surprise, given its topic. *The Patriot* garnered Oscar nominations for cinematography, sound, and original score. In *The Patriot*, the combination of the memory of the American Revolution and the logic of Hollywood moviemaking resulted in a product that dresses a very essentialist story in organicist trappings.

As is often the case with historical films, *The Patriot's* plot is compelling on a personal level but furthers hoary legends (and creates new ones) that historians have been at pains to debunk. Gibson plays Benjamin Martin, a composite of several American Revolutionary War figures, most notably South Carolinian Francis Marion. A wealthy South Carolina planter with African Americans in his employ—rather than under his ownership—Benjamin is called to the South Carolina legislature in 1776 and argues against funding the Continental Army. He dreads violent conflict and its price, which he knows well from his service in the French and Indian War. But the assembly votes for independence, and his dashing eldest son Gabriel (Heath Ledger) enlists. Benjamin takes up the cause once brutal British officer William Tavington (Jason Isaacs) kills Benjamin's second son. He leads a militia in guerrilla tactics, among them using ambushes, taking shelter in uneven terrain, elaborate ruses, and intentionally targeting officers. In doing so, he motivates British General Charles Cornwallis (Tom Wilkinson) to give Tavington license to cruelty. That includes locking the population of a small village, among them Gabriel's sweetheart, into a church before burning it down—an incident borrowed from a Nazi atrocity late in World War II, and far more heinous than anything the British

Figure 4.3. The Patriotic Benjamin Martin. Martin (Mel Gibson) carries the battle standard to inspire his fellow soldiers in Roland Emmerich, dir., *The Patriot*, special ed. (DVD;
Sony Pictures Home Entertainment, 2000).

actually committed during the American Revolution. Gabriel's attempt
at revenge results in his own death at Tavington's hands. Over the
course of the movie, Benjamin's men learn to accept Occam (Jay Arlen
Jones), a slave joining the American cause to gain his liberty. The movie's climactic scene portrays an amalgamation of several real battles, as
Benjamin finally kills Tavington in super slow motion. The subsequent
depiction of the Battle of Yorktown seems tacked on, given that the
main conflict in the film has already been resolved. And therein lies
the central problem of *The Patriot*: the urge to tell a universal story of
familial revenge while also attempting to portray a historical event, the
American Revolution.

The contradiction of *The Patriot* lies in the tensions among Hollywood's desire for a recognizable story along familiar lines—the Hollywood studios are still conservative institutions, now peopled by liberals—and the personnel on the film's creative team, their notions of
historical similitude, and their own perception of the story. *The Patriot*
began as the brainchild of screenwriter Robert Rodat and producer
Mark Gordon. Fresh off their success with the World War II film *Saving
Private Ryan* (1998), they cast about for their next big idea. It didn't take
long. "From the time I was a kid," Rodat later said, "the American Revolution always fascinated me. I've never understood why there wasn't a
movie that had captured it." Rodat's suggestion stirred Gordon, who had
grown up near Williamsburg and Yorktown. Rodat began with Francis

Marion, mixing in details from other historical figures Thomas Sumter, Andrew Pickens, Daniel Morgan, and Elijah Clark, but he eventually decided upon a composite fictional character as the protagonist. *The Patriot's* creators were not out to make a conservative movie. Rodat and Gordon have both contributed to Democratic campaign funds. Despite what may be their liberal personal political proclivities, what appeared on-screen was a story suggesting that the Americans were good, free-dom-loving people who won the war against an evil British military by using guerrilla tactics—rather than a complicated conflict in which many on the American side fought at least partially to preserve slavery and that was won mostly because of long British supply lines and the aid of a very traditional French military.

In line with Hollywood conventions about how to market a movie, the movie's creators wanted to make a film that anyone could relate to. American patriotism, though, doesn't sell well beyond American shores, endangering a crucial component of blockbuster movie revenue. The result was a script that centered around one man's reluctant entry into the war, not on principle, but to defend and, eventually, to avenge his family. Executive producer Gary Levinsohn later argued that "what's so great about these types of stories is that they're really everybody's story. It's America's story, the New World story. It's Australia's, it's South Africa's story. It's for anyone who is forced to defend their children and their beliefs" (thus begging the question whether *The Patriot* should also be for the descendants of loyalists who defended their homes from patriots). But in this movie, nothing about beliefs appears to motivate Benjamin's entry into the war; rather than defending ideals or nation-hood, he fights to defend his family. Writing in the online magazine *Slate*, critic Michael Lind suggested that *The Patriot's* creative team must not understand patriotism at all. As it turns out, Emmerich, Rodat, and Gibson do know what patriotism is, but, as Gibson pointed out, "Mar-tin's not really the patriot; he hasn't got the wider view of things. . . . Martin just goes along to watch his son's back." Emmerich concurred, noting that "this movie is called *The Patriot*, but Benjamin Martin is not a Patriot . . . in the end, he fights not for himself but for his children. He carries the flag at the end to rally the troops not so much out of patrio-tism but as the symbol of his personal struggle." In other words, rather than describing the character played by the big-name actor, the title better refers to his son. But the title *The Patriot* surely would have fared better in audience pre-screenings than *The Patriot's Reluctant Father*.

Nonetheless, contrary to my academic colleagues and other critics, I would argue that *The Patriot* is often a good and occasionally great movie about the American Revolution—wrapped in the forced dramatic mediocrity that marks the Hollywood blockbuster formula. The scenes featuring Benjamin and Gabriel efficiently and poignantly depict the fraught relationship between father and son, one of the central literal and figurative dynamics of the Revolution: Benjamin's frustrated attempt to temper Gabriel's headlong insistence on joining and rejoining the Continental Army, his trying to caution the younger man to be careful, their banter, their chewing an apple using identical movements. Other scenes show the Revolution's misery: a militia man, Rollins, comes home to see the corpses of his family and, in despair, takes his own life; after a pause, Benjamin releases the men to a furlough, and they ride off wordlessly. It captures Revolutionary rage in the fury with which Benjamin attacks the British regulars who were transporting the captive Gabriel, minutes after the death of Benjamin's son Thomas at Tavington's hands, and his sons' horror witnessing their father's bloodlust. It depicts the British quandary in the conflict between Cornwallis's understanding of Britain's goal to reincorporate the colonies into the empire and Tavington's recognition that military reluctance will not win the war. With the major exception of its bizarre and regrettable treatment of slavery, *The Patriot's* first hour and a half beat out any previous film on the Revolution. The Al Pacino vehicle *Revolution* (1985) was more complicated, but it was also a box-office flop. *The Patriot* may be about as good a large-scale movie about the Revolution as we're likely to get, given the economic logic of big-budget movies.

Script changes made the film both more essentialist and more organicist in ways that tell us more about contemporary moviemaking than about the past. *The Patriot's* realistic sets, period costumes, and elaborate battle scenes featuring state-of-the-art computerized special effects cost money. Accordingly, the script was modified to include the elements of blockbusters: limited dialog, easy-to-digest symbols, spectacle (in the form of big battles), and unambiguously positive endings. These changes are evident in the revisions to Rodat's original 1998 script, made after its being picked up by Centropolis Entertainment, director

Figure 4.4. Revolutionary Rage. Mel Gibson shows the violence and rage of the American Revolution in Roland Emmerich, dir., *The Patriot*, special ed. (DVD; Sony Pictures Home Entertainment, 2000).

Emmerich's production company. Rodat's 1999 effort minimized the first draft's enlightening South Carolina assembly debate whether to support the Continental Army, flattening it into the question of Martin's reluctance to fight. He inserted into the second draft the recurring symbol of a ragged American battle flag, which Gabriel first picks up and repairs and Benjamin waves heroically in the film's grand battle scene. Benjamin's killing of Tavington gained considerable melodrama after revision. In the second draft, the Occam character appeared, so as to include an African American fighting for freedom. And between the 1999 script and the final cut, the ending was significantly revised. In the draft, following the Battle of Yorktown, Martin's friend Harry Lee announces the birth of his son—to be named "Robert E." The Confederate Civil War general really was Henry Lee's son, but born in 1807. The deft reference to the unfinished business of slavery lent the script's resolution an ominous tone. The movie eliminates that twist, with Lee naming his son Gabriel. Rodat's original closing scene had Benjamin once again working on a chair, as he had at the movie's opening, thus providing symmetry. The on-screen ending shows Occam leading Benjamin's neighbors to frame a new house to replace the one the British had burned. So here we have a free, Revolutionary-era South Carolina black man, voluntarily building a house for white one! Made for the sake of drawing more people into theaters, such changes also lent the movie mixed ideological messages.

Similar to the challenges that public history sites face, one of the keys for studios to big movie sales is finding common denominators across the ideological spectrum that will offend few prospective customers. *The Patriot* endeavored to portray race in a way that satisfies both essentialist and organicist leanings. For Rodat, writing Gabriel Martin's African American workers as voluntary employees rather than as forced labor transformed the protagonist from a slaveholder, a tough sell nowadays, into a sympathetic figure for the turn of the twenty-first century. This is the same kind of founder that essentialists like the tea party or Glenn Beck like to imagine, as loathing slavery rather than fighting to perpetuate it. The invention of Occam, fighting on the American side for liberty, allows the audience to have its cake and eat it, too: it provides for the inclusion and empowerment of African Americans, as well as the melding of personal and national independence. During the course of production, Rex Ellis, then chair of the Smithsonian's National Museum of American History's cultural history division, convinced Emmerich to move the location of Martin's retreat of his family to a maroon community located on the South Carolina beach. Maroons were formerly enslaved people who had escaped to found their own communities. It's both wonderful and preposterous: wonderful showing that there were small maroon communities at the time, preposterous in that they were, for their own protection, inland, unusually inaccessible, and generally hostile to whites, for all the reasons one might expect. Essentialism is not only about an unambiguous patriotism but also very much about a racialized view of the American Revolution and, by extension, contemporary American society. Organicism imagines a multicultural, multiracial society in which every individual has agency. *The Patriot* manages to give moviegoers both by offering a biracial founding Shangri-la.

The adding of white fantasy slavery lite—all the racial hierarchy, none of the mutual resentment—echoes previous films. British actress Joely Richardson played Charlotte Selton, Martin's sister-in-law turned love interest. She likened her participation in *The Patriot* to a particular classic Hollywood historical drama, a comparison apt in ways that she might not realize. "I watched *Gone with the Wind* as a child again and again. And for me there was that element of fantasy to *The Patriot*," she later said. "It's somehow imprinted on our minds, this idea of the romantic South, the shape that a corset will give you, the flowing skirts.

Figure 4.5. Gone with the Revolution. Charlotte Selton (Joely Richardson) in full plantation garb, flanked by Benjamin's children and her slaves.

When we shot at some of the plantations in South Carolina, there were
people riding up on horses, and carriages coming back and forth, and
I'd rush out in my Scarlett O'Hara kind of dress." For Richardson, getting to dress up like a Southern belle "was a dream come true." To be
charitable, Richardson's failure to realize that not everyone thinks of the
antebellum South as "romantic" may stem from her English upbring-
ing. One can bet that many white people in the audience were equally
in thrall to *The Patriot*'s South-sans-suffering. African American film-
maker Spike Lee was not; he wrote that he and his wife "both came out
of the theater fuming." *The Patriot* no less whitewashes the racial history
of the American South than *Gone with the Wind*, albeit in a turn-of-
the-twenty-first-century fashion. In keeping with mass popular culture
at the time, the 1939 classic portrayed blacks as submissive supporters
of a benevolent slavery system, cheering as their white masters went off
to defend the peculiar institution. *The Patriot*'s representative black is
free by the end of the movie, with nary a scar—but no less deferential
to whites. Watching *The Patriot*, one might think that the Revolutionary
South was nearly one big, happy, biracial community.

   In addition to their inherent essentialism, the *National Treasure* movies and *The Patriot* demonstrate the underlying historical logic of nearly
all fictional movies dealing with the past. Writers and directors take on
subjects about which they are passionate and tend to value what they
define as historical accuracy. Jon Turteltaub and Robert Rodat are no
exceptions. Both harbored an interest in history, and neither desired to

mislead audiences or misrepresent the historical record. They wanted to tell stories about imagined characters and fictitious events that could be manipulated for dramatic effect while still somehow not violating history. Sometimes, of course, to keep to that guideline involved some twisted logic, given the movies' suggestions of such fantastical notions as the founders being connected with the Knights Templar; Benjamin Franklin inventing multicolor, multilens eyeglasses for code breaking; and a glorious underground city of gold concealed beneath Mount Rushmore. Turteltaub hewed to a standard very common to historical fiction and moviemaking, one that affords creative minds nearly endless leeway: "Our rule was that we wouldn't put anything into the movie that we knew was not true." Unless there was indisputable proof that something absolutely did not happen, it's free game. Rodat applied the same logic to Benjamin in *The Patriot* because even in the 1770s there was the possibility for a white South Carolina man to have free black employees, no matter how rare the actual occurrence. Taken to its logical extent, that same standard can be applied to nearly any "historical" movie, even such vapid and intentionally absurd fare as *Abraham Lincoln, Vampire Hunter* (2012). We have no have definitive proof that Lincoln abstained from hunting vampires before his presidency—no denials exist. The problem from a historical point of view is that these eventualities may have been possible, but not probable, therefore giving viewers a skewed view of historical reality. But historical similitude is not what successful moviemaking, essentialism, or organicism is ultimately about.

Perhaps the most conscious effort at an on-screen, organicist portrayal of the American Revolution featured the most prominent stars but resulted in the least public debate. *Liberty's Kids* was neither widely noted nor commented upon, despite its showcasing a regiment of celebrities, among them Dustin Hoffman, Walter Cronkite, Annette Bening, Liam Neeson, Whoopi Goldberg, Michael Douglas, Samuel L. Jackson, Warren Buffett, Billy Crystal, Ben Stiller, Yolanda King, Michael York, and Sylvester Stallone. The forty-part children's animated series was produced by DIC Entertainment, a creator of commercially successful animated children's series that had been criticized for their lack of educational content, and first aired on PBS from 2002 to 2004. It portrays the Revolution from the Boston Tea Party in 1773 through George Washington's inauguration in 1789, from Maine to Mississippi and Paris to Philadelphia, and it deals sympathetically with whigs and loyalists, masters and slaves, men and women, French and English, and European Americans, African Americans, and Native Americans. It addresses not only politics and battles but also major cultural, technological, and social transformations. While *Liberty's Kids* exhibits the aesthetic and narrative limitations of children's television as a genre, it transcends its predecessors and, in some ways, all previous television depictions of the Revolution, such as Disney's live-action adaptation of *Johnny Tremain* (intended for the small and silver screens) or its 1959–1960 live-action *Swamp Fox* series. *Liberty's Kids* clocks in at around fifteen hours (thirteen and a half, not including the opening and closing credits and other features), making it the most sustained filmic treatment ever made on the American Revolution. For better or for worse, it is the broadest television depiction of the American Revolution we are likely to have for a long time. Whether their teachers like it or not, *Liberty's Kids* may provide the basic understanding of the American Revolution for a generation of Americans who watched the show on PBS, independent TV channels, the History Channel, DVD, or the Internet. My girls love it.

Liberty's Kids reveals how contested choices behind the creation of films concerning the American Revolution become fraught with concerns regarding audience and the final product's ideological ramifications. The series reflected the programming philosophy of PBS Kids (the network's children's content division) and much of the sensibility of the man whose idea it was, Kevin O'Donnell, as well as head writer Doug McIntyre. *Liberty's Kids* met multiple objectives for PBS, DIC, and the DIC team. PBS wanted to establish a beachhead in the six- to eleven-year-old viewing cohort to match its strength with pre-school audiences. In addition, the subject matter would play well to PBS's parent institution, the Corporation for Public Broadcasting, whose funding depended upon a Republican-dominated Congress suspicious of its programming, which conservatives had long characterized as being liberal leaning. Soon after George W. Bush was inaugurated, his administration signaled to PBS its unhappiness with what it perceived as the network's more liberal programs. At the 2001 PBS annual meeting, when PBS and DIC unveiled the series to member stations and the public, DIC president Andy Heyward proudly predicted that the series would "inspir[e] young Americans to understand a little more how fortunate we are to be living in such an open democracy," appealing to PBS's ambivalent political patrons. Bush Administration Secretary of Education Rod Paige looked on with pride. For DIC, *Liberty's Kids* bore few of the features that DIC executive Robby London had identified as necessary for a children's series' financial success as it lacked ties to recognizable brands or previously developed property, had no fantasy component, and held little potential for international syndication. In fact, one of the series's characteristics that most pleased PBS about the project was that, as PBS programmer Jennifer Lupinacci put it, the DIC people "were committed to the topic and doing right by their American audience." Although it lacked profitable qualities, in syndication the series could fit into a programming block to satisfy the new Federal Communication Commission rules that required commercial broadcast stations to include more educational programming. Adding *Liberty's Kids* in the block would allow DIC to sell other properties to more stations.

For the show's creators, too, the project went beyond the usual calculation of dollars and cents, syndication and market share. O'Donnell dreamed up the series concept. He was appalled by the boring nature of his daughters' textbooks and used his elder daughter as inspiration for Sarah's character. As a boy, Director Mike Maliani had been dragged to various historical sites by his history-buff father; working on *Liberty's Kids*, he found himself and his father reconnecting and gaining greater respect for each other's avocations. In a departure from DIC's usual casting procedures, Heyward personally lobbied Cronkite to give voice to Franklin; for his part, Cronkite became so engrossed that his main complaint was that "I finish with one script and then I have to wait until the next one to find out what happened." Such was the sense of common purpose that, while praising historical consultant and Pulitzer Prize–winning Jack Rakove's contributions, O'Donnell said that in comparison to the people working directly on it, "for Rakove, [*Liberty's Kids*] was just a job." Lupinacci may have been initially wary of a mainstream production company with a sparse educational programming track record, but she soon learned, much to her pleasure, that "they were not trying to sell chocolate bars in the schoolyard." For both O'Donnell and Maliani, *Liberty's Kids* represented a high point of their careers. It was as well for one of the main writers, Doug McIntyre, a longtime TV veteran (his many credits include episodes of *WKRP in Cincinnati*), amateur historian, and—more to the point here—political conservative who has been a fixture on 2000s Los Angeles talk radio. The combination of their passion for the project and their differing visions made for lively discussion on every scale, from the grander vision of the series to particular bits of dialog.

Liberty's Kids follows the adventures of James Hiller and Sarah Phillips, young fictional "journalists" reporting for Benjamin Franklin's *Pennsylvania Gazette*. As Franklin's apprentice and a committed Yankee, James reports on stories from a patriotic slant. English Sarah, entrusted to Franklin's care during her American sojourn as she seeks her army-officer father, takes the loyalist side in print and in spirited debates with James. Often accompanied on their adventures by the also-fictional pair of Henri, an orphaned French boy, and Moses, Franklin's free black employee, they are somewhere between enterprising reporters chasing stories wherever they might lead and animated, eighteenth-century Forrest Gumps, fortuitously showing up at and sometimes getting caught up in momentous events. Despite the anachronism of investigative reporters (a twentieth-century phenomenon), the series otherwise gamely reflects Revolutionary life and times. Sometimes it does so a little too much, mixing in occasional phrases that might puzzle today's twelve-year-olds, but all in all the series does well in invoking eighteenth-century British North America. The series opens in 1773 with the Boston Tea Party and continues through independence, the war, the Constitutional Convention, and Washington's inaugural. Scenes range from Franklin's negotiations in France and John Paul Jones's victories off the coast of Britain to the Ohio country and from the New Hampshire grants to the lower Mississippi. Of actual historical actors, Benjamin Franklin, George Washington, and Abigail Adams get the most face time, and the series features usual Revolutionary suspects like Thomas Jefferson, John Paul Jones, Paul Revere, and Benedict Arnold. Other, lesser-known personalities abound: Deborah Sampson, Joseph Plumb Martin, Joseph Brant, Elizabeth Freeman, James Armistead, and Sybil Ludington, to name a few. Because the series was animated, this extravaganza could be kept under DIC and PBS's budget.

What ultimately appeared on-screen resulted from cordial but constant negotiations between the PBS's programming arm and the creators at DIC, within DIC, and between DIC and its consultants. PBS

Figure 4.6. Sarah and James Share a Rare Agreeable Moment in *Liberty's Kids: The Complete Series* (DVD; Mill Creek Entertainment, 2013).

got its way most of the time, especially in terms of presenting a diverse and multicultural early America in order to promote a diverse and multicultural present. Lupinacci "very much wanted to have a diverse cast of characters" and found ready allies in O'Donnell and children's media expert UCLA professor Gordon Berry, consulting on the project. They discussed picturing not only Anglos, Native Americans, and African Americans, but also Jews, Latinos, and, from the PBS end, even Asian Americans. Not surprisingly, no Asians made the cut, but *Liberty's Kids* featured episodes on Jewish merchant Moses Michael Hays and on Spanish governor of Louisiana Bernardo de Gálvez, who are absent in all but the most encyclopedic scholarly treatments of the Revolution. In a particularly unsubtle exchange, James remarks to Gálvez, "I can't help but notice the diverse makeup of your army," prompting the governor to note that he commands men from Majorca, Spain, and Cuba, free blacks and mulattos, local colonists, and Indians. More surprisingly, Native Americans took center stage in only two episodes; O'Donnell and McIntyre later regretted not featuring Indians more prominently. One subtle form of portraying diversity that did not appear in scripts but did on storyboards and, eventually, on-screen was the inclusion of women and blacks in crowd scenes, thus showing a more pluralistic early America than previous generations' television had. For specific depictions of minorities, Berry helped DIC's writers think about how children would perceive what they heard and saw. He also provided cover for DIC in their discussions with PBS over content: such was the strength of Berry's reputation that his endorsement of episodes carried great weight with the PBS programmers.

In addition to appealing to a multicultural audience, Lupinacci was very concerned about guns. Philosophically dedicated to non-violent programming, PBS Kids also had a reputation to protect and was mindful of the industry maxim that kids "watch up," that is, younger children will watch programming targeted toward the older children in a show's main projected audience. Lupinacci had no trouble imagining "the number of calls we'd get from moms of Barney-age kids wondering why all of a sudden they're seeing guns on their kids' TV screens." PBS at first floated the possibility that *Liberty's Kids* not show guns at all or at least not show them discharging on-screen. McIntyre, who wanted a traditional narrative of the Revolution and later regretted the exclusion of the Battle of Brandywine, punctured that proposal. As he later put it, DIC "had to make the argument that we didn't outmarch the British, we outshot them." Lupinacci retreated a bit, admitting that "there's no way these stories could be told without guns," but she worked with Maliani and his storyboard artists to "downplay the visuals and sound effects where [guns] were concerned" to emphasize that "the audience would be clear why there was conflict, not distracted by the conflict." Accordingly, there are only a couple of scenes that focus on or even mention particular deaths, such as those of Joseph Warren and John Corbin (the husband of Margaret Corbin, one of several sources of the "Molly Pitcher" image). The irony is that by limiting on-screen violence but chronicling many Revolutionary War battles, *Liberty's Kids* implicitly reinforces an impression of the ennobling passions of war while minimizing the brutal consequences to people fighting for king or country.

Underlying conflicts over the extent to which the final product would be organicist or essentialist erupted over a few key questions.

Voicing aspirations and concerns similar to those of public history professionals trying to interpret the same issue in other venues, the show's creative team had the most trouble wrestling with its depiction of race and slavery. Everyone wanted to portray slavery as the nation's "original sin"—a phrase that came up repeatedly in interviews—and wanted to show African Americans as active players in the Revolution, but how? O'Donnell later recalled one conference call in which he kept everyone on the line for five hours in an effort to hash out how the show would depict slavery. One suggestion, immediately rejected, was not to show slavery at all. Nonetheless, everyone was cautious about how much of the cruelty of slavery should appear in a children's series and wanted to find some sort of balance between portraying slavery's barbarity and showing the human dignity of the enslaved. Berry and PBS pushed for emphasizing the latter, thought McIntyre remained skeptical that such a treatment represented an accurate interpretation of the repressive slave regime. Lupinacci said that PBS "wanted to be able to portray African Americans not as victims, but people." In the planning stages, they decided to lean toward African American agency. The on-screen product ended up even more on the agency end of the spectrum. In what was probably inspired by movies and novels depicting twentieth-century prisons and labor camps, an early episode script described a plantation enclosed by high walls and a white overseer coming into slave quarters to tell the slaves that it was time for lights out. Rakove's objections to those inaccuracies resulted in their removal. Episode by episode, scene by scene, the writers, producers, directors, consultants, and programming people made decisions and moved on.

Negotiations over race got worked out in peculiar ways. Dreaming up the character of Moses represented a masterstroke of threading an African American character through the entire series. For DIC, concerned with narrative structure and keeping kids tuned in, Moses provided a sympathetic adult figure to watch out for Sarah and James while Franklin was in France and allowed viewers to see what became a familiar face in nearly every episode. Moses is noticeably a large, well-built man. Unlike the slightly plump Gálvez and the relatively trim Moses Michael Hays, Moses carries an air of black nearly hyper masculinity. For Lupinacci and PBS, trying to foster appreciation for diversity and self-esteem for all its young viewers, Moses "was a free

Figure 4.7. Phillis Wheatley and Moses in *Liberty's Kids: The Complete Series* (DVD; Mill Creek Entertainment, 2013).

black man, a counterpoint to the characters that would need to be represented as slaves," representing African Americans' contribution to the American founding. For all involved, his appearance as a main character placed an African American as central rather than peripheral to the story. McIntyre first wrote Moses as having been freed by his owner in gratitude for a heroic act. PBS balked. Rather than a black man gaining freedom through white largesse, PBS wanted Moses to have bought his freedom, thereby demonstrating agency. McIntyre objected on the grounds that few Revolutionary-era blacks had the opportunity to buy themselves out of slavery, and having Moses do so would give an erroneous impression of typicality. PBS won. Ironically, when Rakove saw the script, he expressed concerns with the entire premise of a black man being accepted to run a newspaper in 1770s British North America, arguing that it would not be a realistic possibility for at least another couple of decades. None of them, not even Rakove, was aware that at least one black man, Charles Roberts, had a major role in running a newspaper in New Haven and then New York City in the 1760s—and he was an indentured servant, not a slave. In this case, PBS's organicism won out over Rakove's history.

Liberty's Kids features four African Americans: Moses, who bought his freedom; Moses's brother Cato, who escaped to the British for his; James Armistead, whose master allowed him to serve the Continental Army and eventually gain his freedom; and Phillis Wheatley, whose owners granted her freedom. "I have always thought that one person of ability may accomplish great things for the world if he first forms a solid plan and then passionately devotes himself to following it through," Benjamin Franklin writes at beginning of *Liberty's Kids*. The lesson that one might learn from Franklin (who, through his sponsorship of Moses, appears far more anti-slavery than he behaved historically) and from these exemplary African Americans is that anyone with enough gumption can attain her dreams. That's a nice message, but it doesn't square with the hard reality. Contrary to the number long used by historians of 100,000 slaves escaping to the British during the Revolution—Thomas Jefferson's back-of-the-envelope, extrapolations based upon hearsay— recently scholars Cassandra Pybus and Alan Gilbert have, through painstaking research, pegged the number at between a fifth and a third of Jefferson's guesstimate, many of whom died of smallpox in British army camps. In Revolutionary-era America, the number of free African Americans did increase significantly. But so did the number of enslaved people, who by the time of the Constitution's ratification still constituted over 95 percent of the United States's blacks. Roughly 450,000 Americans were enslaved as of 1770, and over 694,000 according to the 1790 federal census (with maybe 60,000 free blacks). The feel-good stories of *Liberty's Kids*, when presented as the only stories, are both better and worse than nothing. They can inspire African American children— or for that matter, any children—showing that everyone has a place in American society. But shown without context, such stories are also damaging. The message that anyone can succeed without displaying the thousands who didn't, or had an entirely different measuring stick of success, is misleading at best.

Liberty's Kids and other film treatments of the Revolution offer up the same twin delusions at the eternal center of American politics and culture: that everyone wants more than anything else to be free, and that everyone can be. Perpetuating these untruths in a depiction of the American Revolutionary era, especially in the context of racial slavery, embeds these myths even more deeply for both white and black viewers' consideration of the past and the present. When I teach an introductory U.S. history course and discuss antebellum slavery, I survey my students to ask how many would have tried to escape if they had been enslaved. Nearly every student raises a hand—compared to strong historical evidence that fewer than 1 percent of enslaved people attempted to escape slavery (a much greater number engaged in intentionally short-term flight, often to visit loved ones). Almost no student raises a hand when asked how many would have come to college if they would never get a chance to go home or see their family again. When I add the possibility that students would be risking torture if they didn't get straight A's and that, regardless of their success, their family might be broken up or brutally punished, no hands remain. And college students represent the same demographic as the enslaved most likely to have tried to escape: young, fairly healthy, bright, independent adults without children. *Liberty's Kids*, by contrast, shows only the plucky and the lucky. *Liberty's Kids* implies that those who remained enslaved did so because of something lacking, in other words, blaming the victims. The consequences for contemporary society can be discerned: if anyone can escape slavery, then anyone can succeed today. That's a nice message for PBS to inspire its young viewers that at its core reinforces the essentialist tenet of a free society of individuals for whom there are no structural racial, cultural, or economic constraints.

Just as *Liberty's Kids* sends mixed messages on race, Sarah's forthright manner has the potential to undermine the show's unstated feminist ambitions. Despite Sarah's "reporting" being pure anachronism, at least it performs a valuable service to young twenty-first-century viewers. She interrogates historical actors, debates them and James, and quills her conclusions for the *Pennsylvania Gazette*. She becomes doubly transformed: grappling with a range of positions and arguments, and intellectually emboldened by the act of exploration. For O'Donnell, young viewers would see a peer gain empowerment through questioning, discovering, and interpreting events for herself. O'Donnell understood this kind of device intuitively from his experience in children's animation. Psychologists are beginning to find evidence that such experiential

Figure 4.8. Assertive Sarah. Sarah challenges Ethan Allen head-on in *Liberty's Kids: The Complete Series* (DVD; Mill Creek Entertainment, 2013).

exploration is the way that many of us in contemporary America absorb and understand history. The fabrication of Sarah as a journalist furthers narrative and educational goals that do not materially contradict the series's purposes. However, to offer Sarah as a paragon for independent, contemporary girls, the writers of *Liberty's Kids* had her behave in ways that would have been abominable for a girl in eighteenth-century British America. True, James and others sometimes caution her, a signal to the audience that her questioning ways were not typical. But Sarah's aberrance from codes of acceptable Revolutionary-era comportment lead to no consequences. In a way, it's corollary to the depiction of African Americans in *Liberty's Kids*, showing a woman who can act and speak for herself—and be accepted for doing so—rather than one who defers to others. To be charitable to the makers of *Liberty's Kids*, perhaps this was a necessary artifact of producing something that would be historical and didactic. Current historians fault these same aspirations in the writing of the nation's first generations of historians and claim to avoid them in our own. It's not that O'Donnell and PBS decided for organicism over accuracy, although that was a result. Rather, their portrayal of Sarah fit their vision of contemporary children's television.

By contrast, the conventions and limits of children's animated television tend to reinforce essentialism. *Liberty's Kids* both follows and flouts them. The medium relies on narrative, on personification of broad and complex historical phenomena, and on moving stories along quickly so as not to tax short attention spans. Unlike much American media fare, in *Liberty's Kids* British accents aren't always associated with evil, and characters with minority accents are not presented as less intelligent than those whose speech sounds more white and proper. Still, *Liberty's Kids* eschews a deeper understanding of broad-based, messy movements in favor of empathy for grand individuals, and it commemorates the struggle for representative government but not the struggle over it. It celebrates heroes without examining the mass of people, preparations, and movements more powerful than any individual. It portrays progress toward racial and gender equality while giving short shrift to the enduring legacy of American society's deep divisions. *Liberty's Kids* reflects the diversity of American faces without the diversity of its ideas. It centers on the national government as opposed to local or state-level controversies, focuses on Washington and a narrow array of military leaders, and contrasts the noble suffering of enlisted men with the pettiness of squabbling politicians. It avoids thorny questions of how government should be structured and, just as crucially, who should do the structuring. To the writers' credit, two episodes depict poor people's plights with great sympathy. A struggling Philadelphia mother has difficulty affording food for her children while merchants hoard goods; a Massachusetts farmer and veteran gets dragged out of court, sobbing, as his farm is ordered repossessed. But in each case, grievants move quickly to rage-induced violence depicted in unsympathetic ways—notwithstanding the more heroic depiction of organized violence unleashed by minutemen and the Continental Army in the name of national independence. In *Liberty's Kids*, to revolt against a king in the name of popular sovereignty might be patriotic, but to question a government that invokes the people as its source of authority is only portrayed as irrational. Nothing could be more essentialist in its upholding an authoritative view of elite founders' wisdom.

While *The Patriot* portrayed the Revolution as theater blockbuster and *Liberty's Kids* presented the Revolution as children's cartoon, the seven-part 2008 HBO miniseries *John Adams* offered the life of a founder through a serious, big-budget biopic for grownups. HBO claimed to have spent $100 million on the series, or nearly $4 for every of its approximately 28 million subscribing households. Actor and producer Tom Hanks, whose Playtone production company had already worked with HBO, had bought the television rights soon after reading David McCullough's book, but the project took time to get off the ground. In July 2005, Playtone trumpeted that shooting would occur that coming fall, winter, and spring in Virginia, activity that Gov. Mark Warner hoped would be worth $60 million to the state in economic development. But casting proved to be a problem. "The actor chosen to play John Adams will be required to play him as a young man as well as a man in his 90s," explained HBO chairman Chris Albrecht, and "a big star probably won't want to give us the large amount of time we need to film the miniseries." In August 2006, Paul Giamatti agreed to play John Adams, and Laura Linney soon signed on as Abigail. Filming took place mostly in Virginia in late winter and spring 2007, making extensive use of Colonial Williamsburg; the French scenes were shot in Hungary. Playtone built full-size replicas of the Adamses' house and the White House on a plot of land outside of Richmond. The gamble paid off: the premier attracted 2.7 million viewers, and subsequent installments averaged 2.3 million. Most critics adored it, as did the Academy of Television Arts & Sciences, lavishing the series with twenty-three Emmy nominations, of which it won a record-breaking thirteen. Between DVD sales, use of the series for subsequent showings, and the boost to the subscription network's reputation for quality programming, *John Adams* proved a long-term boon to HBO's bottom line. McCullough's initially almost whimsical foray into early American history had turned into big Hollywood business.

John Adams presents a fascinating amalgam of essentialism and organicism. Writer Kirk Ellis, director Tom Hooper, and producer Tom Hanks may have had every inclination of showing organic elements of the American Revolution. They wanted to portray the partnership between John and Abigail, to celebrate one of the few founders who opposed slavery (although only privately, rather than publicly), and to

Figure 4.9. John Adams in the Continental Congress. John (Paul Giamiatti) takes on the Congress and the world in his quest for a declaration of independence, in Tom Hooper, dir., *John Adams* (DVD; HBO Video, 2008).

express patriotism as service and sacrifice rather than as knee-jerk militarism. That bent shines through in many telling elements, especially in terms of race. Subtle details indicate an organicist sensibility: crowd scenes always include African American faces, and city scenes pan by exterior walls plastered with fliers offering bounties for capture of runaway slaves. Director Tom Hooper was adamant about showing slavery on-screen, most notably in the Adamses' arrival in Washington, D.C., where they encounter slaves building one of the nation's great symbols, the White House. "Wherever I could bring [slavery] into the story," Hooper said, "I desperately wanted to, and I did seize the opportunities that I had." That scene is especially striking. "Half-fed slaves building our nation's capital," Abigail observes to John. "What possible good can come from such a place?," she asks, as they walk through the unfinished White House. Regardless of their intent, *John Adams* ends up being largely essentialist, anyway. It offers a very sympathetic portrait of its featured founding father, with John as the great mover of independence. It shows politicians as picayune debaters, in contrast to Adams the principled man of action. It puts John or Abigail Adams experiencing events that they had little or nothing to do with, and it foregrounds the

Figure 4.10. "Half-Fed Slaves Building Our Nation's Capital." John and Abigail enter the unfinished White House as enslaved workers look on. Tom Hooper, dir., *John Adams* (DVD; HBO Video, 2008).

Adamses' unease with slavery, though eliding that they did little to fight it. If you like the great man that you're filming—as McCullough, Hanks, Hooper, and Ellis do—it's hard to do great man history any other way. *John Adams* delivered founders chic to its widest audience and furthered its main essentialist thrust of a wise founding father—and mother—who sacrificed comfort for country and valued principle above popularity.

John Adams provides its audience with an Adams's-eye view of Revolutionary America and the early republic, and intentionally so. Screenwriter Kirk Ellis explained that "we would always be favoring Adams' own view of things. We would portray Franklin, Jefferson and the others though Adams' perspective." Benjamin Franklin (Tom Wilkinson) comes across as a witty and wise but somewhat unprincipled rake; Thomas Jefferson (Stephen Dillane) is an undisciplined, naïve, and yet duplicitous dreamer, although his film portrayal is nowhere near as devastating as the picture McCullough painted of him. Nonetheless, John Adams could also be self-critical, and, as many television critics noted, *John Adams* exposes a complex John Adams to the broad audience HBO banked on. He's principled and irascible, brilliant and insecure, and occasionally a little ridiculous. Franklin's famous assessment of John

Adams is borne out over the course of the series: "He means well for his Country, is always an honest Man, often a wise one, but sometimes, and in some things, absolutely out of his senses." The series's greatest triumph lies in Laura Linney's Abigail, the deepest and most nuanced on-screen interpretation of any Revolutionary-era woman. The fleshing out of Abigail was one of the strengths of McCullough's biography, and Ellis did justice to the book in making the series as much about a partnership as about John's individual faults and virtues. Ellis claims that Abigail "was very much his ballast, as he referred to her often." Unlike Franklin's well-known slight, clear on the page, there's no evidence that John ever referred specifically to Abigail as his "ballast." Nonetheless, the metaphor is apt, and one that McCullough used, which is probably where Ellis got it. Still, Linney's Abigail is more glamorous and less independent than the woman staring out of Abigail's eighteenth-century portrait. She is the faithful woman behind the man.

Historians have long discussed the problem of on-screen historical authenticity, and *John Adams* proved a big, juicy, $100-million target. Notwithstanding the filmmakers' desire for verisimilitude, HBO is also in the business of making entertainment and faced the challenge of compressing a very long life and good chunk of history into 501 minutes (closer to 475, excluding each episode's opening and closing credits). Historians and pundits took the miniseries to task for its many omissions, inaccuracies, and fabrications. These included everything from the seemingly trivial, such as the actors' Hollywood-quality teeth, to very serious misinterpretation, such as the series' placing the Battle of Bunker Hill as a motivation for the Continental Congress's decision to form an army under George Washington's command, despite the battle's happening several days afterward. More seriously, the treatment of the Boston Massacre and the subsequent trial forms an easily digested lesson in *John Adams*, that Adams braved the opprobrium of his fellow patriots in his singlehanded defense of British officer Sgt. Thomas Preston and his men. But beyond a few memorable quotations and some of the names, little of that sequence reflects the actual events: Adams was one of three lawyers, all of whom were supported by the Sons of Liberty, who wanted to show that Massachusetts could put on a fair trial. The desire to "get the history right" and varying degrees of success at doing so are fairly typical of film and television production.

Get a DVD of nearly any historical film made since the late 1990s, no matter how egregious its diversions from the historical record, and chances are it will include a special audio track with cast or production principals extolling the creative team's efforts at authenticity or a full-blown documentary on their painstaking efforts to replicate the past. Many historians play what Robert Sklar called "historian cop," citing on-screen offenses. But more interesting is considering why filmmakers make their decisions, given the conventions they work within.

Perhaps the best way to understand *John Adams* as an exercise in history is to recognize it as an amalgam of a TV series and a biopic, with the structural elements and conventions those forms entail. The "biopic"—shorthand for biographical motion picture—had its heyday in Hollywood from the 1930s through the 1950s, when the big Hollywood studios churned out movies depicting the lives of the great and, sometimes, the not so great. During the 1990s, the convention was revived for commercial success and as a star vehicle. Each *John Adams* episode opens with a time and place title—like the old title cards that preceded classic Hollywood biopics. It then moves on to a dramatic visual of an event that both provides a conflict to be resolved and motivates the main characters, in this case, John and Abigail. In order to keep those characters on center stage as well as to keep viewers abreast of important developments, the protagonists become witnesses to events that their historical models not have seen. Events and debates must be compressed, to move things along and keep production costs down. As historians Nancy Isenberg and Andrew Burstein have written, *John Adams* actually repeated many of the same scenes and plotting of *The Adams Chronicles* (1976), a PBS bicentennial series. Kirk Ellis is a thoughtful screenwriter familiar with how to structure movies and films that viewers and producers will recognize (he occasionally teaches screenwriting courses). He utilized all of these devices to give the Adamses life arcs, to shape each episode with a dramatic structure that could bring to life the material he worked with, and to keep the series from sprawling even more than it did. That's a tall order given the Adamses' eventful lives. The biopic and TV conventions led Ellis to place John and Abigail at the center of the action, just as McCullough did, and to tell their story, and that of the American Revolution, from their point of view. The result is another essentialist portrayal of a proud founder.

Those considerations help us better understand the tensions between what Ellis had to accomplish and historians' desires. Many events in or around Boston were central to the Revolution and important elements in the Adams's life. However, John and Abigail were present at only a few. That left the filmmakers with the quandary of how to portray those happenings. Despite the fact that we know John and Abigail through their letters, Ellis nearly eliminated the reading of any correspondence on-screen in favor of dramatization. In keeping with biopic conventions, Ellis and Hanks also decided that the production would show the world from the Adamses' perspective. They came up with a simple answer: stick the Adamses into those events, anyway (perhaps this occurred to Hanks first, having starred in *Forrest Gump*, which improbably places its hero as a central or peripheral figure at all sorts of events). Such scenes fit the biopic conventions, but they also reinforce an essentialist interpretation of a few important people at the center of the Revolution.

John's appearance as a putative witness occurs at several junctures, especially in the first few episodes. "Join or Die" (Episode 1) launches on the evening of what would eventually be called the Boston Massacre. John has arrived home from law work in the country. Hearing alarms, he runs out to find dead men in the street and cradles a dying man in his arms—notwithstanding that the real Adams arrived at the scene after it was cleared. But by scripting the event this way, Ellis allowed viewers to see the massacre's bloody results. More important, John sees them. The episode's conflict is set between John's duties as a lawyer and the violence inherent in having British troops stationed in Boston. Marchers in the subsequent funeral procession walk behind a "Join or Die" banner, totally out of place for Boston in 1770 but part of the graphic design for promoting the series and recognizable to viewers as a symbol of the Revolution, thereby offering valuable foreshadowing. Adams becomes essential to the greater Revolution. The opening sequence of "Independence" (Episode 2) begins on the Adams farm with John tutoring his young son Charles on the finer points of manure composting. A rider streaks by, announcing that British troops have marched on Concord. Adams shoos his family inside, telling them to flee to the woods if there's trouble, mounts up, and hits the road, where he sees the bloody remains of British men and horses and catches up to the American farmers giving chase to the Redcoats. The scene shows

Adams's panic and war's terrible toll. The film compresses real life: Concord is about twenty-five miles northwest of Boston, and Braintree—the site of the Adamses' farm—lies a dozen miles south of Boston. On-screen, John sees carnage resulting from the desperate British march back to Boston—despite the fact that real John actually didn't make that trip for several days, at which point he asked people along the route for their accounts of that bloody day. These sequences provide the dramatic result necessary to convey Adams's motivations for independence because he—and we—see that war has already come.

We might take such scenes as a harmless stretching of the facts. After all, what's important was that British regulars did fire into a Boston crowd, colonist militia and British regulars did engage in combat at Lexington and Concord, and the heroic efforts of Henry Knox's men and their beasts of burden did make a significant impact on the military situation and thus the political decision for independence. *John Adams* does not suggest that the Adamses' roles were decisive in these happenings, and how Abigail and John found out about them is not historically crucial. Nonetheless, in an unstated but quite important way for the perception of viewers, the series's placing the Adamses as witnesses to nearly every crucial event reinforces their centrality to the American Revolution. Other interpretations are more consequential. In conversation with George Washington outside of Boston in 1775, Adams says that he will fight in Congress for more arms and supplies. The problem isn't mentioned again, giving viewers the impression that the issue, apparently, has been resolved because of Adams's doggedness. In the debate on independence in the Continental Congress, Franklin wishes John "good luck" before a particular speech concerning independence as if this will be a duel with John Dickinson, which is how it's portrayed on-screen, rather than as an extended debate among many men. Most historical film productions—that is, ones that aim to relate history—make characters that are composites of multiple actual historical figures, to make them simpler and more easily dramatized. What *John Adams* does is to make the Adamses into composite characters, as well, standing in for every Revolutionary couple and their experiences, as witnesses to the grand scope of the American Revolution. This is essentialism, in which the wisdom of a few founders is substituted for the actions of thousands.

The on-screen John is nothing if not a man for both the eighteenth and the twenty-first centuries. He wears a wig and breeches but, no less than Sarah of *Liberty's Kids*, behaves according to contemporary sensibilities, especially in terms of today's views of class and race. The Adamses' companionate marriage forms the major component of the series's twenty-first-century ethos in that Abigail and John are at least partners (although admittedly she's still the junior partner). Even here, there are some wonderfully appropriate moments, like when the two are reunited in France: they bow formally to each other in front of the servants, emotions held in check. Other actions and omissions bespeak Adamses that Ellis and Hanks would have us believe are just like our neighbors. In *John Adams*, Abigail manages the household and the farm all by herself, even when John is abroad. That looks much more middle-class than showing servants who actually worked in the Adams house-hold, a decision that did not hinge on budget or time constraints, given the prospective cost of having a few extras in the background. The Brit-ish soldiers' trial following the Boston Massacre make John into a police procedural courtroom hero. Adams's actual defense, as McCullough pointed out, did rely partly on a sophisticated interrogation of wit-nesses and evidence. But it also hinged on an explicit denunciation of what the historical Adams characterized as a mob of undesirables, mocking the people the soldiers fired upon as "a motley rabble of saucy boys, negroes and molattoes, Irish teagues and out landish jack tars." That would not be acceptable for a twenty-first-century hero in a mul-ticultural age. Such omissions lead to the misinterpretation that John Adams was just like us. *National Review* movie critic Rebecca Cusey hailed Adams's "truly revolutionary confidence in ordinary Americans, a trust that simple farmers, laborers, and traders could recognize, enact, win, and defend liberty." That's an Adams that John and Abigail, both disdainful of the common white man and holding an even dimmer view of African Americans, would have failed to recognize.

Ultimately, we end up with an essentialist American Revolution and an essential founder from whom Hanks would like to draw liberal polit-ical comparisons. Hanks fits the mold that conservatives have cast as the "Hollywood liberal" (if you want literally a million hits on any Internet search engine, type in "Hanks" and "liberal," and see what comes up). He starred in *Philadelphia* (1993), the first major studio film to feature a gay man as the main protagonist, one that wrestled with the intertwined issues of AIDS, homosexuality, and discrimination. He has supported liberal causes and candidates, most notably narrating the film that introduced Barack Obama at the 2012 Democratic National Convention. And although Hanks was drawn to putting *John Adams* on film at the dawn of the new millennium—his production company inked the deal to the film rights for McCullough's book in Fall 2001—over the course of the production he came to see parallels between Adams's story and latter-day events that fit contemporary liberal political storylines. Hanks was asked in 2007 about his motivation to produce *John Adams*. Referring to the Bush Administration's eagerness to invade Iraq, Hanks opined that "John Adams kept us out of a catastrophic war with France when half the country wanted to go to war, which he knew would destroy us. And because of it he lost a re-election campaign to Thomas Jefferson. I could pull out David McCullough's book and say, 'See? It hasn't changed since 1800.'" At the premier event, Hanks compared Mike Huckabee and Mitt Romney, both then vying for the Republican presidential nomination, to Southern delegates to the Continental Congress, saying, "You can write [in the Declaration of Independence] that all men are created equal—but I'm not giving up my slaves!" Hanks demonstrated that conservatives hold no monopoly on essentialism.

The emphasis on one founder or a pair of founders and their point of view, as opposed to a messy Revolution as a mass movement, results in an essentialist experience. Essentialism presents history as driven by great men and as a story with only one authoritative point of view. Kirk Ellis keeps a much lower profile compared to Hanks, politically and otherwise, although to note that someone draws less media attention than a major movie star is perhaps not saying much. Like Tom Hooper, Ellis has emphasized that "John was the only one of the founders who did not own slaves." I guess that depends upon what one means by "founders": it's a very elite view and surprising, given that Ellis knew about men like Samuel Adams, Thomas Paine, and Alexander Hamilton. But what we end up watching is the story of John as a lion of liberty, not the indispensable man that Washington was, but indispensable nonetheless. Just as today's tea party politicians cast themselves as incorruptible heroes unwilling to compromise, rather than as politicians in the muck of government, *John Adams*'s John Adams is loathe to play ball, whether with what the series portrays as the petty bickering politicians in America or the besotted courtiers of Europe. "Thanks be to God that He gave me stubbornness . . . especially when I know that I am right" is Ellis's favorite John Adams quotation. Ellis also quotes Adams contrasting himself with his Virginia colleague: "Mister Jefferson tells people what they want to hear. I tell them what they need to know" (or at least, that's what Adams told himself). That certitude, while perhaps admirable in people we happen to agree with, is part and parcel of an essentialist understanding of history, exactly the kind of no-questions-answered historical fundamentalism of the tea party and of constitutional originalists. In movies, if the history doesn't match the interpretation, then the history is what is jettisoned, rather than the other way around. To paraphrase the great line from the movie classic *The Man Who Shot Liberty Valance* (1962), when the legend becomes fact, film the legend.

Because filmmakers and even many historians argue that the conventions of television and movies necessitate that broad movements get personified, one might think that on-screen dramatic interpretations of the Revolution must inherently be essentialist. If movements are flattened into heroes, and if the heroes of the Revolution are the bewigged founding fathers, then, the argument goes, the medium is to blame. But that is too easy, letting filmmakers off the hook rather than encouraging creative scripts that can be both dramatic and nuanced. Even if the subject is to be the Revolutionary War, a focus on the soldiers rather than on the generals is entirely possible, as demonstrated by the highly successful film *Glory*—very much a genre movie in its grafting conventions of World War II war films onto the story of a black Civil War regiment. If filmmakers have their hearts set on individuals, they can look to *Revolution* (1985). Admittedly, that movie met with neither critical nor popular acclaim, but *The Patriot* demonstrated that a Revolution movie could focus on players other than Washington or Adams and still do well at the box office. Furthermore, filmmakers can show groups working together instead of only a few heroic individuals. This kind of effort, too, has appeared on-screen for the Revolution. *The Crossing* is a 90-minute, 2000 A&E adaptation of a Howard Fast historical novel depicting the Continental Army's crossing of the Delaware on Christmas night, 1776, to ambush Hessians at Trenton. It features a standard treatment of a heroic George Washington (Jeff Daniels). But it also portrays the bravery and endurance of the Marblehead, Massachusetts, soldiers—nearly all skilled ocean fisherman in their civilian life—who silently rowed boatload after boatload of men, horses, and ordinance across a dark, icy river through a snowstorm. Genres and media can be limiting, but they are not straitjackets.

Beyond profit, movie and TV industry writers and producers value one thing above all else: the story. If the story feels true to them, they reason, audiences will find it compelling. They want recognizable characters, too, all the easier for audiences to relate to. Maybe that's why—whether liberal like Tom Hanks or conservative like Mel Gibson, making popcorn fare like Jon Turteltaub or edutainment like Kevin O'Donnell, organicist interpretations can be harder than essentialist ones. I am not arguing for strictly organicist on-screen products or that moviemakers abandon their time-honed craft for bringing compelling stories to our screens. The trick continues to be in exploring organicism and essentialism in tandem: how to portray persevering generals and heroic slaves, lone tribunes of liberty and boisterous tavern politicians, cruel patriots and suffering loyalists, wise framers and blundering bureaucrats, strident partisans and fearful disaffected, a glorious cause and bone-breaking devastation. And on top of that, to convey that we have different ways of seeing the past. As a historian, I have trouble imagining how to accomplish all those goals in the context of hundreds of pages, and I have no idea how to translate that into something that would not make viewers' eyes glaze over. To blame producers for missing the mark of encapsulating two somewhat incompatible ideologies about our nation's past and future, given the logic of big-budget on-screen entertainment, may be demanding too much. Still, as with history writing, the impossibility of perfection should not prevent us from the attempt. The challenge remains.

5

To Re-create a More Perfect Union

Originalism, the Tea Party, and Reenactors

In January 2011, the new Congress opened with a Republican majority. Republican House of Representatives leaders orchestrated a public reading of the Constitution. Many had gotten elected by tea party activists, railing against what they perceived as the unconstitutionality of President Obama's new healthcare plan. Despite their campaign rhetoric blasting "Obamacare" and thundering that judges should show more fidelity to the Constitution as originally written, they opted not to read the whole document. They skipped parts that had been superseded by amendments or that could be considered offensive. They therefore silently eliminated the "three-fifths clause." It had been negated by the Thirteenth Amendment and, if any constitutional clause would be offensive, that would be the one. When drafting the Constitution, delegates haggled over how many people should be in each House district and who should be counted. They settled on a formula the Continental Congress had used in 1783 when figuring out how much in taxes each state should contribute to the national till. They would count the number of white people (free or indentured servants), exclude Indians who didn't pay taxes, and then add three-fifths of the number of "all other persons." Those "other persons" were the 700,000 slaves, mostly concentrated in the five Southern states. Lest this seem trivial, it was anything but: delegates understood that the balance of power in the House between the number of representatives from Southern and Northern states hinged on how slaves might be counted. The three-fifths compromise ensured Southern states enough votes in the House to stave off attempts to regulate or abolish slavery. That African Americans could be counted as three-fifths of a person would certainly offend most Americans today.

But conservative TV host, best-selling author, and tea party cheerleader Glenn Beck was flabbergasted by the House's excision of the three-fifths clause for an entirely different reason. He bashed congressional Republicans for what he considered historical ignorance. "If slaves in the South were counted as full human beings," Beck said on the air, "[the founders] could never abolish slavery." He ignored the fact that the founders could have opted not to count slaves at all and that slavery ended not because of the founders' intentions but because of the Civil War. Against all evidence, Beck claimed that the three-fifths clause was an attempt to provide for the eventual elimination of slavery, rather than a move to further cast it in stone. Beck's insistence on the founders' innocence concerning slavery might seem puzzling.

However, in the context of America's changing political climate of the twenty-first century, Beck's position makes perfect sense. Beginning haltingly as early as the 1980s, an increasing number of Americans have championed applying an essentialist interpretation of the Revolutionary era to American political problems. They have done so in that most patient of disciplines, the practice of constitutional law, as well as in the most raucous of ways, through political rallies and demonstrations. Beck's giving the founders a pass on that most odious of American institutions, slavery, served to cleanse their public image for the work that he and other essentialists need them to do: to be considered unimpeachable authorities not only on the political issues of their own day but also the legal and cultural ones of our own times. Then, by invoking the founders as their patrons, essentialists on the bench, in the streets, and in the halls of Congress could use the founders' words more authoritatively to buttress their political positions. As the new judicial doctrine of "originalism" and the explosion of the tea party indicate, many Americans want nothing more than to recast the nation in its founders' images. But as the reenactors who spend the most time trying to recreate the Revolution know, that's easier said than done.

One of the more obscure arenas in which the Revolution has always been contested is nonetheless among the most consequential: the nation's courtrooms and law journals. For a century or more after the ratification of the Constitution, jurists and lawyers tried to interpret the Constitution and its amendments according to what they divined the authors intended for that charter to mean. Even though the nation was changing in many ways, doing so made sense. The nation's first generation had written and ratified the document but saw fit to modify it substantially. That Revolutionary cohort did so first with the Bill of Rights, composed of ten amendments, and then with two additional amendments. In response to a particular court case, the Eleventh Amendment (1793) prohibited states from being sued by other states or their citizens. The Twelfth Amendment (1804) was a reaction to the deadlocked 1800 presidential election and provided for different ballots for presidential and vice presidential candidates. Over the next two generations, the Supreme Court provided the central venue for constitutional change with a series of major court decisions. During and after the Civil War, the Thirteenth, Fourteenth, and Fifteenth Amendments guaranteed all citizens freedom, due process of law, and the vote (on paper, anyway). For nearly a half century more, constitutional change came in the courtroom rather than through the amendment process.

Since then, the nation has revised the Constitution in fits and starts. Progressive-era changes included allowing the federal government to tax citizens directly (Sixteenth Amendment, 1913), requiring Senators to be elected by the people at large rather than by state legislatures (Seventeenth Amendment, 1913), prohibiting alcohol production and sales (Eighteenth Amendment, 1917), and granting women the vote (Nineteenth Amendment, 1920). In the throes of the Depression, Americans tinkered again, setting the date for the president to take office and Congress to begin its sessions (Twentieth Amendment, 1933) and repealing Prohibition (Twenty-First Amendment, 1933). Republicans prevented a repetition of Franklin Roosevelt's four presidential electoral victories by limiting presidents to two terms (Twenty-Second Amendment, 1951). Representation and voting became the next major focus of constitutional change, allowing the District of Columbia a say in presidential elections (Twenty-Third Amendment, 1961), banning poll taxes (Twenty-Fourth Amendment, 1964), and extending the vote to eighteen-year-olds (Twenty-Sixth Amendment); meanwhile, the assassination of John F. Kennedy and the threat of nuclear war prompted the development of a more complex succession scheme in case of presidential death (Twenty-Fifth Amendment, 1967). Since then, the only amendment ratified has been the one longest in gestation: forbidding Congress from giving itself a raise without having to face the voters first, originally proposed in 1789 (Twenty-Seventh Amendment, 1992). Debate on the constitutional intentions of the founders has been most intense during those times when, rather than changing the document itself, Americans have had to consider how to interpret the words on the page.

What about those parts of the Constitution that seemed out-of-date but appeared impossible to amend? Beginning in the 1870s, suffragettes—that is, women seeking the right to vote—did not expect a constitutional amendment. They proposed another way of looking at the Constitution: to consider it a living document. To them, the Constitution should be interpreted not in light of what its writers intended but, rather, in the context of what was dictated by changing social, economic, and political realities. Over the course of a few decades, this view, soon to be called "living constitutionalism," became the dominant mode of constitutional interpretation. That shift signaled more than a change of method; it also necessitated a new way of thinking about authority and history. Living constitutionalism implied a break with the founders, no longer relying upon them as the ultimate arbiters of law or investing them with infinite wisdom that prevailed through the ages. In that and in its results, it tended to be an organicist practice and became the underlying philosophy behind the legal victories of the civil rights and women's rights movements. And yet, for most of the twentieth century, living constitutionalism formed the basis for both conservative and liberal jurisprudence. Living constitutionalism suffered from serious logical weaknesses. By unmooring jurisprudence from the founders, its proponents risked drifting out to sea. They would reply that they were still limited by precedent, that is, by the accumulation of previous cases, but critics noted that there was nothing to prevent a majority of Supreme Court justices from what others might perceive as venturing off on a decision bound neither by precedent nor by the founders' intentions. The ultimate danger, then, was that, rather than interpreting the text, living constitutionalists could make up the law and then claim that their new rulings somehow matched changing conditions.

By the 1980s, conservative legal minds had laid the groundwork for a response to living constitutionalism. "Originalism" contains all the elements of essentialism: the notion of history as a knowable, fixed truth; the founders as the ultimate authorities on civic affairs; and for many, though not all of its practitioners, a focus on individual liberty and what they call "traditional values." Originalists appealed to what they called the framers' "original intent," that is, the first intended meaning of the

Constitution as conceived in the eighteenth century. Conservatives were disgusted with a string of Supreme Court decisions affecting broad swaths of American life, rulings that relied on living constitutionalism. The most stinging included *Brown v. Board of Education* (1954), barring legal segregation; *Griswold v. Connecticut* (1965), which established an explicit right to privacy; *Miranda v. Arizona* (1966), forbidding the use of suspect testimony in court unless a suspect had been informed of right to counsel; and *Roe v. Wade* (1973), which forbade states from banning abortion during a pregnancy's first trimester. Conservatives argued that liberal justices were "legislating from the bench," creating law or rights out of whole cloth that did not exist in the text of the Constitution.

Originalist thought assumes that the Constitution has one, fixed, easily discernable meaning—notwithstanding that eighteenth-century Americans thought differently than we do, lived in a different world than we do, understood language differently than we do, and, crucially, often bitterly disagreed among themselves as to what the words meant. Conservative thinkers added an emphasis on private property and personal liberty and mixed in their particular mode of traditional Christian values. Over the last thirty years, originalism has grown from an idea played with in a few law journals to a significant movement, claiming adherents among law professors, practicing lawyers, and judges all the way to the Supreme Court. It's backed by the Federalist Society, an organization bankrolled by wealthy donors that sponsors books and symposia and that helps originalists network to further each others' careers. Originalism has provided the philosophical backbone of several major Supreme Court majority opinions over the last decade. And in its view of the founders and of history, originalism represents judicial essentialism.

Originalism has morphed through several iterations. Most popularly associated in the 1980s with two Reagan Administration officials— Attorney General Ed Meese, and Solicitor General and rejected Supreme Court nominee Robert Bork—by the 1990s originalism had come under attack from liberal and conservative legal minds and from historians of all stripes. It was one thing to contend that the Constitution did not explicitly include a "right to privacy," the linchpin of cases concerning conception and abortion. But for more ambiguous legal questions, originalism proved to be logically unsustainable for the simple reason that there were many founders and they didn't agree. Whose perception of the Constitution should count—the men in the Constitutional Convention (who argued about it in the convention and for decades afterward) or the men who voted in the state conventions that ratified the Constitution? How much weight should be given to the Federalist Papers or other pro-ratification writings—some by men who attended the Constitutional Convention, others not? More problematically, late twentieth-century conservative policy preferences often closely matched those of the Constitution's opponents. Should the Anti-federalists' positions count, especially in their defense of the states' sovereignty? As any historian will tell you, when we actually look carefully at the founding generations' intentions, we find as great a range as in today's politics. In addition, as the 2000s progressed, the claim that liberal Supreme Court justices were more activist than their conservative brethren, and thus straying from the founders' intentions, became increasingly harder to sustain. Recent conservative Supreme Court decisions have overturned a century of relevant precedents and legislative acts, indicating that much of originalists' objection to "judicial activism" had more to do with unwanted results rather than disagreement over the force of precedent. Furthermore, a closer look at the historical record could suggest verdicts diametrically opposed to those actually written by originalists. These include decisions on the role of corporations in public life, which the current Supreme Court has greatly reaffirmed, notwithstanding that the founding generation was deeply ambivalent about corporations and their potential for economic and political power.

The founders' words could not always provide the results that originalist jurists wanted. The second wave of originalism, forcefully articulated from the early 2000s on, reasons that even the framers were not up to their own ideals. After all, the men who attended the Constitutional Convention were politicians trying to get elected, get legislation passed, and make their reputations. So they can't be trusted. Rather, then, this revised originalism points to "original understanding" or "original public meaning," that is, how a typical, reasonable eighteenth-century person would have understood the Constitution. But instead of trying to get a grip on the full worldview of Revolutionary-era people, original understanding as practiced entails a close textual analysis, phrase by phrase and word by word, to find a particular, fixed meaning of the Constitution regardless of context and often contrasting with the documented views of the framers. In this, their method is akin to treating the Constitution as some preachers treat the King James Bible, as holding some one, essential, easily discernible truth, rather than as an imperfect translation with many possible competing interpretations. Originalists have thus dispatched the pesky problem of having to deal with alternate views or, indeed, anyone's actual views. Jurists using original public meaning resort to late eighteenth-century dictionaries and to English law treatises to consider the meaning of almost every word, stitching together interpretations. But those dictionaries were notoriously idiosyncratic, the work of individuals rather than broader surveys of how people perceived the meaning of words. Furthermore, while eighteenth-century Americans did look at English law books, American colonial law had to some extent diverged from English law. Original public understanding scholars risk interpretations divorced from what the framers intended to do, what the ratifiers debated, or common eighteenth-century practice. By just looking at words and phrases without considering the broader context, such analysts may have a great understanding of individual trees with no concept for the forest. Paradoxically, then, original meaning originalists are not bound by what eighteenth-century people actually wanted governance to accomplish.

In contrast to living constitutionalism's potential for straying from constitutional principles, originalists' flaw is to engage in what historian Saul Cornell derides as "historical ventriloquism," making up a hypothetical eighteenth-century man on the street for the purpose of giving him views to legitimate their current ideology. That "reasonable man" on the street is, perforce, a man, and if we assume that this man was a citizen, he is a white man. I'm a white man, and I don't resent white men, nor do I have what conservatives charge as "liberal guilt." Nor do I object to the study of dead white men: my first book was about the white men who founded the nation's first corporations, so when I suggested above that the nation's first generation was very wary of corporations, it was based on considerable knowledge. But what started out as a reasonable assertion—to consider the framers' intention when interpreting the law—can devolve into the elaborate intellectual ritual of taking contemporary ideology, outfitting it in a powdered wig, three-cornered hat, and breeches, and thereby inventing a claim to historical and thus jurisprudential legitimacy. That's a shame, because, by clinging to this logically and historically spurious legal philosophy, originalism's practitioners unnecessarily invite doubt concerning their positions. I don't happen to agree with most of those positions, but I'd be willing to give them more credence were they backed by an intellectually defensible rationale.

The most stunning example of dressing up a contemporary policy in essentialist robes came via the *District of Columbia v. Heller* decision. In that case, the Supreme Court ruled five-to-four to strike down a law regulating handguns in Washington, D.C. The majority opinion was written by original understanding's high priest, Associate Justice Antonin Scalia. Nonetheless, *Heller* was the first Supreme Court decision in the history of the republic to assert that the Constitution's Second Amendment guarantees an individual right to own guns. In that sense, it was a departure from the more than century of jurisprudence on the intersection between the Second Amendment and private gun ownership. It also ducked the historical record of the eighteenth century. Associate Justice John Paul Stevens countered that "a review of the drafting history of the Amendment demonstrates that its Framers *rejected* proposals that would have broadened its coverage to include such uses" as the very ones that Scalia cited as central to the Second Amendment: recreation and individual self-defense rather than guaranteeing freedom from government. Scalia's attempt at legitimacy through enlisting the founders for his decision required what legal scholar Reva Siegal delicately labeled "temporal oddities." Scalia dismissed copious evidence from the founding era, including alternate drafts of the Second Amendment, in favor of sources from more than a hundred years later. In and of itself, that's fine. Justices decide what reasoning and evidence they will use as, for example, Chief Justice Earl Warren did when relying on social psychologists and sociologists when he wrote the decision in *Brown v. Board of Education* to outlaw segregation. In the *Heller* case, Scalia was actually engaging with the Constitution as a living document insofar as his opinion was instrumental in creating a new, individual right to bear arms based upon arguments that had only emerged from the 1970s on. Scalia's assertion of an objective "originalism" led him to claim a legitimacy from the founders for a position no less political than anyone else's.

In the late 2000s, legal scholars devised yet a third iteration of originalism, one that its proponents suggest encompasses the previous two. The two most prominent innovators of this approach, law professors

John McGinnis and Michael Rappaport, labeled their brainchild "original methods originalism." In order to practice either original intent or original public meaning, they argue, contemporary jurists and lawyers should look to how jurists and lawyers at the time of the Constitution applied it. "To find the original intent of the Constitution's enactors," McGinnis and Rappaport argued, "one must look to the interpretative rules that the enactors expected would be employed to understand their words." And "to find what an informed speaker of the language would have understood the Constitution's meaning to be," they suggest, about original public meaning, "that one must look to the interpretive rules that were customarily applied to such a document." The central insight of original methods originalism is that the framers expected the Constitution to be contested in legislatures and courtrooms. To understand the Constitution we must therefore know what basic rules and systems late eighteenth-century Americans expected would be used to put the Constitution in play and to settle debates over it. This naturally begs the question of what method the nation's first generation of jurists would use to apply the Constitution. Not surprisingly, McGinnis and Rappaport suggest that the framers and their contemporaries were themselves originalists. For this strain of originalism, the method is the message.

Unfortunately, original methods originalism raises no fewer questions than it purports to answer. Original methods originalism further compounds the flaws of the other two originalisms: its practitioners have to parse either the minds of the Constitution's framers or of the early republic man on the street through yet another filter, in this case that of eighteenth-century legal scholars. Original methods originalism threatens to devolve into a game of telephone played between a twenty-first-century legal mind and several sets of late eighteenth-century texts. And that McGinnis and Rappaport discovered the originators to be originalists really doesn't tell us much. Those early republic lawyers were looking at a document that they and their colleagues had written and voted on, when the ink was barely dry, so naturally they looked to their own intentions—or at least, what they later claimed they meant. But having a sense that the republic itself was a fragile experiment and believing from history that republics don't last long, anyway, they proposed nothing on how subsequent generations of Americans, or Americans a dozen generations down the road, as we are, would interpret things. That was well beyond their imagination. We could then ask the next question: did the framers expect future generations to perceive the law the same way they did, and be bound by those legal methods? On this, given their belief in the fragility of the republic, they were predictably silent.

As with all exercises in memory, we must note not only what is recalled through originalism but also, just as crucially, what is forgotten. What we choose to let time's undertow take out to sea is no less revealing than what washes up onshore or what we choose to keep afloat. In the 2000s— really since the Cold War began—most American politicians and jurists have conveniently forgotten a central element of American Revolutionary constitutional thought: the fear of a standing army. Colonists' uneasiness with a permanent military ran deep. One stream of their political thought derived from late seventeenth- and early eighteenth-century English political tracts, among them John Locke's *Second Treatise of Government* (source of the phrase "life, liberty, and property") and essayists John Trenchard and Thomas Gordon's *Cato's Letters*. These peripheral writings represented the point of view of English country gentry distrustful of government, wary of power, mystified by finance, and shut out from the opportunities that imperial growth had created for those with better connections or canny enough to see the main chance. And they resonated with colonists alienated from a Britain that disdained them, while Southern colonial planters and Northern merchants became ever more enmeshed in debt to English and Scottish trading houses. From the 1760s on, colonists could make the connection between the military costs of the burgeoning British empire and the national debt that fighting wars and consolidating its victories required. It was a short line to connect the dots between the British sending troops to Boston in 1768 (to defend it from no one in particular), Parliamentary efforts to extract more tax revenue from the colonies, and *Cato's* extended admonishments against the tyrannical dangers of standing armies. Revolutionary-era American political pamphlets were rife with warnings about the dangers of standing armies, leading to a clause in the Constitution forbidding any military appropriation for longer than two years. Notwithstanding the history, the Supreme Court has enabled recent presidents' defense expansions at the expense of congressional oversight of the military.

Originalism may be essentialist in nature, but it has transcended divisions between conservative and liberal legal thinkers. In this, it is similar to the previous practice of living constitutionalism. Prominent liberal legal scholars like Jack Balkin and Akhil Reed Amar appeal to the framers to bolster their own constitutional interpretations. Justice Scalia has claimed that his originalism is neither conservative nor liberal and that "it has nothing to do with what your policy preferences are; it has to do with what you think the Constitution is." He has pointed to several cases in which he joined a majority on the side of what he has characterized as "liberal" positions—although he and fellow originalist Associate Justice Clarence Thomas have spun constitutional interpretations in line with contemporary conservative political positions nearly 90 percent of the time. Scalia's record is perfectly consistent with his claim to be following the intentions of the founding generation: Scalia's written opinions suggest a worldview as little hospitable to women and blacks as that of the founders. Legal scholar Frank B. Cross has scrutinized the difference between individual Supreme Court justices' publicly proclaiming originalism as their guiding philosophy on the one hand, and on the other, using originalism as a method by referring to eighteenth-century sources in their opinions. Analyzing court decisions reaching back to 1952, he found liberal justices citing found-era documents not much less often than conservative ones, even during the 2000s. Furthermore, he reasoned, if originalism truly only relies on the founders' interpretation of their work, rather than the justice's own policy preferences, then one might expect that, when conservative or liberal judges did use originalism, their decisions might be more likely to stray from their ideological bent than when they seemed to use other approaches. But Cross found that "for no justice did originalism appear to cause ideology to dissipate." In other words, even when methodologically relying on the founders, liberals made liberal decisions and conservatives made conservative decisions.

Regardless of its proponents' ideological proclivities, originalism retains an essentialist core. Cross's analysis indicates that originalists are far more committed to preconceived notions of their desired outcomes than to any real interest in the past, no less than they accuse living constitutionalists (liberal or conservative) of doing. Cross also noted a more heavy reliance on the founders' writings, especially *The Federalist*, in big cases, suggesting perhaps that jurists believe a quotation or two of the founders more useful in swaying the public than in determining the legal basis for their decisions. Obama Supreme Court nominee Elena Kagan implicitly admitted as much when she testified in her 2010 confirmation hearings that "we are all originalists." But there is more at work here. As legal theorist Lawrence Solum has pointed out, all originalists share two common ideas. One is that the meaning of the constitution (and its amendments) was fixed at the time of writing, and the other is that interpretation should be limited to that meaning. That investment of authority in the founders, as well as the sense of history as knowable and containing one unambiguous truth, marks originalism as essentialist. Perhaps we may be looking in the wrong place in our digging for the intellectual or philosophical roots of originalism. For Supreme Court Justice David Souter, "behind most dreams of a simpler Constitution there lies a basic human hunger for the certainty and control." These include the certainty of a system of social relations that mirror the values with which Scalia, and many conservatives, identify. That squares with how political scientist Daniel Levin has found originalism practiced by either conservatives or liberals to be more akin to a nostalgic yearning for an authentic, democratic society free from modernism than to a rigorous historical analysis of what the founders may have meant. For them, a purer, more democratic past only waits for us to bring it back to life.

A more popular and short-lived movement to recreate the Revolution also yearned for a more pure present. The tea partiers have made an indelible impact on the contemporary political landscape, but they were preceded by another recent conservative movement seizing upon the American Revolution. In 2005, the self-proclaimed "Minuteman" movement basked in national media and political attention. The Minutemen objected to what they characterized as a flood of illegal immigrants pouring across the Mexican–United States border. Two men working independently of each other galvanized the movement. Former Los Angeles kindergarten teacher Chris Simcox had moved to Tombstone, Arizona, in 2002. Outraged by illegal immigration into the United States in the months after the September 11 attacks, Simcox bought a newspaper weekly, the *Tombstone Tumbleweed*, which he exploited to launch himself as the tribune of anti-immigration efforts. Meanwhile, retired Orange County, California, accountant Jim Gilchrist had founded a web-based endeavor called the Minutemen Project. Both men got their first broader media attention through conservative radio outlets. They eventually hit free publicity pay dirt through Fox News and the promotion of politicians such as Tom Tancredo, a Colorado congressman who had made opposition to illegal immigration his political calling card and who would vie for the 2008 Republican presidential nomination (as with almost all one-issue candidates, his hobbyhorse did not get him far). Despite Minutemen statements to the contrary and their vehement denial of any racial motivation, they were overwhelmingly white, about two-thirds male, and mostly in their fifties or older, reacting—or, perhaps, overreacting—to what Simcox colorfully described as "hordes of illegals running from the bushes." Now as in Revolutionary times, citizen-soldiers came to defend the country against what they perceived as foreign interlopers.

The Minutemen's angst was driven by real anxiety concerning cultural change, but their proposed solutions relied more on emotion than logic or evidence. Although illegal immigrants have by definition broken U.S. law, rounding up and deporting over ten million people, a significant proportion of them relatives or parents of U.S. citizens, would be an impossible task, not to mention cruel and economically disruptive. In a nation of a little over three hundred million inhabitants, forced deportation would require an operation to round up one out of every thirty residents. It would necessitate a massive nationwide manhunt and dragnets that would likely end up violating the rights of citizens and legal immigrants. A combination of patrolling and walling off the 1,933-mile Mexico–U.S. border would be exorbitantly expensive and would antagonize our southern neighbor. Further increasing security at authorized border crossings would slow legitimate international traffic to a standstill, exacting a large cost from border communities and international commerce. Jim Gilchrist argued that illegal immigration was a national security issue because the 9/11 bombers were not legal immigrants. Fair enough, but the 9/11 hijackers entered the country legally, by airplane. Building fences across the Sonoran Desert would have little effect on U.S. vulnerability to Middle East–based terrorism. Immigration policy had became a national-security distraction given that, by 2005, the U.S. National Guard was already stretched in its efforts to support two wars without the extra burden of manning the Mexico–U.S. line. The Minutemen's anger or fear of illegal immigration had not translated into workable policy.

Just like the Revolution's minutemen, their twenty-first-century namesake movement lasted no more than a year or two. The Minutemen's great moment in the Southwestern sun occurred on March 1, 2005, when they converged on Tombstone, Arizona, to deploy a monthlong civilian patrol of the surrounding area, a prime site for illegal border crossings. They claimed to have over a thousand Minutemen present. Journalists described a scene in which the media and other observers (from the American Civil Liberties Union and the Southern Poverty Law Center, among others) outnumbered the estimated one hundred and fifty Minutemen who had made the trip. Nonetheless, Gilchrist could legitimately claim victory: his goal was not to secure temporarily a small stretch of the border but rather to produce political theater that would get noticed. And it did. In a Senate hearing the very next day, both Republicans and Democrats bemoaned the poor state of border security and what they characterized as the Bush Administration's inadequate funding proposal for a very modest increase in border patrol agents. After getting a lot of play on talk shows and from conservative politicians looking for airtime, the Minutemen and their movement faded. Simcox and Gilchrist eventually had a falling out. Simcox's 2010 senatorial primary bid against John McCain was his last major public hurrah. Between a lack of charismatic leaders and the rise of the tea party movement, the Minutemen melted away. As with many single-issue movements in American history, the lack of leadership and infrastructure doomed the Minutemen.

The essentialist invocation of the Revolutionary-era minutemen made political and ideological sense for their 2000s namesakes. Gilchrist and Simcox both emphasized that their followers were civilians, rather than professional military or law enforcement (although, interestingly enough, many of them were retired military or law enforcement officers—just as many of the original minutemen had served in the French and Indian War). That civilian ideal dovetailed with the ethos of another movement that sympathized with the modern Minutemen, the contemporary militia movement, which also invokes early American white men as defenders of a pure, lily-white America against the encroachment of government, on the one hand, and people of color, on the other. And after all, the vast majority of colonial minutemen were white, just like their present-day namesakes. Gilchrist's website claims that his is a "multiethnic" movement, but it is actually overwhelmingly white and, for that matter, overwhelmingly male. Regardless of individuals' protestations that their agenda is not racially or ethnically motivated, the targets of the Minutemen's efforts, should they have come to fruition as policy and law of the land, were Latino people of color. The contemporary Minutemen are claiming the Revolutionary phenomenon of citizens organized to defend their land against an imperial army as an implicit precedent for defending a current international border against an "invasion" of illegal immigrants. Today's Minutemen are thereby asserting an essentialist America, one in which white Americans are the defenders of a land that will be tainted through its figurative browning by ethnic others.

The Minuteman movement offered a preview of a broader and sustained political uprising claiming Revolutionary inspiration: the tea party. The U.S. housing bubble burst in early 2008. That summer, giant investment bank Lehman Brothers failed, and other major financial institutions teetered. To limit long-term economic catastrophe, the Bush Administration pushed successfully for the passage of a $300 billion federal fund to prop up the housing market. In October, President Bush signed a plan for the federal government to buy $700 billion in bad bank assets. Meanwhile, the housing market tanked and, with it, the economy. Unemployment leapt from 5.1 percent in March 2008 to 8.3 percent in February, 2009. To top it all off for many political conservatives, the unthinkable happened: Barack Obama took office in January 2009. Conservative media outlets and even many politicians called Obama a "socialist," questioned his citizenship, and labeled him a Muslim and even a terrorist. Hysteria seeped through all sorts of fissures: in the town where I live, a church with several hundred members held a serious theological debate over whether Obama was in fact the anti-Christ (the answer was "no" by a close margin). On February 18, 2009, the Obama Administration announced another a program to further aid in refinancing mortgages. The next morning, CNBC financial news reporter Rick Santelli, whose Chicago market updates included a rant every week or two, went ballistic on the air, questioning why taxpayer money should go to help "losers" who took out risky mortgages. "We're thinking of having a Chicago Tea Party in July!" he yelled. Santelli fumed that, "if you read our founding fathers, people like Benjamin Franklin and Jefferson . . . What we're doing in this country now is making them roll over in their graves." The video went viral, and within days groups were meeting across the country calling themselves "tea partiers" and "tea party patriots." Tea partiers were energized in their anger at Obama for his background and his policies, especially his healthcare initiative.

No movement happens instantaneously or in a vacuum or can last long without expertise and institutional support. The tea party melds local activists with entrenched political insiders. The tea party chapters that sprouted across the nation in 2009 were new organizations, but the tea partiers' self-image as members of a spontaneous and grassroots movement only tells part of the story. Surveys and interviews have indicated that a large proportion of tea party activists had already been active in conservative political causes. They were continually bolstered by the drumbeat of conservative media outlets, most notably by Fox News's Glenn Beck, who used his highly rated television and radio talk shows, his quickly penned bestsellers, and his web presence to rally the troops. Deep-pocketed, longtime conservative movement insiders seized upon the tea party movement as their chance to team up with local activists to push their own long-term agenda of lowering taxes for the wealthy and reducing government regulation. The most notable of these was FreedomWorks, a Washington-based group funded partly by corporations but largely by extremely rich men like banking scion Richard Mellon Scaife and coal-mining magnates Charles and David Koch and run by lobbyist and former U.S. House majority leader Dick Armey. As early as 2002, Citizens for a Sound Economy, a FreedomWorks precursor, had already registered the internet domain "usteaparty.com." By 2008, FreedomWorks had experimented with websites developed in-house masquerading as grass-roots efforts. FreedomWorks poured literally tens of millions of dollars into training activists and providing logistical support for websites, fundraising, and rallies. The involvement of FreedomWorks, major Republican figures, and Fox News has led to accusations that the tea party movement is "astroturfing," that is, that it's a top-down movement rather than one led by the grass roots. The movement would not have bloomed and survived without dollars and free media attention. Nonetheless, one recent study surveyed polls, sociological reports, and membership data indicating that by the end of 2013, up to a third of Americans sympathized with the tea party, somewhere between six and eight million people could be characterized as "supporters," and core membership in the five major tea party factions totaled over five hundred thousand. That's a lot of people.

The tea partiers' latching onto a Revolutionary-era event and their veneration of the Constitution and the founders begs the question of how they learn about the American Revolution. Much of what tea partiers know of the American Revolution comes from the writings of W. Cleon Skousen. Born in Canada in 1913, Skousen grew up in California and joined the FBI in 1936. He parlayed that job into a professorship at Brigham Young University and a four-year tour as Salt Lake City police chief, getting fired for overzealous enforcement in one of the country's most conservative cities at the height of the Cold War. He then remade himself into a best-selling author and highly paid speaker on the ultra-conservative circuit, leveling anti-communist accusations so outlandish that the FBI kept tabs on him in the early 1960s as potentially dangerous. Meanwhile, he wrote several history books published by his self-established Freeman Institute and launched a program of one-day seminars about the founding and the Constitution. His greatest coup was getting a version of his U.S. history textbook, *The Making of America*, adopted for sale by the 1987 California commission to celebrate the Constitution's bicentennial. The decision drew immediate outrage and was overturned when historians like Jack Rakove, the lone dissenter on the commission, pointed out that the book referred to slaves as "pickanninnies" and asserted that slavery was more of a burden for owners than for slaves. Rakove blasted the volume as "a joke that no self-respecting scholar would think is worth a warm pitcher of spit." Skousen died in 2006 but was rediscovered by Fox host Beck in 2008, who touted Skousen's books and ideas. Skousen's magnum opus, *The Five-Thousand-Year Leap*, became a fixture of the Amazon best-seller list during the summer of 2010. Not one to miss a profit opportunity, Cleon Skousen's nephew Mark Skousen has edited a couple of collections of Benjamin Franklin's writing. The Freeman Institute, now revived as the grandly titled National Center for Constitutional Studies (NCCS) and run out of an activist's barn in a remote corner of Idaho, annually offers hundreds of one-day seminars to eager tea partiers across the country.

Promoted on tea party websites and at tea party events, NCCS seminars function to confirm tea partiers' worldview and to provide them with unambiguous historical and ideological ammunition rather more than to stimulate thinking or invite discussion. The seminars are primarily a guided tour through a fifty-four-page, black-and-white illustrated workbook titled "The Making of America," based upon Skousen's longer textbook of the same name. I attended one in April, 2011, held in the auditorium of a nearby high school. Between twenty-five and thirty of us—all white, mostly adults, but with a few kids brought by their parents—were scattered among the room's several hundred red fabric foldup seats. The NCCS has a stable of volunteer speakers whose expenses get reimbursed and who often bunk with the local organizers during their stay. Our seminar leader perfectly fit the NCCS mold: Charlie Brown, a well-mannered white man in his fifties, a real estate manager (i.e., someone who serves as the professional landlord for house and apartment owners), and father of eight children. He had been a nearly anonymous candidate in the 2008 Arizona Republican gubernatorial primary. The seminar consisted of Brown speaking at the front of the room, leading us through the workbook. This format of a lecturer telling attendees the one-word answers to write into their books was revealing in and of itself; there was no room for discussion or varying opinions. When participants queried him about particular points in the material, Brown several times responded, "I've been asked that in seminars before. I don't know the answer." Gaining additional knowledge apparently had not occurred to him. Rather than promoting a thoughtful exploration of history's complexity, a curiosity about the past, or a sense of the past as a foreign country, this was history as catechism.

The lecture and book offer the patina of intellectual legitimacy to a grab bag of borrowed assertions, strange ideas, cherry-picked quotations, and outright mischaracterizations too long to catalog. The book offers no sense of competing interpretations, only a linear narrative with one-word blanks to be filled in over the course of the seminar, with a handy answer key in back. History is thus presented as a text with simple, correct answers, much like the way the Bible is presented in fundamentalist religion, lending credence to historian Jill Lepore's accusation that the tea partiers view the past through what she aptly labeled "historical fundamentalism." Consider the alternatives: essays and short answers, matching, even true-false responses might stimulate additional discussion and questioning, but fill-in-the-blanks with an answer key allow no such possibilities. And the blanks were cleverly chosen to avoid interpretational nuance. For example, a list of Revolutionary War battles includes a blank for each under the column "Winner." The Battle of Breed's Hill (popularly known as the Battle of Bunker Hill) is omitted, despite being one of the war's most famous battles. But really, it couldn't be included given the question-and-answer, winner-take-all format. To do so would be to invite debate on a topic, military history, that some attendees might know well enough to point out that the battle could be construed as a victory for the redcoats, who took the field but suffered enormous casualties, or the rebels, who retreated but demonstrated discipline and showed that they could stand up to the British army. The elision of easily controvertible assertions is necessary to this ur-essentialist history in its promotion of history as an enterprise in uncovering and using a knowable and certain truth. The content itself relates a story of decline from the original wisdom of the God-inspired founding fathers. Skousen's tea party popularity stems from his appeal to both religious conservatives and economic libertarians, sugarcoating an essentialist past in an intellectually easy-to-swallow package.

The Making of America places all governance along a continuum from tyranny and civil law, which it equates with "ruler's law," at one end and democratic chaos at the other. Republicanism and common law, which it equates with "people's law," represents the happy medium. The United States actually uses a hybrid of civil law (an overarching law, in our case, the Constitution, applied in jurisprudence) and common law (law by the accumulation of judicial precedents), but that kind of nuance is absent here. The book's historical section opens with a survey of Old Testament law. It suggests that the Angles were descended from the ancient Israelites and established English common law, and it portrays free-market capitalism as "natural law." Skousen then claims that the divinely inspired founders fomented the Revolution and that the Declaration of Independence and Constitution derived from biblical law. Here we find founders primarily anguished over whether to regulate interstate commerce—notwithstanding that the chaos of interstate commerce under the Articles of Confederation was one of the main motivations for the Constitutional Convention. Lessons about the original Constitution include examples of how subsequent presidential actions and Supreme Court decisions have eroded the power of the Congress and the states. Some amendments are quoted with little comment, such as the Thirteenth Amendment (banning slavery) and the Nineteenth Amendment (granting women the vote). Others are dealt with at length, lovingly or loathingly. The Sixteenth Amendment (allowing personal income taxes) and the Seventeenth Amendment (requiring popular election of senators in place of appointment by state legislatures) come in for especial opprobrium, with criticism centering on how they allegedly violate the founders' vision. Not addressed is why, if the founders wanted to bind future generations, *The Making of America* praises their wisdom in providing an easier path to amendments than the United States' previous governing document, the Articles of Confederation. But this is Skousen and the tea partiers' essentialist vision of the founders: a God-inspired, nearly unanimous group of men whose timeless words and actions are inviolate.

Despite these logical and historical failings, there is something about the tea partiers' view of the American Revolution that we must take seriously and, indeed, learn from. Historians of all political persuasions and liberal pundits have fulminated at length at how the tea partiers' American Revolution appears so much different from the historical American Revolution. I largely agree with those criticisms. I find the tea partiers' anti-intellectualism off-putting at best and downright dangerous when it comes to denying basic facts, thus preventing rational discourse concerning the serious challenges the nation confronts. I deeply disagree with their preferred policies, which, ironically, have greatly contributed to upward distribution of wealth over the last thirty years at their expense as well as the erosion of the possibility of their social mobility. Still, of all the symbols, groups, and incidents in U.S. or even world history, they picked the Boston Tea Party as being particularly resonant of their own complaints. We must come to grips with the significance of their selection of the Boston Tea Party in particular and the American Revolution in general as their political forebears. Further, if I as a historian am to expect the general public to look with a discerning eye at the historical interpretations we see every day and to consider what can be learned from those interpretations, it is also my responsibility as a historian to consider public interpretations with an open mind. I say this not only because historians should set a public example for how to think about history; I also say it because, heaven forfend, historians (myself included) might actually learn something.

Just as telling of what the tea partiers chose is what they didn't. Evocation of the Boston Tea Party was one among many possibilities. Every generation of Americans has featured the disgruntled and dissenters. Every movement has cooked its own salsa of rants and rights, jeremiads and justice, pettiness and politics, zeal and zealotry, hopes and horrors. In Pennsylvania in the 1780s and 1790s, farmers closed major roads for months at a time to protest waves of foreclosures caused by a combination of high taxes, low money supply, and government policies that appeared to enrich speculators at the expense of common people. Farmers in central Massachusetts closed courthouses in 1786 with a similar purpose. Slave revolts occurred in Virginia in 1800, 1822, and 1831 and in Louisiana in 1811 and 1835–1838. Much of the abolitionist and women's suffrage movements consisted of political activism. So did the Grange movement of small farmers in the 1870s, the farmers' alliances of the 1880s, and the populists of the 1890s. Tens of thousands of workers brought national transportation to a standstill during the Great Railroad Strike of 1877, and 340,000 workers walked off the job during the Great Southwest Railroad Strike of 1886. Over 900,000 voters cast their ballots for Socialist Party presidential candidate Eugene Debs in 1912, and again in 1920. In 1932, 43,000 World War I veterans and family members marched on Washington to demand immediate payment of government-promised compensation. The black civil rights movement of the 1950s and 1960s in turn inspired the women's movement, the Native American movement, and eventually the gay rights movement, and the anti–Vietnam War protests were among the most widespread in the nation's annals. American history could be written as a continuous series of protests, during copious times and fallow, during peace and war, during times of political strife and relative consensus. Nearly all of these movements clothed themselves in the flag and quoted the words of the founders. Protesting the political status quo is as American as apple pie.

But nearly all of these protests are celebrated by the left side of the political spectrum, the same politicians, historians, moviemakers, and institutions that promote an organicist view of the Revolution. What such movements hold in common is a challenge to power structures and powerful people internal to the British colonies and then the United States. For every abolitionist, there were ten slaveholders and another twenty white Americans who would have owned slaves if only they could have afforded them. For every dollar that union members raised to support strikers, American corporate leaders had ten in the bank, and other American businesses and often the state and federal governments were willing to put in twenty to defend their interests. One of the central ways that governmental and corporate leaders—American and around the world—have defended themselves in the court of public opinion is by painting social movements as inspired and even controlled by outsiders, regardless of the evidence. My favorite personal example is at my own university, where even after 57 percent of the entire faculty filled out cards asking for a vote to unionize, administrators who had spent only a year or two at the institution still characterized the unionization movement as consisting of a few agitators controlled by the union's national affiliate. One would think that such a rhetorical strategy would be deemed absurd, but its continued use indicates that it strikes a chord with many Americans who live under the illusion that Americans advance themselves only through individual action while collective action is suspect, foreign. The sense that social movements that have happened after American independence must be the work of outsiders, that they are somehow un-American, made them beyond choice for tea partiers.

The selection of the Boston Tea Party makes perfect sense as the chosen metaphor for a contemporary essentialist movement. It was a social protest, engaging ordinary citizens, but it did not contest American civil authority. Because the Boston Tea Party occurred before independence, that demonstration did not challenge the founders or any of the structures they put into place. So, unlike all the other movements I mentioned above, for the modern tea partiers to identify with the historical tea party is perfectly consistent with an essentialist view of the founders and the founding as beyond reproach. It raises no questions about the propriety of the structures put in place by the Revolutionary generation, in keeping with the essentialist position of an infallible founding. Rather, the tea party was one of the few protests that was endorsed by Revolutionary leaders. As historian Alfred Young has noted, calling the event a "tea party" further dulls its radical edges. Well past the turn of the nineteenth century, the event was little commemorated, and when it was, it was as "the affair of the tea." But its reinvention in the 1820s and

1830s as a "tea party" made the event seem less like an angry yet stern crowd destroying ships full of private property in brazen resistance to civil authority and more like a costumed, egalitarian prank. After all, we don't see many contemporary tea partiers, and certainly not their well-heeled sponsors, suggesting the destruction of anyone's private property. That the original tea party participants came from many walks of life further serves today's tea partiers in their claim that theirs is a grass-roots movement. Another crucial similarity between the historical and contemporary tea parties is that, unlike most social movements, which attempt to craft a better future, these both attempted to resist further erosion in their way of life.

Skousen's story of American decline resonates deeply with how tea partiers interpret their own experience. Consider the demographic of the tea partiers. They are primarily white, middle-aged or older, mostly male but with many female activists, middle-class or better financially, somewhat better educated than the general population, and predominantly religious conservatives but also including a strong contingent of libertarians. They perceive that they live in a world of diminishing returns despite their having followed the rules. Over the last thirty years, while the economy has grown, real wages for most Americans have stagnated, especially for those fitting the tea party profile. Worse, despite their American dream for a better life for their children, their offsprings' opportunities have dried up. Studies of elite private colleges have demonstrated that the use of diversity in admission decisions has led to the laudable result of more ethnic and racial minority students, but between the increase in those students and international students, the children of white middle-class families, especially men, have had a harder go at getting in. Meanwhile, as states cut back on public higher education funding, that avenue to advancement has become increasingly difficult to navigate. Tea partiers' rage against immigrants and foreigners is misplaced and often cruel: migrant farm workers haven't taken the jobs of native-born Americans. Those have gone to foreign students and the call workers, factory workers, accountants, paralegals, and medical coders in Mexico, Indonesia, China, and India. Nor are people of color to blame for federal deficits, at least, not any more than white people. Nonetheless, tea partiers' rage is real. With the increased difficulty of getting an education in America for middle- and lower-class whites, their future appears foreclosed to them. For some in the Great Recession, they've had their present foreclosed, too—houses included. Meanwhile, they see the institutions that used to protect their interests, especially state and federal governments, abandon them. What they have left is their vision of a past when things were better: their traditions, their heritage, their religion, and their history—in other words, much of what gives life meaning. They're not giving that up without a fight—nor should we expect them to.

We could ponder the economic frustrations of the tea partiers in light of those of eastern New Englanders in the 1770s. As Gary Nash has demonstrated, Boston's economy stagnated from the 1750s through the 1770s. Instead of economic opportunity, Boston attracted British army regiments, which were placed there in 1768 to keep an eye on Bostonians, not to secure the colony; Boston wasn't at risk of attack. British soldiers drew low salaries but were allowed to take on work in their free hours, meaning that their presence resulted in lower wages for Bostonians because the soldiers' room and board was paid for, so they could afford to work for cheap. The "lobsterbacks," so called because of their red uniforms, made a point of mustering loudly on the Boston Commons when the locals were at church and carousing partly out of the joy of antagonizing those New England "jonathans," as they mocked the locals for their biblical naming patterns and dour social habits (for example, theaters were banned in Boston until 1790). The surrounding area had fared little better. In towns like Concord that had been settled by whites for a hundred years or more, farmers labored to eke out a living on increasingly exhausted soil that had never been all that fruitful. Generations of carving up farms for multiple sons had resulted in plots that left little margin for poor harvests or market gluts. Many energetic young men looked west, but to areas far enough from the city that transportation costs ate much of the profit of any surpluses they could produce. And those who stayed were frustrated: historian Robert Gross has argued that the high rate of pregnancies before marriage resulted from the conscious strategy of younger couples' forcing their parents' hand to provide them either with land or with cash to buy their own farms elsewhere. Meanwhile, the British empire seemed to be prospering, and Britons looked down on provincial Americans. Maybe today's tea partiers' rage isn't so different from that of their namesakes.

The tea party movement is primarily a white movement, another reason why tea partiers identify with those white colonists. As historian Jill Lepore has written, tea partiers see a white American Revolution. There is no better proof of this than a January 2011 Tennessee tea party demand that in elementary schools and high schools all the founders must be portrayed without faults despite evidence of their slaveholding. As spokesperson Hal Rounds put it, the tea partiers wanted to combat "an awful lot of made-up criticism about, for instance, the founders intruding on the Indians or having slaves or being hypocrites in one way or another." Of course, even many of the founders accused each other of being hypocrites on slavery, the Northerners because Southerners held slaves but spoke about freedom, and the Southerners because Northerners talked about the evils of slavery while profiting from commerce and consuming products dependent upon slavery. That's beside the point. Two elements are at work here. One is that tea party movement does overlap somewhat with other groups, like the John Birch Society, that clearly includes racists. The second is that the tea partiers inherit a long strain of suspicion toward people of color—perhaps partly from those New England farmers and Boston city dwellers. We should not confuse all Massachusetts anti-slavery with racial tolerance. In an eloquent assertion of human equality, the Massachusetts General Court issued a judgment in 1780 outlawing slavery. But that was not necessarily a sign of broader forward racial thinking: the ban stuck also because white Massachusites assumed that the result would be fewer Africans imported in their midst. It may have been somewhat akin to anti-immigration thought in contemporary America—like the Minutemen—in that white Revolutionary New Englanders thought of eliminating slavery as a way of reducing the number of Africans in their ranks. Then as now, many pine for a whiter America.

The tea partiers' choice of a name, veneration of the founding fathers, and what they learn at NCCS seminars about the supposed Anglo-Saxon origins of American freedom become of a piece: they all imply a republic in which whiteness is the preferred norm. Race may have played a role in the current tea party's origins: if we really do date the movement's beginnings to late winter of 2009, then it appeared within a month or two of Barack Obama's first presidential inauguration. In addition to political conservatism, an element uniting tea partiers is their deep loathing for the first black president, an enmity that appears to have a racial tinge. Hatred of political opponents is nothing new, nor does it require a racial component. In at least one white Mississippi high school, students cheered when they heard the news that President John F. Kennedy had been shot. Nixon held enemies in great contempt. Liberals derided Reagan, and conservatives vilified Clinton. But none of them ever charged their enemies with being foreign, exotic, cultur-ally un-American. This is not to say that tea partiers are overt racists. African American Herman Cain was one of the short-term tea party darlings during the 2012 Republican presidential primaries, in contrast to the deep disapproval of Cain by non–tea party Republicans. In lon-ger interviews, tea partiers have denied the suggestion that their poli-tics are racially motivated, and they have expressed dismay that they are perceived as harboring racial animus. Nonetheless, several extensive surveys have indicated subtle but unmistakeable hints that tea partiers tend to be much more likely than other white Americans to blame black people for black people's misfortunes more than white people for theirs and to be less charitable to blacks than to whites. "Even as we account for conservatism and partisanship," political scientist Christopher S. Parker concluded of a broad 2010 survey, "support for the Tea Party remains a valid predictor of racial resentment." If history is cultural pol-itics by another name, holding up the white founding fathers as heroes speaks volumes about racial attitudes.

As much as race, tea partiers' rally around resentment of taxes. The tea partiers' adoption of the Revolutionary slogan "No taxation without representation" made much more sense as an analogy to 2008 and 2009 politics than its critics have been willing to admit. Numerous histori-ans and pundits have pointedly remarked that tea partiers are in fact represented: the tea partiers are U.S. citizens, the vast majority of them are registered to vote, and so, the logic goes, they are most certainly rep-resented. Eighteenth-century British critics made a similar argument about the taxation without representation slogan in the 1760s and 1770s. In today's United States, we're used to redistricting every ten years, so that at least when we vote for members of the House of Representatives, each person's vote is roughly equal (senatorial representation, though, is skewed: Wyoming has two senators for a half-million people, Cali-fornia two senators for thirty-three million). Not so in 1700s Britain, whose parliamentary districts were centuries old, despite significant changes in the overall population and its geographic distribution. The population of districts commonly referred to as "rotten boroughs" had dwindled so low that as few as a dozen voters selected their representatives to the House of Commons, that is, the lower house of Parliament. Other districts consisted of land wholly owned by one person and thus were called "pocket boroughs," that is, in the pocket of whoever held them. Meanwhile, some newer, growing cities like Manchester had no representation at all. In 1765 British ministerial official Thomas Whately replied to colonists that as few as a tenth of Britons got to vote for members of Parliament but that they and colonists were "virtually represented": in other words, every member of Parliament took into account all the subjects' interests, regardless of whether or not those subjects had gotten the chance to vote.

Lest we think this sounds absurd—as it did to 1760s colonial American writers like James Otis and John Dickinson—tea partiers were not wholly wrong in 2009 when they charged that the current political system didn't really represent them, either. Both the Republicans and the Democrats chose their candidates for Congress through caucuses or primaries that involved a small number of party stalwarts. Even to get to that point, potential candidates had to have a great deal of money, support of party leaders, name recognition, or some combination of the three. Before the tea party explosion of 2009, tea partiers had little say in the nomination process. Once legislators get in office, the national legislative process is almost entirely disjointed from the lives of the vast majority of Americans. Americans continue to live with the fiction of one person, one vote because that is technically the case at the moment of an election, when we go into the booth, make our choices, and wait for the results to be posted on the TV, the Internet, or the local paper. But, given that there's now on average one member of the House of Representatives for every 690,000 people, and one senator for every 3,000,000 people, it's increasingly hard to argue that anyone's view is heard beyond the lobbyists, political consultants, corporate executives, and extremely wealthy individuals who manage to capture the ear of officeholders. Just like colonial Americans, we're virtually represented. Since 2009, tea party activists have dominated many Republican primaries, and, because there are many House districts drawn with

Republican majorities, from 2011 on the House of Representatives has had a sizable tea party caucus. But in 2009, tea partiers were not wrong to see a federal government that did not represent their views.

Policy-wise, the tea party has made a facile and convenient but ultimately incorrect connection between the Revolution's principled positions concerning the nature of particular taxes and their own continuing aversion to any taxes whatsoever. This antipathy to taxation of any sort, rather than only to specific measures, comes from our particular historical moment. In 1985, conservative Grover Norquist founded the Americans for Tax Reform, a lobbying and advocacy group opposed to all taxes and just about all government. He launched his movement by trying to purge the Republican Party of moderates—what he called RINO's, "Republicans in name only"—thus moving it to the right. Norquist initiated Americans for Tax Reform's "no-tax pledge," committing its signers not to raise or enact new taxes in any way, which has become a necessary commitment for surviving Republican electoral primaries. By 2009, every Republican in Congress was a signatory. The tea party's rage came as a godsend to Norquist and other long-term movement conservatives like Stephen Moore, who founded the anti-tax Club for Growth, and Jim DeMint, the tea-party-friendly South Carolinian who in 2013 left the Senate to became head of the Heritage Foundation. It was but a short hop between colonial protests of imperial taxes and contemporary conservative opposition to all taxes. This blanket resistance formed a key link as well as the most obvious contradiction between wealthy conservatives on the one hand, who have little personal need for public services or aid, and the tea partiers, many of whom are recipients of farm subsidies, veterans' benefits, Social Security, and Medicaid. Essentialism works for the tea party because the Revolutionaries' aversion to certain kinds of taxes is poorly understood enough for tea partiers to co-opt it as a hostility to all forms of government revenue.

In sum, the tea partiers' anger does echo in eerie ways that of many white, yeoman farmers in the Revolution: alienation from a political process that they feel does not represent them, suspicion of metropolitan and colonial elites that disdain them, fear of people that don't look like them, and a religious faith in their own righteousness. They also share a rage at a government that props up powerful corporations. Among the current tea partiers' greatest bugbears are what they perceive as need-less government bailouts of big banks and the auto industry. In 1773, the original tea partiers were reacting to a policy that actually reduced taxes on imported tea so that colonists would forgo smuggled tea in favor of the legal, East India Company variety. That is, they were reacting against not only their lack of say in government policy but also to a policy that propped up a big corporation (the East India Company) in which they had no direct interest. For many Americans, that anger continued through the 1780s and into the 1790s. In the 1780s, some rural residents resorted to forcibly blocking roads and closing courts to prevent fore-closures—most famously in what later became known as "Shays' Rebel-lion"—but found that, like today's tea partiers, they were more likely to be effective through the ballot box than in the streets. Tea partiers, too, are angry about the ways that metropolitan political and economic elites appear to be abusing government to line their own pockets and sneer-ing at them, to boot. That is a historical interpretation of the original tea party and of the Revolution, and though not nuanced or meticulous, it is nonetheless an important insight that seems to have largely passed by the academy. When tea partiers say they are "taking back America," they mean that in two senses: "taking back" chronologically to a better time in their imagination, and reclaiming it for the middle-class white men who now feel powerless to stem the march of time.

Meanwhile, another set of white folks has found a different essen-tialist vehicle for recalling the Revolution, but they differ strongly with the tea party on what the Revolution means. They, too, are generally politically conservative, especially on such issues as the right to bear arms. They're not seeking to become modern minutemen or a mod-ern tea party; rather, they want to re-create the entire War of Indepen-dence. American Revolutionary War reenactors hearken back to what they conceive of as a purer, more patriotic, and more earnest time. And yet they resist much of the current essentialist political cant. In order to get a better sense of their rituals, I attended a battle reenactment orga-nized by the Continental Line, which is the nation's largest consortium of Revolutionary War reenactors or, as they call themselves, "living his-torians." They gathered on a brilliantly sunny July Saturday at a remote farm in Pennsylvania's Pocono Mountains. Despite its being far from any major metropolitan area—over two hours' drive from New York or

Philadelphia, well off any major highway, and with no public transportation—the event drew hundreds of living historians, scores of vendors (the people who sell things to the reenactors, called according to eighteenth-century military parlance "sutlers"), and thousands of observers and hangers-on. This being such a big weekend and such a spacious site, it attracted a wide range of units: Continentals, state militia, Royal regiments, loyalists, Hessians, Native Americans, artillery, and cavalry. Units are self-organized, and most of them belong to one of a few umbrella organizations that coordinate the larger events. Because of its grand scale as the Continental Line's biggest event of the summer, units are loathe to miss it. What I found was a group of people whose dedication to the Revolution had ideological implications, but they want contemporary Americans to draw much different lessons from it than do originalists or tea partiers.

Unlike those movements, reenacting the American Revolutionary War has not attracted great numbers. Probably fewer than ten thousand people in the whole country actively engage in Revolutionary reenactment. It's costly: clothing, a gun, and other equipment for those in the uniformed ranks can easily run upwards of $1,000. Some soldiers pay more than that just for a firearm. One drawing point of militia companies as opposed to Continental Army units beyond the loosey-goosey attitude toward discipline is that, because most militia didn't have regular uniforms, the clothing can be much cheaper. Although some reenactors join up after seeing a parade or reenactment, especially young men enticed by the snappy British uniforms, most came to it through social connections. Like one middle-aged white man I talked to who works as a correctional officer in southern New Jersey, some are gun enthusiasts excited by actually being able to use old guns in their original context (although, as I had to explain to one of my daughters, they don't use live ammunition). He got hooked by one of his buddies who was a reenactor. Many who had no interest in guns or the Revolution tried it after being asked by a friend and ended up enchanted. Others come to it through family, having an interested father or brother. All were history buffs when they started or became ones, and my conversations with them almost invariably included tips on books that they found particularly edifying. To most Americans, and to me before I went to reenactments and started talking to living historians, it seems like an alien and perhaps even aberrant activity: playing soldier for the weekend, refighting without bullets a war of a bygone age. It is a romanticized recreation of the past. Some of the soldiers pretend to "die" on the battlefield, but none of the reenactors mimicks ailments like dysentery or infection, suffers from frostbite or malnourishment, or is involuntarily absent from his family for months or even years at a time. Wanting to understand the Revolution is nice, but why not just go camping and bring a book?

But Revolutionary War reenacting holds charms that people who scoff at it might not realize. Reenacting is an intensely social and sociable activity, much more so with the Revolutionary War than with Civil War reenactment, which tends to draw more single men. A very large proportion of the people I saw had come as a family. Wives and husbands, sons and daughters from babies to college age to wizened veterans. A few are even third-generation reenactors. They tend to stick with one regiment, so each reenactment also functions as a reunion—especially for those who have relocated but still travel to events to be with their buddies. I had a great conversation with Second New Jersey Regiment soldiers. Being New Jersey born and bred myself, I approached them during their preappointed lunch break between battles (real wars are more poorly scheduled). Under their tent they had laid a out a grandly tantalizing spread of loaves, cheeses, sausages, pickles, and non-tropical fruits they hacked at with their knives. The soldiers greeted me graciously and even dressed me up and took a picture of me. They were enjoying breaking bread together, the summer's day, and each other's company with a camaraderie rare in the frenetic anomie of contemporary America. Escapism on a daily basis might be harmful, but retreating into another century for a few weekends a year, with no cable television, no texting, no errands, no Facebook, no news, no email, no work, no traffic, no smartphone, but lots of time in a bucolic setting with family and friends, with no agenda but a few musters and a battle or two in which no one gets hurt besides the occasional twisted ankle sounds downright therapeutic, and many reenactors perceive what they do exactly that way. Rather than Revolution as politics, it's Revolution as lifestyle.

Revolutionary War reenactors are partly nostalgic, partly genuinely interested in what they and other reenactors call "living history," most evident in their never-ending quest for their version of historical veri-similitude. As historical film consultant Riley Flynn, who works with reenactors on a regular basis, has remarked, "If you rub two re-enactors together, you will get an argument over authenticity." That authenticity is usually channeled into material culture and military ritual. As thoughtful reenactors concede, both quests are quixotic. One recounted to me a conversation he had with his regimental commander. A hand-sewn shirt is superior to one stitched together by machine. But what of the thread—hand spun or machine spun? Was the fabric handwoven or machine made? Even if it is wool or linen (unlikely to be cotton, expensive stuff in the eighteenth century), was the wool hand sheared, and from what sheep variety? How was it dyed? The degrees of authenticity are endless. The same goes for reenacting battles. Unless the reenactors are fully trained, with the right numbers of troops, using live ammunition, on the same battlefield landscaped to be just like it had been, with the same weather, having marched so far the day before on eighteenth-century rations, it will never be truly authentic. Some reenactors are more starry-eyed than others. Minutes after I had a conversation with a young militia member who rhapsodized about how Revolutionary-era "people made things to last" and "really sacrificed for the war," another uniformed fellow knowingly confided that "military contractors back then made shoddy stuff, too," and "a lot of farmers were war profiteers and were willing to sell their grain to whatever army was marching by." Furthermore, Revolutionary War reenactors are still twenty-first-century people. Some units, especially the ones with younger members, include women in the lines as full soldiers, a matter of some controversy. On the whole, they are a fairly laid-back lot. You can turn back the calendar to an earlier season, but that won't turn back time, and the reenactors I talked to did not delude themselves otherwise.

Reenacting the American Revolution seems less overtly political than reenacting the Civil War, but in the end, it still has deep ideological implications. The vast majority of Civil War reenactors do so as Confederates, with the potential (and sometimes actual) baggage in terms of defending slavery or "states' rights," which serves in contemporary American political culture as a catchphrase for conservative political causes ranging from the dismantling of desegregation to resistance to the Obama healthcare plan. Several reenactors told me

Figure 5.1. A Battle of Authenticity. Spectators in baseball caps in the foreground crowd against gabbing British regulars, while a motley group of Continental and militia reenactors casually prepares for combat.

that the Civil War reenacting's image as a stalking horse for latter-day political positions turned them off. Nonetheless, although there are a handful of well-known African reenactors and regiments, the reenactors and the audience at the Revolutionary reenactment I attended were overwhelmingly white. That lack of racial diversity should not be surprising. In the northeast—by necessity the main area of reenactments—most African Americans live in urban areas and so have little connection to camping, and few live in the rural or suburban towns where reenactments take place. African American historical nostalgia in the United States is mostly limited to the Civil Rights era, one of the few times when African American fortunes seemed to be looking up. Just as much, Revolutionary War reenactors tend not to dwell on the fact that most white revolutionaries were engaged in a war ostensibly for liberty while few of them wanted to extend that freedom to the blacks that they or their neighbors held in bondage, in every state of the union. While different from those Confederate reenactors who identify with a cause that explicitly fought to retain slavery, they're still recreating a movement that resulted in perpetuating human bondage. I do not mean to imply in any way that they are racist, but the activity that they engage in nonetheless can be perceived in racial terms. One person's essentialist nostalgia may coincide with another's painful, repressed memory.

Nonetheless, unlike most other ways that the American Revolution is memorialized in American culture, the reenactors' Revolution has components mixing an organicist interest in common people with an essentialist nostalgia for the simpler life that they associate with the past. They indulge their passion not for great men but for regular people making deep sacrifices. Most Revolutionary War reenactors come from places where they grew up among battlefields and historic sites or visited Colonial Williamsburg as kids, and so have an emotional connection to the period. Many camped as boy scouts. Some are descended from Revolutionary War soldiers. They're all history buffs. So, for them, joining up and participating in a regiment is a chance to celebrate and explore what many of them perceive to be a fairly apolitical event, the American Revolution (of course, I'm arguing very much otherwise). Says reenactor Mike Brown, "It is my way to honor [my ancestors'] efforts and sacrifices in our nation's independence from tyranny and unequal rights as Englishmen in a remote land." Some also cite traditional gender roles, traditional mores, and a more genuine and simpler work ethic and time. Meanwhile, they are intent on busting the myths that too often the people who watch them hold. Sometimes those have to do with particular details or tactics regarding battles, campaigns, commanders, or equipment; at other times, with broader issues regarding the war or the Revolution. Although many reenactors have reverence for their favorite Revolutionary War commanders, they do not fall into the trap of idolizing the leaders at the expense of the thousands of ordinary people who fought the war on both sides. That consideration of class, and the tribulations of everyday people, sets essentialist living historians apart from originalists and tea partiers.

Furthermore, reenactors limit their recreation of the Revolution to their own cultural realm, rather than extending it to politics. In my conversations with Revolutionary reenactors, they removed their reenacting from any connection with contemporary politics. As longtime reenactor Kevin Young put it, referring to politicians and activists across the political spectrum, and pointedly to the tea partiers, "Think people today would risk their lives for 'The Tea Party?' Todays' politicians & activists would have been eaten for lunch by those with a real cause!" That sentiment was unanimous: to a man, every Revolutionary reenactor that I talked to spoke with great disdain about the phenomenon of what Thomas Paine memorably scorned as "sunshine patriots": those who evoke the tea parties, minutemen, and midnight rides without being willing to undergo long-term deprivation for, and possibly to die for, their patriotic principles. Reenactors passionately recount the real sacrifices that soldiers and their family made for cause and country, in contrast to today's reluctance to sacrifice anything. Reenactors also decried what they perceived as deep historical ignorance. Matt Murphy, from the New Jersey Second Regiment, emailed me that "I would love to take some Tea Party people, travel back in time with them and have them speak to the real soldiers of the Revolution. I bet they'd lay back on their much of their rhetoric!" And finally, living historians rail against politicians glorying in the nation's heroic Revolutionary past but skimping on the resources necessary to preserve it. Many reenactments are hosted on location by state and local historical societies whose never-generous federal and state funding has been sliced to the bone. One reenactor fumed that keeping a small site open would require only "funding equal to a big politico's night out on the town. Politicians don't give a hoot'n holler about history. Some say they do because it sounds good at election time, but in my book 'actions speak louder than words'!" Reenactors will never approach true authenticity. They know that other essentialists will miss the mark, too, only in different ways.

We as Americans cannot turn back the clock any more than reenactors can, but we also find it impossible to abandon those parts of the American past that function as common touchstones. As the reenactors' language and admissions about their own activities and those of their fellow essentialists suggest, they, originalists, and tea partiers have all been engaged in acts of selective memory. Organicism is no less selective, only in different ways. Trying to bring back the Revolutionary era, whether through policy or through physical recreation, cannot be done without either doing violence to the past, undoing much of what we value about the present, or both. Originalists and tea partiers choose to ignore those parts of the past that contradict their politics in their efforts to roll back parts of the present that scare them. For their part, reenactors stow their smartphones in their cars as they unpack their soldiers' gear to spend weekends in conscious denial of the Revolutionary War's deprivation and disease. But they all hearken back to the Revolution because it provides a communal emotional touchpoint for what they think of as the nation's ideals, for who belongs, for what being a citizen means, and for the nature of the compact between citizens and the government. As their example suggests, just as organicists and essentialists differ, essentialists differ among themselves about the answers to the nation's pressing political and cultural questions; organicists, too, come in many flavors. Re-creating contemporary America along Revolutionary lines is impossible, but over the last decade some Americans have found trying to do so irresistible. If originalists, tea partiers, and reenactors are representative of this yearning, then we can expect that, if Americans continue to do so in the future, their debates over the meanings of the American Revolution will be no less contentious than those in the opening years of the twenty-first century.

Conclusion

What I hope you as the reader take away from this volume is to think of it as a prompt for deeper consideration for when you encounter the American Revolution. When politicians speak of "the wisdom of the founding fathers" or working toward a "more perfect union," note how they are framing a debate concerning history and the relationship between the past and the present. When you read a book interpreting the Revolution as a conflict among Americans or as a grand cause for national freedom, think about what the author is implying in terms of class, diversity, and national unity today. When a museum depicts the story of an African American who escaped to freedom or unveils a glowing exhibit of a famous white founder's faultless life, know that its curators are engaged in a conversation about both which past to emphasize and about how we idealize citizens today. When a movie casts a strong Revolutionary-era patriotic woman or an evil, effeminate British man, watch for how it is portraying preferred gender roles for today's citizens and nation. When a political movement invokes Revolutionary symbols, consider those symbols' emotional and ideological resonances. Just as the nation changes over time, so does how we interpret and use the past. This book is not meant to be the definitive statement on our contested memory of the American Revolution but rather a call for a more explicit, conscious understanding going forward of the ways that we use those memories and the stakes involved.

Although I've used the concepts of essentialism and organicism as a way to understand contemporary invocations of the American Revolution, we must be cautious in applying them to other realms of memory or national discussion. Transferring any model from one phenomena to another risks distorting our understanding of both. While essentialist interpretations are usually conservative and organicist usually liberal, that is not always the case. There's a strong correlation between liberal political rhetoric and organicism and between conservative political speech and essentialism, but as we have seen, political liberals have made essentialist movies and written essentialist books, while conservatives have written organicist court decisions and screenplays. Americans imbue events other than the American Revolution with sets of meanings different from how they view the nation's founding event. The collective memory of the Civil War, the Progressive era, World War II, the Cold War, and the civil rights movement may be no less contentious but have become split on different fault lines than our debated recollection of the Revolution. Accordingly, projecting essentialism and organicism on our memory of other historical processes may miss the mark. These characterizations of the memory of the Revolution nonetheless provide a useful conceptualization for how we have debated the nation's founding era in the years past the turn of the twenty-first century, and in doing so, for how we are continuing to dispute the values at the center of the American experience: liberty, equality, community, commitment, and, not least, the pursuit of happiness.

Political invocations, public history, and on-screen treatments of the American Revolution tend to pick the most palatable common elements of essentialism and organicism. But there's another element to the American Revolution that few sites emphasize, and fewer dare to bring up its implications for contemporary America: the degree to which the American Revolution demanded great risk and sacrifice not only from those who took up arms but also from all who took up the cause. Over the last fifteen years, with the popularity of television shows like *The Simpsons*, *Seinfeld*, and *The Daily Show* and journalistic parodies like the *Onion*, and the postmodern challenge to age-old ideas, men's earnest choices to march to war against the redcoats seem foreign to most of us, whether those reasons were to fight for republican principles, to defend home and hearth, or because it was the only job they could get. The idea that many Americans did the same to defend the Crown's right to continue imperial government of the colonies is more alien still. Historian Sarah Purcell has argued that the first generation of U.S. citizens remembered the Revolution primarily as a war, with all the heartache, pain, and trauma that years of large-scale and interpersonal violence entail. Of all the treatments I read, watched, or walked through, few portrayed the

American Revolution as anything less than gloriously successful. The first white house exhibit at least noted that the Revolution had not freed all Americans. Nonetheless, even that installation forms part of a logical tourist flow from the Philadelphia Visitors Center to the Liberty Bell to Independence Hall, still providing a narrative that resulted in freedom. As the grumblings of reenactors indicates, little in today's memory of the Revolution recalls the sacrifice in blood, in money, in privation, and in destruction. The major exception is in the more organicist writings of historians like Ray Raphael, author of *A People's History of the American Revolution* (inspired by Howard Zinn's *A People's History of the United States*). But that doesn't make much of a dent in the polished facade of collective memory we have made for ourselves.

We must also recognize that both essentialists and organicists comfort themselves with unexamined conventional wisdom about the American Revolution that falls apart upon the most cursory examination. To square the contemporary mainstream ideals of racial and gender equality with what they see as eternal founding principles, essentialists argue that emancipation and even women's rights stem from the American Revolution. For example, in a column lamenting historians' dim view of the film *The Patriot*, conservative culture warrior David Horowitz praised the film for "forcefully embrac[ing] the idea that the American revolution and black freedom is one continuum." Gordon Wood has made a similar claim, arguing that the American Revolution made ending of slavery possible. Look, they can point out, the Constitution allowed for the elimination of the slave trade after 1808. Similarly, when organicists paint the struggle for Civil Rights as "perfecting the union" or portray one free black character as representative of all Revolutionary-era African Americans, they perpetuate a mirror image of the same myth: that the seeds of twenty-first-century equality were planted by the likes of Thomas Jefferson and John Adams, and furthermore, that one person, if he or she wanted something hard enough, can always overcome the racial, gender, and economic barriers to success that eighteenth-century people faced or that people face today. As with the essentialists, there is just enough of this assertion to make it sound plausible. In 2003, when the highest court in Massachusetts decided that same-sex marriage could not be legally barred, the majority opinion cited its 1780 constitution guaranteeing "inalienable rights" to all citizens. No politicians or major films or national best sellers challenge this fundamental tenet of the national faith shared by essentialists and organicists.

The idea that the American Revolution planted the seed of emancipation is an easily testable proposition. If what historian Bernard Bailyn has celebrated as the Revolutionary "contagion of liberty" led to the end of slavery, we would expect the freedom-inspired United States to have banned human bondage before the British empire. But that's not so. A 1772 court case in England effectively led to the end of slavery in the British isles—well ahead of the time when any American was openly advocating independence. Britain peacefully outlawed slavery in the rest of its empire in 1837, a full generation before the white populations of eleven American states used the words of the Declaration of Independence and the Constitution to justify their bloody rebellion to keep slavery, at the cost of potentially ripping apart the union. Admittedly, egalitarian Revolutionary ideas inspired Northern states to immediate or gradual emancipation, but certainly not the Southern ones. Nonetheless, historians Paul Finkelman and David Waldstreicher have soundly demonstrated that much of the Constitution was written with an eye on how to maintain slavery. The later outlawing of the slave trade occurred with white Virginians' blessing, but not because they wanted to free their black slaves. Rather, Virginia had a labor surplus, and the ban on slave importation provided Virginia a captive internal market (in all the senses of that term), propping up prices as Virginian slaveholders sold their human property downriver. Abolitionists' use of Revolutionary words was politically expedient but didn't actually do the job. African Americans' freedom required a war and three constitutional amendments in the 1860s, and full citizenship took another century. That wasn't the work of the founders. It was a repudiation of one of the central pillars of the founders' work: a republic built on slavery.

Despite their common deficiencies, proponents of organicism and essentialism have each contributed greatly to American civic life through their use of the American Revolution. For many years only organicist interpretations valued mass activism as one of the Revolution's legacies. We should not be surprised: denigration of groups threatening the status quo in any way had been a natural consequence the increasing conservatism of politics and media over the last twenty years. During the 2008 presidential election campaign Sarah Palin sneered at Barack Obama's experience as a community organizer. With the rise of tea party politics, that attitude has changed dramatically, and for the better. Less than a year after Palin's taunt, tea partiers bragged about their movement as being primarily from the grass roots, and at this writing still do, despite the considerable boost they've been given from millions in Super PAC money, the support of billionaires, and the cheerleading of a major cable network. Surveys indicate that tea party supporters are far more likely to contact their member of Congress or state representatives, to know the process by which bills become law, to go to rallies, and to engage in other forms of civic activism than most citizens, even those who express affiliation with either of the two major parties. The recovery of the American Revolution not only as the province of elite founders but also as a movement of the people brings us both closer to understanding the American Revolution and closer to living one of the goals of its more radical participants, namely, a broadly participatory citizenship.

The organicist emphasis on a multicultural Revolution, too, has brought more Americans into the political process and the greater democratic project that is the United States. Avenging the Ancestors Coalition was formed in the fight to effect an interpretation of the first white house that would emphasize the African Americans who lived on the site; it has since reawakened African American activism concerning other historical sites in Philadelphia. The DNA evidence regarding Thomas Jefferson's paternity of most of Sally Hemings's children has resulted in detente and in some cases growing affection between Thomas Jefferson's black descendants and his white ones. These might seem like baby steps toward interracial understanding, but even the smallest step is better than none at all. For a long time, common wisdom among public history professionals—or at least, white ones—has been that reminding African Americans of slavery's past would only result in further shame. But doing so has actually resulted in frank conversations from which all sides benefit far more than the tacit mutual silence those discussions had displaced. At the same time, the insistence that women participated in the Revolution no less than men can be equally beneficial. I've talked to a number of female college students who trace their interest in the Revolution to their watching Sarah on *Liberty's Kids*. My daughters, too, want to know more about the Revolution, about history, and about how our nation works today through their watching *Liberty's Kids* and reading the Felicity Merriman books of the American Girl line of dolls and stories. That's because, as problematic as those works may be as history, my daughters can see a little of themselves reflected in the nation's formative event.

These combined developments show that, despite their mutually exclusive underlying assumptions, we can recast the essentialist and organicist Revolutionary narratives. We can explore a more complicated, more multivocal, more messy Revolution, one with multitudes within multitudes, one that transcends the narrow interpretations of both essentialists and organicists. James Madison was against the Bill of Rights before he pushed it through, and he and Alexander Hamilton later debated the meanings of what they had written in the Constitution. Evangelicals in Virginia fought for religious freedom. African Americans wrote, protested, and ran for freedom or protected their families by forgoing the risk. Small farmers and urban laborers challenged their social superiors for political and ideological control of the new governments. Probably a fifth of free Americans opposed the revolution, and up to another two-fifths were what people then called "disaffected," meaning that they took neither side. There were over two and a half million people on North America's Eastern Seaboard during the American Revolutionary era; each one had a story.

We should be mindful when we see the Revolution and its many figures in so many facets of our lives because, each time we encounter it, we are encountering a bid for political and cultural legitimacy. Accordingly, it is not only important that we continue to read and research to understand the American Revolution better. It is also incumbent upon those of us who want to be active citizens to gauge the difference between contemporary evocations and more diligently researched history. We can then be informed rather than manipulated by those who use the Revolution for their own purposes, and we can reclaim the Revolution as a vital lesson and force for furthering the American experiment. Widespread acceptance of such critical thinking in the face of a broader American culture that avoids discussions of gender, race, and class may not reflect realistic expectations, but it may not be too much to ask. The charge should be taken up by academic and public historians, by filmmakers and candidates, and by the public at large if the United States is to understand its past and better address its future.

Meanwhile, don't expect Americans to stop debating the American Revolution. Perhaps the rise in interest in the Revolution that appears to have begun from the late 1990s will dissipate somewhat in the coming years. When we look back, fads seem like they should have been easy to distinguish from longer-term trends (remember pet rocks?). When you're in the middle of one, it's much harder to tell. But as I write this conclusion in 2013, there's still a lot to come. The Museum of the American Revolution continues to limp along in an old facility while raising millions for a new 118,000-square-foot building to go up in Philadelphia, which has yet to break ground. Similarly, the new American Revolution Museum at Yorktown is still in the planning stages. Mount Vernon has announced the opening of a new archive and library, the result of a $106 million fund-raising campaign. The stream of best-selling books on the American Revolution runs unabated. It will likely continue to flow, as publishers push what they perceive as sure-fire commercial successes for comparatively reasonable investments. Perhaps readers might be less willing to pry open their wallets for yet another Franklin or Washington biography, but there are always new angles to write from and new mountains to conquer (for example, the Battle of Bunker Hill, the subject of Nathaniel Philbrick's 2013 best seller). Authors will be further aided by the digitization of many of the founders papers, with most of those of the big six—Washington, Franklin, Adams, Jefferson, Hamilton, and Madison—already fully searchable at a single website. Networks have aired major series roughly relating to the Revolution: Fox's *Sleepy Hollow* (I know, Washington Irving's story doesn't take place during the Revolution, but in this series, it does) and AMC's *Washington's Spies*, renamed *Turn*, were slated for broadcast. Politicians seem unlikely to abandon Revolutionary-era references anytime soon. As they say in the biz, this show's got legs.

Essentialism particularly appears to be gaining steam as it becomes further institutionalized. That's not the same as winning the greater battle. As philosopher Olivier Roy has pointed out, conservatives cleave ever more tightly to an idealized, fundamental past exactly when their core values seem most imperiled. America's electing a fairly liberal, black president, passing laws legalizing same-sex marriage, allowing gays in the military, and restricting religious expression on the part of schools and state and local governments—all suggest that essentialism may be a rearguard action. One study of tea party focus groups indicated that they were motivated more than anything else by fear and by the impression that they had already lost America. Nonetheless, with originalism being touted across the legal ideological spectrum and taught in law schools, it may be the primary method of constitutional interpretation for the next generation of jurists. It's the dominant interpretive philosophy of the Federalist Society, an extremely well funded conservative organization of forty thousand judges, scholars, and lawyers, which funds forums and law school chapters. That momentum will entrench originalism, at least in its conservative form, for decades to come. Even though Glenn Beck's star has slightly faded since he went supernova in 2009, the tea party shows no signs of abating. Tea partiers will continue to elect members to the House of Representatives and to statehouses as long as many districts remain firmly in Republican hands; tea party activists can dominate the primaries that are the de facto Republican selection process in those districts. Such successes will ensure that candidates will continue to chase tea partiers' votes in local and national media outlets. The movement has even spawned a low-budget TV series, *Courage, New Hampshire*, available on DVD and streaming over the Internet. And now tea partiers can make the pilgrimage to the Boston Tea Party Ships & Museum, to baptize themselves into Revolutionary fervor by throwing empty crates into Boston's Fort Point Channel. Essentialism's increased currency seems to accrue interest judicial appointment by judicial appointment, election by election, book by book.

And that's often the way a nation's collective memory works. It is a recursive process. This year's TV series gets immortalized next year on DVD, the History Channel, and Netflix. Books displayed at the front of a bookstore one season get passed around to friends and relatives in subsequent seasons, eventually sold to yet new owners at garage sales or church fund-raisers. Law students become judges whose opinions their former classmates scour for clues on how to present their cases or law professors who varnish and then pass on the pearls of insight they received. Political activists take a one-day seminar, teach their children what they learned, and put it up on their websites to attract potential like minds to their cause. Candidates appeal to those potential supporters, offering them a return to the glorious past that they've learned about. Lessons get reinforced by politicians and the media pundits who enable them while trolling for ratings. Many historical sites offer tourist families what they want to see, lest their expectations be so upset that they decide to spend their vacation dollars at theme parks offering bigger thrills, fewer challenges, and more sugary treats for the kids. As psychologists and sociologists tell us, we're less likely to give full credence to facts and ideas that run counter to our preconceived notions. Like all collective memories, our national memory has become a feedback loop, in which what goes in differs little from what goes out. Major changes occur rarely, and only in step with broader cultural changes that also happen slowly rather than abruptly.

Meanwhile, as the previous chapters suggest, though collective memory is always contested, our memory of the American Revolution has been subjected to an increasingly earnest tug-of-war. Each side seems more and more dug in, and less and less willing to compromise, on what it considers crucial American ideals. That unwavering commitment mirrors the nation's ever-more-unbridgeable ideological divide, a growing rift resulting from a variety of technological, cultural, and social developments. The ability of people to select what they read, hear, and experience has accelerated since the turn of the millennium. With our brains constantly bathing in a stream of soundbites, posts, and tweets, we segregate ourselves into communities of folk who share the same values that we hold. Facebook, Twitter, and other social media sites let us make small communities of like-minded people who can repost and retweet the blog entries and clips that we agree with, and we take less and less time to seek out the outlets that promote points of view different from our own. The availability of scores of cable channels allows viewers to choose those most closely matching their political preferences. Hosts and pundits can cater to ever narrower slices of the electorate. Using demographic and marketing techniques, political consultants have carved most federal and state electoral districts into single-party strongholds. And what they don't accomplish by design, their constituents do themselves: evidence increasingly indicates that Americans tend to move to areas where there are more people who share their values. Members of Congress now rarely mix socially across party lines, spending more time in fundraisers or in their home districts and less time on Capitol Hill, and so can more easily demonize their colleagues across the aisle with whom they have no casual human relationships. We have drawn our battle lines, verbal muskets at the ready.

At the same time, some of the moderating facets of American society have disappeared or faded. From World War II through 1972, the national draft forced two generations of men into units where they'd have to encounter, and fight alongside, men of different backgrounds and ideas, forming bonds that overcame smaller differences; today's smaller, all-volunteer army is much more homogenous. The advent of cable and then Internet streaming broke the media dominance of the three major TV broadcast networks, whose middle-of-the-road programming had been designed to appeal to the greatest number of people and whose licenses required they give equal time to content promoting differing political points of view. The 1990s loosening of political campaign regulation, combined with the 2010 Supreme Court decision *Citizens United v. Federal Election Commission*, has released a flood of political spending through political action committees that has transformed the campaign cycle from a onetime rinse to a continuous spin. Those organizations, in turn, promote ideological ends, weakening the Republican and Democratic Parties as big-tent political organizations. The rise of megachurches and the growing ranks of the unchurched have accompanied the shrinking of national religious denominations that served as umbrellas for a wide range of theological and social thinking. Cheap airfare and investment in amusement parks and professional and major college athletic facilities has led to an increase in leisure and sports tourism at the expense of road trips to historical sites and national parks. We live in the same country but can inhabit different conceptual universes. That's why your American Revolution and my American Revolution may be two entirely different creatures, and the American Revolution of the person next door still another.

I, too, live a life mostly sheltered from divergent opinions, but my experiences in researching and writing this book have tempered my previous assurances. As an academic historian, my career interest in issues related to social class has led to contacts largely with organicist historians. I work mostly with liberals at a public university, where my activities helping establish our faculty union and negotiate its first contract resulted in my socializing with people considered liberals even among the professoriate. Although I grew up in a reformed Jewish household, my wife and I chose to join a Unitarian Universalist congregation partly because we felt more ideologically comfortable in that very liberal denomination than in the local reformed Jewish synagogue. I read the *New York Times* and the *New Yorker*, follow a few liberal political blogs, and would watch *The Daily Show* if I had the time to do it. There was one instance during the course of my research that I had trouble relating to people beyond my preferred ideological cocoon. When attending the *Making of America* seminar, I shied away from doing interviews, for fear of being perceived as a spy or from affecting the way the seminar would be taught. But I admired that people would take a Saturday out of their busy lives to learn about the nation's history, something that few of us would undertake. Talking to public history professionals, moviemakers, authors, and reenactors, I grew to value even more their dedication to doing history according to the standards of their profession: they do so because of their passion for it. I began to see more clearly the gaps in my own thinking about what's important about the American Revolution, as well as to appreciate the achievements of Revolutionaries despite their shortcomings.

I've also learned to accept that debate over the American Revolution will take place in different ways depending upon the medium in which it is depicted. Although hope springs eternal, we should not expect historical discussion on the American Revolution or, for that matter, any complex historical process to take the form of factually accurate, deeply nuanced, properly sourced, logically sound, civil debate across the spectrum of mass culture. As I've argued in this book, each delivery method has its inherent tropes, expectations, and ideologies and so will necessarily offer interpretations considered appropriate according to the industry's prevailing practices. Scholars (including me) would like moviemakers, politicians, activists, and judges to have a better sense of history and how it works. What we usually mean by "better," of course, means "more like how we do it." But given the last two hundred years, any exhortation on my part for them to do so would be no more realistic than my expecting this book to get me elected president or to gross more than $50 million on its opening weekend. Our vocations have different purposes and differing logics. Like most historians, I'd like to think my work is good history, but I know it's lousy politics. As Joseph Ellis has said about effecting social change through writing about the

American Revolution, "If you want to change the world, get out of the eighteenth century. We need you here." Nearly rarer than unicorns is the social change that occurs because of a book covering events in centuries gone by, and not much more common is the political speech or movie that delves into historical complexity because of a historian's insight. Professionals in other lines of work do not have the responsibility to do history the way academics do, and they would be failures in their industry if they did. We can continue to press them to tell the story better, but in the end, they're telling their own stories about the past.

Only through recognizing each other's best intentions can we move the conversation on the American Revolution, and therefore these United States, forward in a way that we all may participate and learn from each other. Historians and many other observers deplore Americans' evergreen desire to contest the American Revolution through politics and popular culture. Let's not fight, they suggest, let's share the nation's founding symbols. But I think that we should continue to debate the nation's origins. At least the American Revolution gives us a common set of characters, settings, and events. That civic vocabulary allows for debate through a rhetorical shorthand. The point in a democracy is not for us to agree on everything. But we can have discussions if at least we're speaking the same conceptual language. The American Revolution was a capacious enough process that, ever since, Americans have found new ways to invoke its people and words to consider issues that the founders never addressed or to rethink them in ways that the founders never envisioned. I hope that, in another two centuries, the debate will be just as lively as it is today. In the meantime, consider your own American Revolution. Chances are, somewhere tucked inside will be your American hopes and dreams. Share them.

In the course of researching and writing this book, I consulted a wide range of articles from scholarly journals and the popular press, books both about the American Revolution and other topics, online resources, DVDs, and computer databases, and I used a range of methods. Rather than list everything I consulted, I would like to guide readers through my thought process in this essay and point them to further reading on the range of topics that this book addresses. This is just a basic introduction to major works in various fields and to others that I've consulted. Many of these areas have been the subject of shelves of volumes and sheaves of academic articles.

Memory, and especially collective memory, has become an increasingly studied topic. Its heritage, though, goes back way further, to the work of the French sociologist Maurice Halbwachs in 1925, available in English in Maurice Halbwachs, *On Collective Memory*, trans. Lewis A. Coser, Heritage of Sociology (Chicago: University of Chicago Press, 1992). Other major works include Pierre Nora, *Realms of Memory: Rethinking the French Past*, trans. Lawrence D. Kritzman, European Perspectives (New York: Columbia University Press, 1996); Yael Zerubavel, *Recovered Roots: Collective Memory and the Making of Israeli National Tradition* (Chicago: University of Chicago Press, 1995); and Michel-Rolph Trouillot, *Silencing the Past: Power and the Production of History* (Boston: Beacon Press, 1995). More than any other scholar, Jeffrey Olick has been responsible for more recent theorizing in the field, for example, in "Collective Memory: The Two Cultures," *Sociological Theory* 17 (1999): 333–348, and "'Collective Memory': A Memoir and Prospect," *Memory Studies* 1 (2008): 23–29. For a good general overview, see Geoffrey Cubitt, *History and Memory* (New York: Manchester University Press, 2008).

Scholars of American memory have been particularly fruitful, among them David Lowenthal, *The Past Is a Foreign Country* (Cambridge:

Cambridge University Press, 1985); Michael G. Kammen, *Mystic Chords of Memory: The Transformation of Tradition in American Culture*, 1st ed. (New York: Knopf, 1991); George Lipsitz, *Time Passages: Collective Memory and American Popular Culture* (Minneapolis: University of Minnesota Press, 1990); and David Glassberg, *Sense of History: The Place of the Past in American Life*, illustrated ed. (Amherst: University of Massachusetts Press, 2001). Roy Rosenzweig and David P. Thelen surveyed a broad range of Americans to see how they perceive the past and their relation to it in *The Presence of the Past: Popular Uses of History in American Life* (New York: Columbia University Press, 1998). John Bodnar's *Remaking America: Public Memory, Commemoration, and Patriotism in the Twentieth Century* (Princeton, N.J.: Princeton University Press, 1993) is a particularly useful consideration of public history that applies the concepts of "official" and "vernacular" history, refined from Susan G. Davis, *Parades and Power: Street Theatre in Nineteenth-Century Philadelphia* (Philadelphia: Temple University Press, 1986), and complemented by Kirk Savage, *Monument Wars: Washington, D.C., the National Mall, and the Transformation of the Memorial Landscape*, 1st ed. (Berkeley: University of California Press, 2009). On the topic of wars, George H. Roeder analyzed how the Roosevelt Administration tried to shape American perception of World War II in *The Censored War: American Visual Experience during World War Two* (New Haven, Conn.: Yale University Press, 1993).

The general topic of the memory of the American Revolution has long been a matter of scholarly interest. Among the major works are Wesley Frank Craven, *The Legend of the Founding Fathers* (Ithaca, N.Y.: Cornell University Press, 1965); Catherine L. Albanese, *Sons of the Fathers: The Civil Religion of the American Revolution* (Philadelphia: Temple University Press, 1976); Michael G. Kammen, *A Season of Youth: The American Revolution and the Historical Imagination*, 1st ed. (New York: Knopf, 1978); David Hackett Fischer, *Liberty and Freedom: A Visual History of America's Founding Ideas* (New York: Oxford University Press, 2005); and Richard B. Bernstein, *The Founding Fathers Reconsidered* (New York: Oxford University Press, 2009). Kyle Ward provides interesting materials in *History in the Making: An Absorbing Look at How American History Has Changed in the Telling over the Last 200 Years* (New York: New Press, 2007). Although written for middle- and high-school-age students, Steven H. Jaffe, *Who Were the Founding Fathers?: Two Hundred Years of Reinventing American History*, 1st ed. (New York: H. Holt & Co., 1996), delivers an excellent brief overview. More recently, two books have demonstrated the degree to which the first generations after the Revolution shaped its memory. François Furstenberg, *In the Name of the Father: Washington's Legacy, Slavery, and the Making of a Nation* (New York: Penguin Press, 2006), investigates the original founders chic in the early national worship of George Washington; a series of authors consider various topics in Michael McDonnell, Clare Corbould, Frances M. Clarke, and W. Fitzhugh Brundage, eds. *Remembering the Revolution: Memory, History, and Nation-Making from Independence to the Civil War* (Amherst: University of Massachusetts Press, 2013).

The intersection of nationalism and memory has also been much considered. The quotation from Ernest Renan comes from his famous 1884 lecture, "What Is a Nation?," in *Nation and Narration*, by Homi K. Bhabha, trans. Martin Thom (London: Routledge, 1990), 8–22. Benedict Anderson's idea of the nation as an "imagined community" has been the basis for much discussion since his *Imagined Communities: Reflections on the Origin and Spread of Nationalism* (London: Verso, 1983), as has Ernest Gellner, *Nations and Nationalism*, New Perspectives on the Past (Ithaca, N.Y.: Cornell University Press, 1983). Michael Billig investigated the ubiquity of national symbols, including those of memory, in *Banal Nationalism* (London: Sage, 1995). For a good overview of recent debates in the field, consult Graham Day and Andrew Thompson, *Theorizing Nationalism* (New York: Palgrave Macmillan, 2004). Particularly useful volumes on the ways that controversy over national memories constitute debates over nationalism include Michael E. Geisler, *National Symbols, Fractured Identities: Contesting the National Narrative* (Lebanon, N.H.: University Press of New England, 2005); David Brown, *Contemporary Nationalism: Civic, Ethnocultural, and Multicultural Politics* (London and New York: Routledge, 2000); Susana Carvalho and François Gemenne, eds., *Nations and Their Histories: Constructions and Representations* (New York: Palgrave Macmillan, 2009); and John R. Gillis, ed., *Commemorations: The Politics of National Identity* (Princeton, N.J.: Princeton University Press, 1996). Alon Confino explained how national collective memory can contain "common denominators" of two or more competing ideologies in "Collective Memory and Culture History: Problems of Method," *American Historical Review* 102 (1997): 1386–1403.

Much of this work is at the intersection of nationalism and multiculturalism. Essentialism reflects a more thickly shared culture, ethnosymbolically based nationalism that implicitly emphasizes whiteness, militarism, and patriarchy, as outlined by Anthony D. Smith, *The Nation in History: Historiographical Debates about Ethnicity and Nationalism*, Menahem Stern Jerusalem Lectures (Hanover, N.H.: University Press of New England, 2000). Yael Tamir's model of nationalism in *Liberal Nationalism*, Studies in Moral, Political, and Legal Philosophy (Princeton, N.J: Princeton University Press, 1993), exhibiting a more thinly shared culture but offering room for multiple ethnicities, better describes the kind of nationalism that organicists espouse. Among multiculturalism's critiques, some friendlier than others, are David Hollinger's (that its categories are too rigid or so socially constructed as to be meaningless and that it fails to account for multiethnic people) in *Postethnic America: Beyond Multiculturalism* (New York: Basic Books, 1995); and Anne Phillips's (that it further privileges gendered cultural norms) in *Multiculturalism without Culture* (Princeton, N.J.: Princeton University Press, 2007).

About the reflexivity (or lack thereof) of American history as practiced, see a fascinating round-table discussion titled "Self and Subject" in the *Journal of American History* 89, no. 1 (June 2002): 17–53. Considered more broadly in the context of what American historians have called the "objectivity" problem, see Peter Novick, *That Noble Dream: The "Objectivity Question" and the American Historical Profession*, Ideas in Context (Cambridge: Cambridge University Press, 1988); and Ian Tyrrell, *Historians in Public: The Practice of American History, 1890–1970* (Chicago: University of Chicago Press, 2005).

There are many indices of increased ideological polarization in American life. Among the most rigorous investigations of them is "Partisan Polarization Surges in Bush, Obama Years," Trends in American Values: 1987–2012, Pew Research Center for the People and the Press, June 4, 2012 (www.people-press.org/2012/06/04/partisan-polarization-surges-in-bush-obama-years). There's much chicken-and-egg debate about the relationship between gerrymandering and partisanship; for a recent consideration, see Nolan McCarty, Keith T. Poole, and Howard Rosenthal, "Does Gerrymandering Cause Polarization?," *American Journal of Political Science* 53, no. 3 (2009): 666–680. Their website also offers considerable data on this issue at "The Polarization of the Congressional Parties," *Voteview.com*, updated January 19, 2014 (http://voteview.com/political_polarization.asp). Adam Liptak offers a useful survey of the scholarship concerning the political leanings of judges in "A Sign of the Court's Polarization: Choice of Clerks," *New York Times*, September 6, 2010, sec. U.S. / Politics (www.nytimes.com/2010/09/07/us/politics/07clerks.html).

To analyze presidential campaign speech, I harvested speeches from a variety of sources. Transcripts for the major party nominees from 1952 through 1996 are available on the CD-ROM *The Annenberg/Pew Archive of Presidential Campaign Discourse* (Philadelphia: Annenberg School for Communication, 2000). I collected speeches from the 2000 and 2004 elections by downloading the archived campaign websites available through the *Internet Archive Wayback Machine* (http://archive.org/web/web.php), as well as from searches of published transcripts through LexisNexis. For the 2008 campaign, I downloaded the full text of speeches from *ProCon.org* (http://2008election.procon.org; there is a resource page for each candidate that includes the full text of speeches). The *American Presidency Project*, administered by John Woolley and Gerhard Peters, archived candidates 2012 speeches in "2012 Presidential Election Documents" (www.presidency.ucsb.edu/2012_election.php#axzz2fvBGpIuV). After running a Mac OS Automator macro to strip everything into plain text files, I imported them into the TAMS Analyzer program (http://tamsys.sourceforge.net), creating a total corpus of 6,912,612 words. I used TAMS for an initial pass of automated coding but then went through each identified reference to ensure that it was relevant. The graphs were composed in Microsoft Excel using data exported from TAMS.

Thomas Fleming's "Channelling George Washington" column appears intermittently on the *History News Network* (www.hnn.us); the particular one in question is "Channelling George Washington: First in Their Hearts," *History News Network*, January 31, 2011 (www.hnn.us/articles/136006.html). Although the National Rifle Association has never released demographic breakdowns of its membership, much anecdotal evidence indicates that its membership is overwhelmingly white and male, including Robert Farago, "Rick Ector: Why the NRA Doesn't Include Blacks," *The Truth about Guns.com*, April 25, 2012 (www.thetruthaboutguns.com/2012/04/robert-farago/rick-ector-why-the-nra-doesnt-include-blacks/). For elaboration on the Polish Constitution of 1791, see Tadeusz N. Cieplak, "Church and State in People's Poland," *Polish American Studies* 26, no. 2 (October 1, 1969): 15–30. Many scholars have considered the role of religion in the nation's founding, most notably Frank Lambert, *The Founding Fathers and the Place of Religion in America* (Princeton, N.J.: Princeton University Press, 2003); Jon Meacham, *American Gospel: God, the Founding Fathers, and the Making of a Nation*, 1st ed. (New York: Random House, 2006); and John Fea, *Was America Founded as a Christian Nation?: A Historical Introduction* (Louisville, Ky.: Westminster John Knox Press, 2011).

Of "dog-whistle" politics, see Robert E. Goodin and Michael Saward, "Dog Whistles and Democratic Mandates," *Political Quarterly* 76, no. 4 (October 2005): 471–476; and, for a rebuttal, see Andrew Ferguson, "The Dog Whistle and Other Liberal Tropes," *Commentary* 133, no. 3 (March 2012): 63–64. However, as noted by Matthew Gentzkow and Jesse M. Shapiro, politicians of both parties use coded phrases in equal measure; see their supplement to "What Drives Media Slant? Evidence from U.S. Daily Newspapers," *Econometrica* 78, no. 1 (2010): 35–71. For how white Americans often frame language in seemingly non-racial terms—but with racial ramifications—see Eduardo Bonilla-Silva, *Racism without Racists: Color-Blind Racism and the Persistence of Racial Inequality in America*, 4th ed. (Lanham, Md.: Rowman & Littlefield, 2013). The standard work on Americans' racialized perceptions of public assistance is Martin Gilens, *Why Americans Hate Welfare: Race, Media, and the Politics of Antipoverty Policy*, Studies in Communication, Media, and Public Opinion, 1st ed. (Chicago: University of Chicago Press, 2000), while Alex Gould-Werth and H. Luke Shaefer indicate that whites are more likely to apply for and receive unemployment insurance than are people of color in "Unemployment Insurance Participation by Education and by Race and Ethnicity," *Monthly Labor Review* (October 2012): 28–41. As noted by "Partisan Polarization Surges in Bush, Obama Years," *Trends in American Values: 1987–2012*, Pew Research Center for the People and the Press, June 4, 2012 (www.people-press.org/2012/06/04/

partisan-polarization-surges-in-bush-obama-years), support for public assistance of the poor has declined during the 2000s.

A number of observers have weighed in on "founders chic." Evan Thomas coined the term in Evan Thomas, "Founders Chic: Live from Philadelphia," *Newsweek* 138, no. 2 (July 9, 2001): 48–51. Among the historians to weigh in are David Waldstreicher, "Founders Chic as Culture War," *Radical History Review* 84 (2002): 185–194; and Jeffrey L. Pasley, "Publick Occurrences: Federalist Chic," *Common-Place*, vol. 2, no. 2 (2002) (www.common-place.org/publick/200202.shtml), both of whom see it as primarily a conservative phenomenon. Allan Kulikoff argues that this is merely a new phase in Americans' continued debate over the Revolution in "The Founding Fathers: Best Sellers! TV Stars! Punctual Plumbers!," *Journal of the Historical Society*, 5, no. 2 (2005): 155–187, as does Francis D. Cogliano in "Founders Chic," *History* 90, no. 299 (2005): 411–419. Some have debated the extent of the trend, including Fitzhugh Brundage, "Remembering the Revolution: Individual and Collective Memories in the Twentieth Century" (presented at the Organization of American Historians Annual Conference, Milwaukee, April 2012). H. W. Brands credited the fine writing of founders-chic authors, although he lamented that founders chic leads us to rely on the founders rather than on ourselves in "Founders Chic: Our Reverence for the Fathers Has Gotten Out of Hand," *Atlantic Monthly* 292, no. 2 (September 2003): 101–110.

Joseph Ellis, one of the main practitioners of founders chic, mentioned in an email to me the extent and accessibility of the founders' papers, a development cited by other authors as well. For a critique of the longtime exclusive choice of founding fathers for major federally subsidized editing projects—as opposed to projects focusing on women or slaves, for example—see Jesse Lemisch, "The American Revolution Bicentennial and the Papers of Great White Men: A Preliminary Critique of Current Documentary Publication Programs and Some Alternative Proposals," *AHA Newsletter* 9 (November 1971): 7–21. Susan Currie and Donna Lee Brien noted that biographies in particular have always sold well in "Mythbusting Publishing: Questioning the 'Runaway Popularity' of Published Biography and Other Life Writing," *M/C Journal*, vol. 11, no. 4 (2008) (http://journal.media-culture.org.au/index.php/mcjournal/article/view/43).

For the best considerations of how academic historians have written about the Revolution, see Gwenda Morgan, *The Debate on the American Revolution* (Manchester: Manchester University Press, 2007); and Alfred Fabian Young and Gregory H. Nobles, *Whose American Revolution Was It?: Historians Interpret the Founding* (New York: New York University Press, 2011). Much of my list of Revolution-related best sellers (1990s–2010) comes through the generosity of Thomas J. Brown, who compiled it while looking for Civil War–related ones for his introduction to the collection he edited, *Remixing the Civil War: Meditations on the Sesquicentennial* (Baltimore: Johns Hopkins University Press, 2011). I only included those from the non-fiction, hardcover lists. I found more recent ones through the same source Brown mined, "Adult *New York Times* Best Seller Listings," *Hawes Publications* (www.hawes.com/pastlist.htm), which retains *New York Times* best-seller lists going back to the 1950s. My method for selecting prominent academic titles was far more haphazard: I chose books from prominent authors, published by commercial presses, that addressed topics roughly in line with the best-selling trends, in addition to books that won major awards, either academic or trade. While I was unable to obtain even general sales figures for most books, volumes for a few books, like David McCullough's *John Adams* (New York: Simon & Schuster, 2001), were widely reported. Woody Holton and David Waldstreicher kindly shared general numbers and their general takes on their work vis-à-vis founders chic by email. To analyze the books, I purchased Amazon Kindle versions to be able to search them electronically and also used the DeDRM plug-in for Calibre, an e-book management program, to convert the books into text format and import them into Zotero (a bibliographic management program) so I could search all of them simultaneously.

Glenn Beck reacted to Palin's failure to choose her "favorite Founding Father" on "Beck Weighs In on Sarah Palin's Fox Debut," *O'Reilly Factor*, Fox News Network (January 15, 2010). David McCullough has been the subject of many interviews. Among the more in-depth ones are Bob Hoover, "David McCullough: America's Historian, Pittsburgh Son," *Pittsburgh Post-Gazette*, December 30, 2001; and Todd Leopold, "David McCullough Brings 'John Adams' to Life," *CNN.com*, June 7, 2001   (http://web.archive.org/web/20010609152137/http://www.cnn.com/2001/SHOWBIZ/books/06/07/david.mccullough/index.html).

For Ron Chernow's thoughts, see Kenneth T. Jackson and Valerie Paley, "An Interview with Ron Chernow," *New-York Journal of American History*, Spring 2004, 59–65; and Will Swift, "Ron Chernow, 2013 BIO Award Winner, Talks about His Work," *Biographers International Organization*, 2013 (http://biographersinternational.org/tbc/chernow). For a particularly critical take on Chernow's portrayal of Hamilton, see William Hogeland, "Inventing Alexander Hamilton," in *Inventing American History* (Cambridge, Mass.: MIT Press, 2009), 1–44. For a longer view, consult Stephen F. Knott, *Alexander Hamilton and the Persistence of Myth*, American Political Thought (Lawrence: University Press of Kansas, 2002). The Walter Isaacson quotation I used comes from his interview with Ed Nawotka, "Ben Franklin: A Man for All Seasons," *Publishers Weekly*, May 12, 2003, 56. The *Marion Star* headline comes from May 3, 1913, as quoted in Eric F. Goldman, "The Origins of Beard's Economic Interpretation of the Constitution," *Journal of the History of Ideas* 13, no. 2 (April 1952): 245. Cokie Roberts revealed some of her thoughts to Mark Silver in "Cokie Roberts on the Founding Mothers," *U.S. News and World Report*, April 26, 2004. For a revealing portrait of Woody Holton, see "Holton's Rebellion," *Richmond Style Weekly*, April 16, 2008; for Holton in his own words, consult "Ask the Author: Woody Holton, Unruly Origins," *Common-Place*, vol. 8, no. 4 (July 2008) (www.common-place.org/vol-08/no-04/author/). Alfred S. Young discussed history with Sarah M. S. Pearsall for "Hidden in Plain Sight: A Conversation with Alfred S. Young about *Masquerade*," *Common-Place*, vol. 5, no. 4 (July 2005) (www.common-place.org/vol-05/no-04/author).

For more about Annette Gordon-Reed and her thought process, see Vicki Hambleton, "An Interview with Annette Gordon-Reed," *Footsteps Magazine*, n.d. (www.footstepsmagazine.com/SallyArticle.asp); Deborah Solomon, "Questions for Annette Gordon-Reed: History Lesson," *New York Times*, December 5, 2008; and "Our Live Chat with Annette Gordon-Reed," *New Yorker Blogs*, February 1, 2010. Jon Meacham defended his work in David Daley, "Jon Meacham: I'm Not Letting Thomas Jefferson off the Hook," *Salon*, November 17, 2012. In Jill O'Neill, "Interview with Gordon S. Wood," *History News Network*, February 15, 2010, Gordon Wood shared his thoughts; Gary B. Nash took Wood's scholarship to task in "Also There at the Creation: Going beyond Gordon S. Wood," *William and Mary Quarterly* 44 (1987):

602–611. Colin Gordon noted the ideological implications of historical scholarship in "Crafting a Usable Past: Consensus, Ideology, and
Historians of the American Revolution," *William and Mary Quarterly*
46 (1989): 671–695; for more on the politicization of the professoriate,
see Neil Gross and Solon Simmons, "The Social and Political Views
of American Professors," working paper, 2007 (http://citeseerx.ist.psu.
edu/viewdoc/download?doi=10.1.1.147.6141&rep=rep1&type=pdf&a=bi
&pagenumber=1&w=100).

Much ink and many electrons have been devoted to the Jefferson-
Hemings issue. Among the most enlightening about the DNA revela-
tions and its aftermath are Joseph J. Ellis, "Jefferson: Post-DNA," *Wil-
liam and Mary Quarterly* 57 (2000): 125–138; Dianne Swann-Wright
et. al., "Report of the Research Committee on Thomas Jefferson and
Sally Hemings" (Charlottesville, Va.: Thomas Jefferson Memorial Foun-
dation, January 2000); Lewis Lord, "The Tom-and-Sally Miniseries
(Cont.): Rallying around the Founding Father," *U.S. News and World
Report*, January 18, 1999; Leef Smith, "Jeffersons Split over Hemings
Descendants," *Washington Post*, May 17, 1999; and Shannon Lanier and
Jane Feldman, *Jefferson's Children: The Story of One American Fam-
ily* (New York: Random House, 2002). For a flavor of the debate over
Henry Wiencek's *An Imperfect God: George Washington, His Slaves, and
the Creation of America* (New York: Farrar, Straus & Giroux, 2003), see
Lisa Provence, "Mr. Jefferson's Greed: New Book Challenges Image of
Reluctant Slaveholder," *Hook* (Charlottesville), October 18, 2012; Beth
McMurtrie, "The Controversial Contradictions of Thomas Jefferson,"
Chronicle of Higher Education, November 12, 2012; Katie Kilkenny, "The
Debate over Thomas Jefferson's Slaves Rages On," *Brow Beat: Slate's Cul-
ture Blog*, November 21, 2012; Jennifer Schuessler, "Henry Wiencek's
'Master of the Mountain' Irks Historians," *New York Times*, November
11, 2012; and "Who Is the Real Thomas Jefferson?: A Heated Op-Ed War
among Historians Is Picking Up Where Two Controversial New Biographies Left Off This Fall," *Salon*, December 3, 2012.

Multiple historians and other observers have noted the challenges in
bringing history to life in the movies or on television. The most useful
include S. Anderson, "History TV and Popular Memory," in *Television
Histories: Shaping Collective Memory in the Media Age*, ed. G. R. Edgerton and Peter C. Rollins (Lexington: University Press of Kentucky, 2001),

19–36; *Past Imperfect: History according to the Movies*, Mark C. Carnes, general ed. (New York: H. Holt, 1995); Robert Brent Toplin, *History by Hollywood: The Use and Abuse of the American Past* (Urbana: University of Illinois Press, 1996), and *Reel History: In Defense of Hollywood*, illustrated ed. (Lawrence: University Press of Kansas, 2002); Natalie Zemon Davis, *Slaves on Screen: Film and Historical Vision* (Cambridge, Mass.: Harvard University Press, 2002); Marnie Hughes-Warrington, *History Goes to the Movies: Studying History on Film* (New York: Routledge, 2006); and Peter C. Rollins, *The Columbia Companion to American History on Film: How the Movies Have Portrayed the American Past* (New York: Columbia University Press, 2006). Neil Longley York considered the intersection of history, fiction, and film in the portrayal of one event in *Fiction as Fact: The Horse Soldiers and Popular* Memory (Kent, Ohio: Kent University Press, 2001). Film historian Robert Sklar coined the term "historian cop" in "Review: Historical Films: Scofflaws and the Historian-Cop," *Reviews in American History* 25 (1997): 346–350.

Among the most insightful sources concerning movies on the American Revolution in particular are Jamie Malanowski, "The Revolutionary War Is Lost on Hollywood," *New York Times*, July 2, 2000; Cotten Seiler, "The American Revolution," in *The Columbia Companion to American History on Film: How Movies Have Portrayed the American Past*, ed. Peter C. Rollins (New York: Columbia University Press, 2003), 49–57; Mark Glancy, "The War of Independence in Feature Films: *The Patriot* (2000) and the 'Special Relationship' between Hollywood and Britain," *Historical Journal of Film, Radio and Television* 25 (2005): 523–545; Nancy L. Rhoden, "Patriots, Villains, and the Quest for Liberty: How American Film Has Depicted the American Revolution," *Canadian Review of American Studies* 37 (2007): 205–238; and John E. O'Conner, "The American Revolution on Screen: *Drums along the Mohawk* and *The Patriot*," in *Why We Fought: America's Wars in Film and History*, ed. Peter C. Rollins and John E. O'Conner (Lexington: University Press of Kentucky, 2008), 41–62.

For reaction to the Dodge Challenger commercial, see Jim Henry, "George Washington, NASCAR Dad, Drives a Dodge Challenger (That's Made in Canada)," *CBS News Money Watch*, July 17, 2010; and Amy Gardner, "Tea Party Movement's Energy, Anger Make It Target for Admakers," *Washington Post*, July 6, 2010.

All movie earnings and ticket sales numbers are from the website Box Office Mojo (www.boxofficemojo.com); the Internet Movie Database (www.imdb.com) is also an essential source for basic movie research.

The venerable bible of screenwriting, first released in 1979 and now in its fourth edition, remains Syd Field, *Screenplay: The Foundations of Screenwriting*, rev. ed. (New York: Delta, 2005). The collection *Movie Blockbusters*, ed. Julian Stringer (New York: Routledge, 2003), provides a variety of views on the internal logic of big-budget movies, including those of Thomas Schatz, "The New Hollywood," 15–44, and Michael Allen, "Talking about a Revolution: The Blockbuster as Industrial Advertisement," 101–113. For another take on internal thinking, see Gary S. Lynn, *Blockbusters: The Five Keys to Developing Great New Products*, 1st ed. (New York: HarperBusiness, 2002). Carina Chocano noted *National Treasure*'s commercial tie-ins in "Bankrupt 'National Treasure,'" *Los Angeles Times*, November 19, 2004. For Jon Turteltaub's thoughts, see "Interview: Jon Turteltaub from *National Treasure 2: Book of Secrets*," May 8, 2008 (www.fanbolt.com/interview-jon-turteltaub-from-national-treasure-2-book-of-secrets); and April McIntyre, "Director Jon Turteltaub Talks National Treasure: Book of Secrets," May 16, 2008 (www.monstersandcritics.com/dvd/features/article_1397003.php/Director_Jon_Turteltaub_talks_National_Treasure_Book_of_Secrets). As with any DVD of a movie produced since the advent of DVDs, see also the two-disc collectors' versions for Jon Turteltaub's director's commentaries and the "making of" featurettes for both *National Treasure* and *National Treasure 2: Book of Secrets* (Buena Vista Home Entertainment / Touchstone, 2007, 2008).

Similarly with *The Patriot*, a place to start is with the DVD (Roland Emmerich, dir., *The Patriot*, special ed. [Sony Pictures Home Entertainment, 2000]) and with its sanctioned publication (Suzanne Fritz and Rachel Aberly, *"The Patriot": The Official Companion* [London: Carlton, 2000]). Lucinda Moore also provides an insider view in "Capturing America's Fight for Freedom: The Making of 'The Patriot,'" *Smithsonian Magazine*, July 1, 2000. For more on the Smithsonian's role in the movie, see Jacqueline Trescott, "Smithsonian's 'Patriot' Gains: With a Role in Mel Gibson Film, Museum Trades Expertise for Access to New Venue," *Washington Post*, February 13, 2000. Among the many public reactions to *The Patriot* are Nanciann Cherry, "Gibson Delivers Rousing

Entertainment," *Toledo Blade,* June 30, 2000; Godfrey Cheshire, "The Patriot: Mel Smokes Redcoats!," *New York Press,* July 5, 2000; David Hackett Fischer, "Hubris, but No History," *New York Times,* July 1, 2000; Spike Lee, "Sound Off!," *Hollywood Reporter,* July 6, 2000; Michael Lind, "Unpatriotic," *Slate,* July 28, 2000; Christopher Tookey, "The Patriot," *Mail Online,* July 2000. For more on Mel Gibson's views on *The Patriot,* see Tom Dunkel, "Mel Gibson Pops an American Myth," *George,* July 2000, 70–71, 100–102. For draft scripts of *The Patriot,* as well as many other films, see *The Daily Script* (www.dailyscript.com). In order to gauge the political leanings of Hollywood personages, I followed the money. All contributions to federal campaigns are registered and tracked by the Federal Election Commission, which hosts a searchable database at www.fec.gov ("Campaign Finance Disclosure Portal").

Liberty's Kids has been re-released on DVD as *Liberty's Kids: The Complete Series* (Mill Creek Entertainment, 2013); also instructive is Brian Ward, *A Revolutionary Tale: A Look Back at "Liberty's Kids"* (DVD; DIC Entertainment, 2008). For a fuller consideration of the series, see Andrew M. Schocket, "Little Founders on the Small Screen: Interpreting a Multicultural American Revolution for Children's Television," *Journal of American Studies* 45 (2011): 145–163. My interpretation of *Liberty's Kids* especially relies on conversations with Jennifer Lupinacci, Mike Maliani, Doug McIntyre, Kevin O'Donnell, and Jack Rakove. Among other treatments of the series, see Kathryn Shattuck, "Voices of Freedom, and of Its Anchors," *New York Times,* November 10, 2002; and Jill Lepore, who in "No More Kings," *Common-Place,* vol. 2, no. 1 (October 2001), compared it to *Schoolhouse Rock.* For perspective on that production, see E. Engstrom, "*Schoolhouse Rock*: Cartoons as Education," *Journal of Popular Film and Television* 23, no. 3 (1995): 98–105.

The role of PBS was central in the series's development. For more on PBS and its political and programming dilemmas, consult Kim McAvoy, "Public Broadcasters go on Offense," *Broadcasting and Cable* 124, no. 51 (December 19, 1994): 48; Irvin Molotsky, "One Tough Bird, after All; How Public Broadcasting Survived the Attacks of Conservatives," *New York Times,* November 27, 1997; and L. Simensky, "Programming Children's Television: The PBS Model," in *The Children's Television Community,* ed. J. Alison Bryant (Mahwah, N.J.: Lawrence Erlbaum Associates, 2007), 131–146. For a DIC Entertainment executive's take on making TV for kids, see Robby London, "Producing Children's Television," in *The Children's Television Community*, ed. J. Alison Bryant (Mahwah, N.J.: Lawrence Erlbaum Associates, 2007), 80–81. DIC and PBS trumpeted their partnership in "DIC Entertainment and PBS Announce the Debut of 'Liberty's Kids,' A Revolutionary Animated Series; Walter Cronkite to Portray Benjamin Franklin," *PR Newswire*, June 23, 2001.

Mimi White analyzes a character very similar to (if slightly older than) Sara and describes the portrayal as multicultural postfeminist in "Masculinity and Femininity in Television's Historical Fictions: 'Young Indiana Jones Chronicles' and 'Dr. Quinn, Medicine Woman,'" in *Television Histories: Collective Memory in the Media Age*, ed. Gary R. Edgerton and Peter C. Rollins (Lexington: University Press of Kentucky, 2001), 37–58. For more on children's TV and how it is programmed and received, see Anjali Pandey, "'Scatterbrained Apes' and 'Mangy Fools': Lexicalizations of Ideology in Children's Animated Movies," *Simile* 1, no. 3 (2001): 1–14; and Tony Wilson, *Watching Television: Hermeneutics, Reception, and Popular Culture* (Cambridge, Mass.: Polity Press, 1993), 33–39.

For *John Adams*, too, the place to start is with the DVDs; see Tom Hooper, *John Adams* (HBO Video, 2008), which includes the series and various features. For more on the thoughts of the creators of the series, see Michael Fleming, "Hanks and HBO Team on 'Adams,'" *Daily Variety*, November 5, 2001; Dipayan Gupta, "'John Adams' Premiere: Talking to Paul Giamatti, Tom Hanks and David McCullough," *Huffington Post*, March 28, 2008; "Kirk Ellis—Writer of HBO John Adams Series—Interview," YouTube, 2008 (http://youtu.be/ujwgW2UeTbc); Gerald D. Swick, "Kirk Ellis Interview on HBO's John Adams," *Armchair General Magazine*, March 14, 2008; Bill Steigerwald, "John Adams—The Movie: An Interview with David McCullough," *The Doc Is In: A Current Event Blog*, March 13, 2008 (www.thedocisin.net/?p=3747); Peter Travers, "Tom Hanks," *Rolling Stone*, November 15, 2007, 130–135; and "Tom Hanks Talks Revolution," *New York Daily News*, March 5, 2008.

Among the most insightful of the wide public reactions to *John Adams* by popular critics are Anne Becker, "John Adams Brings HBO Best Miniseries Debut since 2004," *Broadcasting and Cable*, March 18, 2008; Rebecca Cusey, "The Lawyer Who Saved America," *National Review Online*, March14, 2008; Barry Garron, "HBO's John Adams a Masterpiece," *Reuters*, March 14, 2008; Lane Lambert, "HBO Miniseries:

Honest Look at 18th Century, Bad Teeth and All: Adams Unplugged,"
Quincy (Mass.) Patriot Ledger, May 19, 2007; Matt Malone, "A Man for
All Seasons," *America: The National Catholic Weekly*, March 24, 2008;
Kent Sepkowitz, "For Teeth and for Country," *Slate*, March 17, 2008;
Tom Shales, "John Adams," Second to None," *Washington Post*, March
15, 2008; Ira Stoll, "Bring Forth the Tar and Feathers," *New York Sun*,
March 11, 2008; Steven Uhles, "Liberal vs. Conservative Battle Is Traced
to Its Roots in 'Adams,'" *Augusta Chronicle*, June 12, 2008. Jill Lepore
weighed in on the series in "The Divider: In an HBO Miniseries, John
Adams Is the Indispensable Man," *New Yorker*, March 17, 2008. For the
most detailed evaluation of *John Adams*'s historical authenticity, see
the series of relevant posts on J. L. Bell's blog, *Boston 1775* (http://bos-
ton1775.blogspot.com). The two extended scholarly treatments of Hollywood biopics are George Frederick Custen, *Bio/Pics: How Hollywood
Constructed Public History* (New Brunswick, N.J.: Rutgers University
Press, 1992); and Dennis Bingham, *Whose Lives Are They Anyway?: The
Biopic as Contemporary Film Genre* (New Brunswick, N.J.: Rutgers University Press, 2010).

Numerous scholars have considered the connections among place,
meaning, and memory. John Bodnar most fully developed the contrast between "official" and "vernacular" interpretations in *Remaking
America: Public Memory, Commemoration, and Patriotism in the Twentieth Century* (Princeton, N.J.: Princeton University Press, 1993), while
Pierre Nora distinguished between "dominant" and "dominated" *lieux
de mémoires* in *Realms of Memory: Rethinking the French Past*, trans.
Lawrence D. Kritzman, European Perspectives (New York: Columbia
University Press, 1996). Among the many interesting works in this area
are James Oliver Horton and Lois E. Horton, eds., *Slavery and Public
History: The Tough Stuff of American Memory* (Chapel Hill: University
of North Carolina Press, 2006); Kirk Savage, *Monument Wars: Washington, D.C., the National Mall, and the Transformation of the Memorial Landscape* (Berkeley: University of California Press, 2009); Marita
Sturken, *Tourists of History: Memory, Kitsch, and Consumerism from
Oklahoma City to Ground Zero* (Durham, N.C.: Duke University Press,
2007); and Thomas A. Chambers, *Memories of War: Visiting Battle-
grounds and Bonefields in the Early American Republic* (Ithaca, N.Y.:
Cornell University Press, 2012). Concerning more recent controversies,

consult Edward T. Linenthal and Tom Engelhardt, *History Wars: The Enola Gay and Other Battles for the American Past* (New York: Holt Paperbacks, 1996). For consideration of these issues in various spaces across the globe, see Daniel J. Walkowitz and Lisa Maya Knauer, eds., *Contested Histories in Public Space: Memory, Race, and Nation* (Durham, N.C.: Duke University Press, 2009).

The acknowledged and much debated ur-text of historical interpretation in national parks is Freeman Tilden, *Interpreting Our Heritage*, 4th ed., expanded and updated (Chapel Hill: University of North Carolina Press, 2007). For a recent evaluation of National Park Service (NPS) efforts and needs, see Anne Mitchell Whisnant et al., *Imperiled Promise: The State of History in the National Park Service* (Bloomington, Ind.: Organization of American Historians, 2011). Charlotte Mires traced the interpretation of the nation's first capital building in *Independence Hall in American Memory* (Philadelphia: University of Pennsylvania Press, 2002). For some visitor impressions, see Yen Le et al., "Independence National Historical Park Visitor Study: Summer 2007," Visitor Services Project, Report no. 195 (Moscow: University of Idaho, Department of Conservation Social Sciences, Park Studies Unit, June 2008). The NPS put together a specific strategy outlined in the "Independence National Historical Park Long-Range Interpretive Plan" (Philadelphia: Independence National Historical Park Interpretation and Visitor Services, December 2007). For another view, see Michael B. Chornesky, "Visceral History: Interpreting Independence National Historical Park," *Hindsight Graduate History Journal* (California State University, Fresno, Department of History), vol. 2 (2008).

The Liberty Bell Center and president's house controversies were largely intertwined. For the building of the Liberty Bell Center, see Richard Sommer et al., *Liberty Bell Center: Bohlin, Cywinski, Jackson*, ed. Rodolphe El-Khoury (San Rafael, Calif., and New York: Oro Editions, 2006). Edward Lawler, Jr., uncovered the history of the presidents' house site in "The President's House in Philadelphia: The Rediscovery of a Lost Landmark," *Pennsylvania Magazine of History and Biography* 126 (2002): 5–95, and "The President's House Revisited," *Pennsylvania Magazine of History and Biography* 129 (2005): 371–410. Doris Devine Fanelli offered a sympathetic view of the NPS's work on the site in "History, Commemoration, and an Interdisciplinary Approach to Interpreting the President's House Site," *Pennsylvania Magazine of History and Biography* 129 (2005): 445–460; Jill Ogline's was somewhat less favorable in "'Creating Dissonance for the Visitor': The Heart of the Liberty Bell Controversy," *Public Historian* 26 (2004): 49–58. There is an explanation of the funding process for the site in "Pennsylvania Governor Rendell Recommends DRPA Funding for Completion of the President's House Site; Funding Tied to Grant from Delaware River Port Authority," *PR Newswire*, January 22, 2009. Gary B. Nash told his side of the story in *The Liberty Bell* (New Haven, Conn.: Yale University Press, 2010) and in "For Whom Will the Liberty Bell Toll? From Controversy to Cooperation," in *Slavery and Public History: The Tough Stuff of American Memory*, ed. James Oliver Horton and Lois E. Horton (Chapel Hill: University of North Carolina Press, 2006), pp. 75–102. For a mostly favorable take, see Edward Rothstein, "The President's House in Philadelphia— Museum Review," *New York Times*, December 14, 2010. For essentialist blowback to reinterpreting the site, see Erick Stakelbeck, "Smearing George Washington," *FrontPageMagazine.com*, January 17, 2003 (http://archive.frontpagemag.com/readArticle.aspx?ARTID=20243); and Michael J. Lewis, "Trashing the President's House," *Commentary*, April 2011. Avenging the Ancestors Coalition (ATAC) keeps an archive of its position papers and activities at http://avengingtheancestors.com. Nathaniel Lee noted the ongoing African American celebration of the site in "Slavery Memorial Marks First Anniversary," *Philadelphia Tribune*, December 16, 2011. For the site's technical difficulties, see Stephen Salisbury, "Faulty Video Screens at President's House Being Replaced," *Philadelphia Inquirer*, February 29, 2012.

Considerations of the National Constitution Center include Gary Gately, "High-Tech Meets History in a More Perfect Union," *Chicago Tribune*, July 13, 2003; and Mariah Zeisberg, "A New Framing? Constitutional Representation at Philadelphia's National Constitution Center," *Perspectives on Politics* 6 (2008): 553–568. To get a flavor of Historic Philadelphia's stories, read Sandra Mackenzie Lloyd, ed., *Patriots, Pirates, Heroes and Spies: Stories from Historic Philadelphia* (New York: Grosset & Dunlap, 2008).

For Mount Vernon's history and its recent building spree, see Scott E. Casper, *Sarah Johnson's Mount Vernon: The Forgotten History of an American Shrine* (New York: Hill & Wang, 2008); GWWO, Inc./

Architects and Mount Vernon Ladies Association, *Integrity, Civility, Ingenuity: A Reflection of George Washington: The Making of the Ford Orientation Center and the Donald W. Reynolds Museum and Education Center at Mount Vernon* (Baltimore: Creo Press, 2007); and Jacqueline Trescott, "Fleshing Out a Founding Father: Mount Vernon Additions Provide New Entree to George Washington's World," *Washington Post*, October 24, 2006. Marc Leepson traced the history of Jefferson's mountain retreat in *Saving Monticello: The Levy Family's Epic Quest to Rescue the House That Jefferson Built* (New York: Free Press, 2001). For characterizations of Monticello's recent efforts to better interpret slavery, consult Edward Rothstein, "Smithsonian and Monticello Exhibitions on Jefferson's Slaves," *New York Times*, January 26, 2012; and Jacqueline Trescott, 'Smithsonian and Monticello Collaborating on Jefferson and Slavery Exhibition," *Washington Post*, blog, August 30, 2011. Patricia West provides a broader consideration of historical houses in *Domesticating History: The Political Origins of America's House Museums* (Washington, D.C.: Smithsonian Institution Press, 1999).

Colonial Williamsburg (CW) has been the subject of two full-length studies and a significant portion of a third: see Richard Handler and Eric Gable, *The New History in an Old Museum: Creating the Past at Colonial Williamsburg* (Durham, N.C.: Duke University Press, 1997); Anders Greenspan, *Creating Colonial Williamsburg: The Restoration of Virginia's Eighteenth-Century Capital*, 2nd ed. (Chapel Hill: University of North Carolina Press, 2009); and Scott Magelssen, *Living History Museums: Undoing History through Performance* (Lanham, Md.: Scarecrow Press, 2007). James Oliver Horton analyzed the CW auction in "Slavery in American History: An Uncomfortable National Dialogue," in *Slavery and Public History: The Tough Stuff of American Memory*, ed. by James Oliver Horton and Lois E. Horton (Chapel Hill: University of North Carolina Press, 2006), 35–56. For continued coverage of Colonial Williamsburg's efforts to interpret slavery, see "'Slave Auction' Divides Crowd in Williamsburg," *Baltimore Sun*, October 11, 1994; Dan Eggen, "In Williamsburg, the Painful Reality of Slavery," *Washington Post*, July 7, 1999; and J. Freedom du Lac, "Slavery Is a Tough Role, Hard Sell at Colonial Williamsburg," *Washington Post*, March 8, 2013. For the official word on CW's new street theater approach, see James Horn, "A Look at the Revolutionary City: The Colonial Williamsburg Official History and Citizenship Site," *Colonial Williamsburg Journal*, Spring 2006; and Lloyd Dobyns, "Revolutionary City: The Colonial Williamsburg Official History and Citizenship Site," *Colonial Williamsburg Journal*, Autumn 2006. William E. White considers CW's Internet presence in "Opening the Digital Door: Colonial Williamsburg Online," *OAH Magazine of History* 25 (2011): 37–41.

Several authors have floated the idea that memory can be inherently nationalistic and conservative, including Wesley Frank Craven and Michael Kammen in the American context and, in a more international one, James V. Wertsch in "Deep Memory and Narrative Templates: Conservative Forces in Collective Memory," in *Memory and Political Change*, ed. Aleida Assmann and Linda Shortt, Palgrave McMillan Memory Studies (New York: Palgrave Macmillan, 2012), 173–185. For detailed coverage of the Minutemen movement, see David Holthouse, "Minutemen, Other Anti-immigrant Militia Groups Stake Out Arizona Border," *Intelligence Report*, no. 118: "Ten Years of Terror" (Montgomery, Ala.: Southern Poverty Law Center, Summer 2005); and Michael Leahy, "Crossing the Line," *Washington Post*, March 19, 2006.

For a good overview of the academic debates concerning the tea party, consult Debra A. Miller, ed., *The Tea Party Movement*, Current Controversies (Detroit, Mich.: Greenhaven Press, 2012). Jill Lepore compared the current tea party movement to the original one and argued that tea partiers' racialized view of American history amounts to "historical fundamentalism" in *The Whites of Their Eyes: The Tea Party's Revolution and the Battle over American History* (Princeton, N.J.: Princeton University Press, 2010). For the tea party's corporate lineage, see Amanda Fallin, Rachel Grana, and Stanton A. Glantz, "'To Quarterback behind the Scenes, Third-Party Efforts': The Tobacco Industry and the Tea Party," *Tobacco Control, Online First* (February 20, 2013), doi:10.1136/tobaccocontrol-2012-050815. Among the most rigorous treatments of the role of race in tea party activism is Eric D. Knowles et al., "Race, Ideology, and the Tea Party: A Longitudinal Study," *PLoS ONE*, vol. 8, no. 6 (June 25, 2013). For an analysis of tea party focus groups, see Stan Greenberg, James Carville, and Erica Seifert, "Inside the GOP: Report on Focus Groups with Evangelical, Tea Party, and Moderate Republicans" (Washington, D.C.: Democracy Corps, October 13, 2013). Anthony R. DiMaggio argues that the tea party is primarily an "astroturf" and media-hyped movement in *The Rise of the Tea Party: Political Discontent and Corporate Media in the Age of Obama* (New York: Monthly Review Press, 2011), while Theda Skocpol and Vanessa Williamson also found significant grassroots support in *The Tea Party and the Remaking of Republican Conservatism* (New York: Oxford University Press, 2012). For an account of Glenn Beck's discovery of Cleon Skousen, see Alexander Zaitchik, "Meet the Man Who Changed Glenn Beck's Life," *Salon*, September 16, 2009. A recent rigorous study of tea party support, membership, geography, and affiliation is in Devin Burghart, "The Status of the Tea Party Movement, Part II: Membership, Support and Sympathy by the Numbers" (Kansas City, Mo.: Institute for Research and Education on Human Rights, January 21, 2014).

On the topic of the decreased economic diversity for college students, both in terms of admissions and attainment, consult Karen Fischer, "Top Colleges Admit Fewer Low-Income Students," *Chronicle of Higher Education*, May 2, 2008; José F. Moreno, Daryl G. Smith, et al., "Using Multiple Lenses: An Examination of the Economic and Racial/Ethnic Diversity of College Students" (San Francisco: James Irvine Foundation; Washington, D.C.: Association of American Colleges and Universities, July 2006); Sara Hebel, "The Graduation Gap," *Chronicle of Higher Education*, March 23, 2007; and Andrew Howard Nichols, "Developing 20/20 Vision on the 2020 Degree Attainment Goal: The Threat of Income Based Inequality in Education" (Washington, D.C.: Pell Institute for the Study of Opportunity in Higher Education, May 2011).

There's a vast and growing literature on originalism. For the best recent summary, see Lawrence B. Solum, "What Is Originalism? The Evolution of Contemporary Originalist Theory," *SSRN: Social Service Research Network*, April 28, 2011 (http://papers.ssrn.com/sol3/papers.cfm?abstract_id=1825543). John O. McGinnis and Michael B. Rappaport make their case for original methods originalism in "Original Methods Originalism: A New Theory of Interpretation and the Case against Construction," *SSRN: Social Science Research Network*, May 19, 2009 (http://papers.ssrn.com/sol3/papers.cfm?abstract_id=1407274). The longer-term ebbs and flows of living constitutionalism and originalism have been charted in Adam Winkler, "A Revolution Too Soon: Woman Suffragists and the Living Constitution," *New York University*

Law Review, vol. 76 (2001); and Howard Gillman, "The Collapse of Constitutional Originalism and the Rise of the Notion of the 'Living Constitution' in the Course of American State-Building," *Studies in American Political Development* 11 (1997): 191–247. Essentialist originalism has marched hand in hand with the growth of the Federalist Society, investigated in Ralph G. Neas, "The Federalist Society: From Obscurity to Power" (Washington, D.C.: People for the American Way Foundation, August 2001); Jonathan Riehl, "The Federalist Society and Movement Conservatism: How a Fractious Coalition on the Right Is Changing Constitutional Law and the Way We Talk and Think about It" (Ph.D. diss., University of North Carolina, 2007); Steven Michael Teles, *The Rise of the Conservative Legal Movement: The Battle for Control of the Law*, Princeton Studies in American Politics (Princeton, N.J.: Princeton University Press, 2008); and Michael Avery, *The Federalist Society: How Conservatives Took the Law Back from Liberals* (Nashville, Tenn.: Vanderbilt University Press, 2013). Reva Siegal wrote a devastating critique in "Dead or Alive: Originalism as Popular Constitutionalism in *Heller*," *Harvard Law Review*, 122 (2008): 191–245. Frank Cross's analysis appears in *The Failed Promise of Originalism* (Stanford, Calif.: Stanford Law Books, an imprint of Stanford University Press, 2013).

For one of the first uses of the term "originalism," and still one of its clearest critiques, see Paul Brest, "The Misconceived Quest for the Original Understanding," *Boston University Law Review*, vol. 60 (1980). Historians have been particularly skeptical of what we commonly refer to as "law office history" and originalism, in particular, including Jack N. Rakove, *Original Meanings: Politics and Ideas in the Making of the Constitution* (New York: Knopf, 1997), 3–23; Saul Cornell, "*Heller*, New Originalism, and Law Office History: Meet the New Boss, Same as the Old Boss," *UCLA Law Review* 56 (2008): 1095, and "New Originalism: A Constitutional Scam," *Dissent*, May 3, 2011; R. B. Bernstein, "The Constitution as an Exploding Cigar and Other Historian's Heresies about a Constitutional Orthodoxy," *New York Law School Law Review*, vol. 55 (2010); and Jill Lepore, "The Commandments: The Constitution and Its Worshippers," *New Yorker*, January 17, 2011.

Although there's little rigorous output particularly on Revolutionary War reenactors, there's excellent work on the living historians recreating other events, including Tony Horwitz, *Confederates in the Attic:*

Dispatches from the Unfinished Civil War, 1st ed. (New York: Pantheon Books, 1998); Karsten R. Stueber, "The Psychological Basis of Historical Explanation: Reenactment, Simulation, and the Fusion of Horizons," *History and Theory* 41 (2002): 25–42; Jenny Thompson, *War Games: Inside the World of Twentieth-Century War Reenactors* (Washington, D.C.: Smithsonian Institution Press, 2004); and Stephen Gapps, "Mobile Monuments: A View of Historical Reenactment and Authenticity from inside the Costume Cupboard of History," *Rethinking History* 13 (2009): 395–409.

For coverage of the Boston Tea Party Ships & Museum, see Jody Feinberg, "A New and Better Boston Tea Party Ships and Museum Returns after an 11-Year Hiatus," *Quincy (Mass.) Patriot Ledger*, June 23, 2012; Kailani Koenig-Muenster, "New Boston Tea Party Museum Opens to a Different World," *Boston Globe*, June 26, 2012; and Edward Rothstein, "Boston Tea Party Ships & Museum Reopens with New Exhibits," *New York Times*, July 3, 2012.

The strongest accounts of the Somerset decision are in Seymour Drescher, *The Mighty Experiment: Free Labor vs. Slavery in British Emancipation* (New York: Oxford University Press, 2002); and Christopher Leslie Brown, *Moral Capital: Foundations of British Abolitionism* (Chapel Hill: University of North Carolina Press, 2006). For the idea that the Revolution made the abolition of slavery possible, see David Horowitz, "Our Nation's Heritage Is under Attack in Our Classrooms, So Why Doesn't Anybody Care?," *Jewish World Review*, July 12, 2000; and Gordon S. Wood, *The Radicalism of the American Revolution* (New York: Vintage Books, 1993), 7. For the Revolution's "contagion of liberty," see Bernard Bailyn, *The Ideological Origins of the American Revolution* (Cambridge, Mass.: Belknap Press of Harvard University Press, 1967), 230–320. Paul Finkelman has noted the centrality of slavery to the early American law in *Slavery and the Founders: Race and Liberty in the Age of Jefferson* (Armonk, N.Y.: M. E. Sharpe, 1996), and David Waldstreicher demonstrated slavery's centrality to the Constitution in *Slavery's Constitution: From Revolution to Ratification*, 1st ed. (New York: Hill & Wang, 2009).

Sarah J. Purcell argued that the trauma of the American Revolution has been greatly underestimated in *Sealed with Blood: War, Sacrifice, and Memory in Revolutionary America* (Philadelphia: University of Pennsylvania Press, 2010), as has John Phillips Resch in *Suffering Soldiers: Revolutionary War Veterans, Moral Sentiment, and Political Culture in the Early Republic* (Amherst: University of Massachusetts Press, 1999).

For Olivier Roy's analysis of modern fundamentalism and its roots, see *Holy Ignorance: When Religion and Culture Part Ways*, Comparative Politics and International Studies Series (New York: Columbia University Press, 2010). One study that notes the interaction between the production of collective memory and its evolution is Eyal Zandbwerg, Oren Meyers, and Motti Neiger, "Past Continuous: Newsworthiness and the Shaping of Collective Memory," *Critical Studies in Media Communication* 29 (2012): 65–79.

Andrew M. Schocket is Director of American Culture Studies and Associate Professor of History and American Culture Studies at Bowling Green State University, and the author of *Founding Corporate Power in Early National Philadelphia.*